Antiques
How to Identify and
Collect Them

Mr. Cowie was the Founder
of THE INTERNATIONAL ANTIQUES YEARBOOK

Antiques:

How to Identify and Collect Them

by Donald Cowie

CASTLE BOOKS ★ NEW YORK

for Ruth alone

Contents

What This Book Is About 9

Acknowledgments 11

1 Furniture 15

2 Ceramics and Glass 30

3 Silver and Jewelry 43

4 Objets D'Art 58

5 Bygones 70

6 European 88

7 Oriental 109

8 Victoriana 121

9 Carpets and Textiles 135

10 Pictures 143

11 Books 154

12 Coins 161

13 Childish Things 170

14 Fakes 176

15 Buying and Selling 183

Bibliography 195

Index 199

What This Book Is About

Twenty-one years ago I founded the British publication *Antiques Yearbook* largely because I could not myself find in the bookshops and libraries what I wanted to know about the kind of antiques that were still available in the shops. Most of the books were either too superficial or dealt with articles that could only be found in museums. My publication did become very popular just because it provided the information wanted by the average man, tersely and often light-heartedly presented.

I soon found that my best readers were Americans. They wanted to learn and they were never what the British call "stuffy." My annual book thus became increasingly U.S.-orientated; and what I have now done is extract the plums and the essence from the knowledge I thus acquired and write it down in a book whose aim is to teach the reader about antiques, yes, but primarily about the antiques that are still available for general collecting: and for one of the best financial investments ever known to man.

DONALD COWIE

9

Acknowledgments

THE author acknowledges with grateful thanks illustrations that have been made available to him for this book by the following: Messrs. Aabenraa Antikvitetshandel, Denmark; Asprey & Company, London; H. Bukowski Konsthandel, Stockholm, Sweden; Bluett & Sons, London; Martin Breslauer, London; Dr. H. G. Bunke, Munich, Germany; H. W. Keil, Broadway, England; Sydney L. Moss, London; Nystad Antiquairs, Lochem, Holland; W. H. Patterson, London; Perez, London; P. J. Radford, Denmead, England; Mrs. Violet Wood, Ousden, England.

The section on ship models first appeared in *The Antiques Dealer* for July 1968, that on prints in *The Antiques Journal,* September 1968, and part of that on firearms in *The Antiques Journal of May* 1969.

This book would not have appeared but for the encouragement of the author's wife, Ruth Mary Cowie, and his son, Peter Duff Cowie.

*Antiques
How to Identify and
Collect Them*

1

Furniture

Definition and Identification

Antique furniture can be defined as movable contents of a household or room, particularly tables, chairs and receptacles, made prior to the year 1830 and authentic of its period.

There are some experts who prefer to say "over one hundred years old" rather than "made prior to the year 1830." This enables the public to collect as antique what was made in Victorian times, and will eventually enable them to collect as antique what was made in our own time (if they do not do so already).

But purists believe, and probably rightly, that our modern machine age, which started about 1830 after the Industrial Revolution, is incapable of producing such beautiful and well-made articles as the former ages of the handcraftsmen.

Since 1830 the only furniture that can equal the products of preceding centuries are reproductions or fakes, with a thin smattering of "arty-crafty" articles made in specialized workshops of noncommercial artists who are out of tune with the feelings and requirements of the age.

Reasonable restoration is allowed in a "genuine" antique. This includes regilding and renewal of plates in period lookingglasses, regilding of gilt chairs and other furniture (provided the underframe is left in the original state), replacement of missing or damaged feet if of the same character as the original, replacement of missing or damaged plinths if ditto, replacement of missing loose leaves from eighteenth- and nineteenth-century dining tables, and replacement of original marble tops or brasses.

What completely destroys the value of a piece of antique furniture is restoration beyond a certain point. This can be defined in various ways. Thus any form of "marriage" between two articles is out. And reductions in depth or size of any piece are fatal. An antique is similarly ruined when it was originally plain and has since been carved, inlaid, or cross-banded.

Similarly, mirrors must not have had the original designs altered or new pediment tops applied, nor must they have been given decorated glass borders or panels which were not originally there.

Solid plinths must not have been altered to bracket feet and vice versa, while painted furniture must not have been entirely repainted.

But how can it be determined that a piece of furniture was made prior to 1830?

The only acid test, of course, is a documented history or provenance of the piece, such as an original invoice for its making accompanied by a detailed record of its ownership since then. There are in existence just a few pieces that can be exactly traced back in this way, and they will be mainly found in the great museums.

The usual test is examination by an expert, whose knowledge and, even more important, instinct are derived from handling and examining antiques over many years. It is a fact that he acquires such a flair that he can tell age and authenticity of an article almost as soon as he enters the room in which it has been placed. "Something tells him"; and this instinct is confirmed by a practical examination which most saliently incurs turning the piece on its back or crawling under it and looking for new wood in the carcass, new screws and nails and joints and glue.

The question "Is it an antique?" is therefore ideally answered by provenance, i.e., a study of the history of the piece since it was made. But since this is rarely possible, and forged provenances are not unknown, the expert looks for (a) style (the general appearance of the article and its design, which should be right of its period), then (b) age of wood, screws, nails, glue, which again should be in period after allowing for reasonable restoration work, and (c) surface, sometimes called patination, which should be deep, rich, and never too clean but embodying the dirt of the years in the very luster of the polish.

After which it should be remembered that none of the above methods is infallible. The piece may be a perfect reproduction: so much for the style test. Its materials may have been taken from genuine antique sources or manufactured according to ancient recipes, even to the glue. The patination may be correct as to period because the wood was taken from a genuine but larger article, for example from a backside-polished church pew to make the reproduction of a seventeenth-century joint stool.

All the same, the best judges of antiques are those who have developed an instinct, remembering that the forgers very often make the following mistakes:

(a) Not getting their sizes quite right, such as making a "Sheraton" sideboard just a little too light in weight and narrow in width, or a "Chippendale" chair rather more suited to modern behinds than to those of the broad-beamed gentry of the eighteenth century.

(b) Scamping matters of final detail, such as the finish of the underpart of frames and the runners of drawers. (Therefore always turn the piece upside down and study those parts with torch and magnifying glass.)

Even so, it is necessary to remember that most articles of antique furniture have been restored and in particular at some period may have been given new underparts and backs and drawerrunners, and that this does not destroy the value and authenticity of the piece so long as it has not been carried too far.

Wormholes: In spite of the lurid stories about fakers at work with blunderbusses to pepper their newborns with period perforations, it is still an advantage to find evidence of worming in furniture. All wood but the hardest mahogany is bound to attract the attention of the worm at some period of its life. The wormholes can of course be tested for authenticity by tracing them through the wood. Faked holes go straight in. The real ones meander.

An antique is genuine, it has been said, only if it is authentic of its period. But how does one determine and recognize the period?

(Courtesy of H. W. Keil, Tudor House, Broadway, England.)

A really early piece of English oak furniture: A chest with domed top and joints that have been through-morticed and pegged: made about 1450 in the north of England probably.

Well, to start at the beginning, plain and ungainly oak such as a narrow old board with plain splayed legs like that of modern Scandinavian furniture *could be* very ancient indeed or pre-Tudor, especially if the grain of the oak appears in diagonal splashes on the surface.

A linen-fold pattern can date carved work as fifteenth or sixteenth century.

More elaborate articles of carved oak—chests, chairs, cupboards, stools—with elaborate architectural designs in inlaid work *could be* Tudor.

Such furniture more heavily elaborated, as with the bulbous legs of tables, *could be* late Elizabethan.

The words "could be" are italicized because there cannot be much left on the general market of genuine sixteenth and early seventeenth-century oak furniture. The expert will most frequently identify pieces that seem to be of the period as later copies, which, indeed, have been made right through the centuries up to the present day. All so-called antique furniture continued to be made, quite legitimately and without any intent to deceive, long after its originating period.

By studying these matters carefully it should be possible to tell of an oak joint stool said to be Elizabethan that it was probably made in the early eighteenth century in Lancashire to the order of a great house, and there preserved for at least a century (otherwise its feet would not be in such good order) and afterwards used in a farmhouse (marks of milk churns on the top).

This diagnosis does not necessarily make the joint stool any less valuable or desirable provided that it is a beautiful, well-made piece of furniture, and it would probably not have been preserved if it had been ugly. The human race has its faults but does tend to cherish what is beautiful and good.

Then if the furniture is of dark old wood but lightish in weight and construction, with applied ornaments, and silk or velvet upholstery, and turned work on the legs, it *could be* Jacobean. Especially if a gateleg table is extremely heavy and obviously very old, and has legs of really elaborate turned work, it could be of this period when the gateleg as such first became popular.

Then if furniture is of oak but drab and straight up and down and leather-seated and backed, it *could be* Cromwellian.

If it is like the Jacobean type described above but still lighter in weight, feminine and fantastic, and walnut (which is now used more and more) and especially if the original feet have been restored after being completely eaten away by the worm and/or floor damp, then it *could be* Carolean.

Note that the earliest marquetry and japanning was of the period about 1675 to 1680 (in England).

If the oak, walnut, lacquer, or marquetry furniture is plain in design it *may be* of the William and Mary period, especially if a Dutch influence can be discerned and there are pear-shaped handles.

But if the furniture is plain and heavy and mahogany as well as walnut and oak, with stoutly bowed cabriole legs and curved backs but not fine carving and any great elaboration of design thereon, it *could be* Queen Anne.

If it is of basic design like Queen Anne but transmogrified by fine carving and elaborate chair slats in the backs it *could be* early Chippendale.

Thus we come to the period when styles are named after designers rather than monarchs, although it should be remembered that the designers whose names became popular were rarely the actual makers of the furniture, especially of the specimens that have come down to us. Because the macintosh was named after its originating Scotsman it does not follow that all rainwear since has been made by him or his firm.

All the same, if the mahogany has a design reminiscent of the Oriental pagoda, with much trelliswork and exquisitely narrow or flat proportions, it *could be* Chinese Chippendale.

Should the furniture be delicate and curving as against the Chippendale solidity and straightness, with turned and reeded legs and shield backs and balloon and hoop backs, and especially should the wood be satinwood, then it *could be* lovely Hepplewhite.

Should it be mahogany with delicate inlays and oval or serpentine fronts, much use of yellow crossbanding, or painted beechwood, and with oval or circular decorations and handles, then it *could* belong to the Sheraton school of design.

And with straight legs and a classical urn, plaque, medallion, vase, and/or looped swag somewhere represented in the decoration, sometimes with painted panels—the general style of the familiar pinewood mantelpiece—then it *could be* attributed to the so-called Adam period.

Then if rosewood, flat and architectural in design, embellished with brass feet and latticed brass grills and edge beading, it *could be* Regency, and, when heavier in design, early Victorian.

On the whole a piece has "quality" and was made by an important or skilled London cabinetmaker when it is very beautiful, exact in proportions, and delicate in method of execution.

On the whole it is "country" or "provincial" when marred by clumsiness or lack of adherence to the original published designs of Chippendale, Hepplewhite, Sheraton and the other great eighteenth and early nineteenth century cabinetmakers.

Observe a typical "Chippendale style" chair in a modern antique shop. It is very beautiful, but the carved and vase-shaped slat in the back is not elaborate, and the carving is not sharp, and the legs are not cabriole and claw-and-ball but straight and plain. It is good but "country," made in the late eighteenth or early nineteenth century for furnishing purposes in part imitation of the Chippendale best and to meet the requirements of the growing middleclass of merchants and small gentry. Or maybe it was made only yesterday by some very clever fakers who work in Florence.

Access to the three great design books of the eighteenth century are essential if the reader is indelibly to remember the differences between the schools and if he is to recognize quality, which in eighteenth-century furniture can be defined as closeness of adherence to those designs.

The books are: Thomas Chippendale's *The Gentleman and Cabinet Maker's Director,* 1754; Thomas Sheraton's *The Cabinetmaker and Upholsterers' Drawing Book,* 1790; George Hepplewhite's *Cabinetmaker and Upholsterer's Guide,* 1788; and the Adam brothers' *Works of Architecture.*

Lessons from Chairs

What has been said so far is, however, very general and the product of years of experience. For the tyro there is almost too much to learn in antiques (as in any other subject).

(Courtesy of H. W. Keil, Tudor House, Broadway, England.)

A very rare Elizabethan joint stool made towards the end of the sixteenth century. Special features are the lovely, thin and molded top, the fluted legs, and the carved rail. A classic of early English furniture.

Are there no short cuts to essential knowledge? Yes, there are; and the answer is specialization. It is a very good idea to concentrate on one particular article. It will then be not so difficult to find out a lot about it.

In furniture the best object for the specialist is the chair. This is an article that shows, better than any other, the marks of its period. It can be acquired not too expensively and it is always useful. There is no more evocative a history of English furniture, in particular, than a collection of chairs.

The earliest chairs in such a collection would be typical specimens of what is known as "turners' work." Dating in rare, valuable cases from as far back as the fifteenth century, they would consist of pieces of turned wood joined together to form a seat, legs, sides, and back. Survivals of this form today are the kitchen and Windsor chairs. It has been presumed that the first English chair was a three-legged stool. Craftsmen in the High Wycombe district particularly had the idea of using the turned legs to make a back and sides for the stool. The apotheosis of this work was the Gothic-backed Windsor of the late eighteenth and early nineteenth century, very valuable now—but still made in the same district as were those original crude stools.

We find next in a chair collection what is called "joiners' work." The medieval chest of oak was used as a seat, then given arms and a back to make a typical box chair, mainly for the use of the head of the house (and the throne of early kings). The joiners also made the X-shaped chair, copying Saracen furniture seen on the Crusades, which was itself descended from the earliest chairs of all, those of the ancient Egyptians.

Out of the Tudor oak chair made by the joiners came the Yorkshire chair, that is still familiar to us today with its hooped rails to lighten the back, and with the frequent carving of a bearded head on the top rail. There are many variations of this oaken type, and a particularly nice example is the chair which has the back pierced by three arcaded openings between two turned balusters on a center rail.

Upholstery as such began about 1610 with the simple padding of those armless oak chairs known as farthingales, because they were built for the accommodation of females in large hooped petticoats. The Jacobeans hung frills from brass studs under and around mainly red velvet seats. The grim Cromwellians made do with leather. The Caroleans developed ornate upholstery; and out of the X-chair, padded and covered with satin and velvet, came the Knole type of chair and settee.

Foreign craftsmen were chiefly responsible for the Charles II type of chair that started off the walnut period (which is roughly dated from 1660 to about 1720). These were elaborately carved in a soft English walnut that is too often sadly wormed, and sometimes they had cane seats. The legs and stretchers were turned fantastically. The backs of these chairs steadily rose in height, and towards the end of the period they had plain padded backs and seats.

It is worth noting that about 1690 the stretchers ceased to extend from leg to leg and met instead at a point crowned by a finial under the center of the seat.

About 1700 the cabriole leg appeared, from Italy via France, and dominated chair design for some fifty years. Meanwhile backs and legs became curved and broad. The claw-and-ball foot appeared about 1710, with escallop shell carving on knees and seat rails approximately between 1710 and 1720.

Walnut ceased to be the most popular wood more or less at the year 1720, for the reason that mahogany then became available with the opening up of overseas colonies; and in the development of mahogany furniture Thomas Chippendale and his school were chiefly responsible for the outstanding characteristics, as can be seen by a perusal of the *Gentleman & Cabinetmaker's Director*. These characteristics were: Use of mahogany; cabriole legs; exquisitely carved ribband-backs and ladder-backs; finally adaptation of Chinese motifs.

Between 1760 and 1785, however, Robert Adam's classical ideas superseded those of the Chippendale school. Legs of chairs began to taper; backs became shield-shaped or oval with three feathers carved, or lyre-shaped, or looped. Hepplewhite's book interpreted the Adam style with considerable influence.

Then Sheraton's writings equally influenced the characteristic *fin de siècle* style and the loveliest English chairs of all, fragile in appearance but not in strength, often in painted or japanned beech, small and square-backed with vase-shaped or lattice back, very lovely then, but surviving hopelessly debauched in the drawing-room chair of Edwardian times.

Finally we have the Regency style of Thomas Hope, George Smith, and others, influenced by the French taste under the Napoleonic empire, sabered legs, ormolu cross-banding, rosewood as well as mahogany, even gilded heads of sphinxes at the end of arms. These were nicest of all in simple bedroom forms, black japanned beech wood with sabered legs, cane seats and a modicum of gilt decoration.

During the Victorian period the chair exhibited all the vigor and vulgarity of our first machine age. Never before were so many weird chairs made and never before were they made with such insensitivity and lack of style. Just a few of the curiosities of that period may be worth collecting, such as the more delicate examples of chairs made in papier-mâché. These were made by hand, without that fatal machine-turning and planing.

"Sheraton" and "Hepplewhite"

Thus it is not too difficult to acquire a smattering of knowledge about what is now regarded as the best period of English antique furniture, that of the late eighteenth and early nineteenth centuries. But it is very difficult to go further and to understand the subject thoroughly. Little effort has been made to present it as a subject for academic or scientific study. The greatest experts still tend to rely upon instinct rather than a code of laws.

Until quite recently it was common for collectors and dealers to speak of "Sheraton" this and "Hepplewhite" that, as if the furniture was actually made by craftsmen of those names.

Therefore it is necessary to clarify carefully some ideas about this most important of periods. At the end of the eighteenth century there were perhaps three hundred separate cabinetmakers' workshops in London, and probably an equal number in the provinces that turned out similar if cruder work. One London firm alone, Seddons of of Aldersgate Street, employed some four hundred craftsmen, and carried a larger stock than almost any similar firm today.

Unlike French furniture, the products of these makers were not stamped (save for those of Gillows). Sometimes labels to advertise their firms were stuck by makers on the insides of drawers, but there are no labels extant with such names as Chippendale, Sheraton, Hepplewhite, Vile, and Cobb. As said before, the only texts for this subject are the famous "pattern books," and, in the words of a leading authority, "No single piece of furniture has in fact been identified as having been made by either Hepplewhite or Sheraton, and curiously few extant pieces are directly or closely related to their book models."

(Courtesy of H. W. Keil, Tudor House, Broadway, England.)
A very fine Elizabethan withdraw refectory table in oak. The bulbs are superbly large, and the carved frieze is beautiful. Date: about 1580-1590.

Hepplewhite himself was apparently a poor cabinetmaker who worked in Cripplegate, which was not a fashionable quarter.

Sheraton was a trained cabinetmaker, but "lived," if that is the word, by his "exertions as an author." Adam Black, subsequently founder of the publishing house, describes in his *Memoirs* how he worked for Sheraton in his youth:

"He lived in an obscure street, his house half shop, half dwelling house, and looked himself like a worn-out Methodist minister, with threadbare black coat . . . My host seemed a good man, with some talent. He had been a cabinetmaker, was now author and publisher, teacher of drawing, and, I believe, occasional preacher. I was with him for about a week, engaged in some wretched work, writing a few articles, and trying to put his shop in order, working among dirt and bugs, for which I was remunerated with half a guinea. Miserable as the pay was, I was half-ashamed to take it from the poor man."

Other testimonies point to Sheraton as a very accomplished artist and observer, who codified or crystallized the practice of his day in cabinetmaking. He was like the poet who at once puts the aspirations of his age into words and creates his age in the same lovely sentence —but, unlike Shakespeare and Tennyson, he did not know how to conduct his business.

Hepplewhite must have been a similar near-genius. He won posthumously an immortal fame that mocks at his contemporary failure.

Sheraton and Hepplewhite did not make the furniture that is given their name today, unlike Chippendale, whose actual hand has been more or less plausibly assigned to certain extant pieces.

They were indeed similar to the architect-authors of those builders' books that are used by the constructors of ordinary houses. They did not invent the styles and methods, nor did they use them in practical work themselves. They just made a poor living and a mocking fame-after-death by providing the elaborate pattern books from which others could extract outlines and ideas.

Then they were fortunate to live and work at the same time as a revolution in aesthetic taste. Adam and others had encouraged this revolution by rediscovering the beauty of the Roman orders and other classical art forms. Many humble cabinetmakers, whose names are still unknown, had translated this revolution into terms of furniture. Hepplewhite and Sheraton in their pattern books elaborated these new styles and put them on paper, Hepplewhite first and faithfully, Sheraton second and derivatory from Hepplewhite but with more straining after impracticable originality.

Sheraton in his later *Cabinet Dictionary* acted similarly for the distorted classical pastiche that was to be the Regency or Empire style.

The names of other cabinetmakers or artists who published pattern books might equally have become famous, for example, those of C. H. Tatham, Henry Hope, Ackermann, Whitaker, Nicholson, or indeed those of the real cabinetmakers of the period such as George Seddon, Richard Gillow, John McLean, George Oakley, Thomas Chippendale the Younger, William Ince, and John Mayhew. But by the chancefulness of history these, who did the actual work, were fated to remain unknown save to a few antiquarian scholars.

Thus the real inspirer of the Regency style in England was a certain Henry Holland, architect to the Prince of Wales, who encouraged Tatham to study and collect ancient sculptures in Rome, and then designed the true Regency furniture for Carlton House, Sloane Place, and Southill.

For better or for worse the names of Hepplewhite and Sheraton have become indelibly associated with certain types of English furniture. "Hepplewhite" furniture displays the first impact of the eighteenth-century classical rediscoveries upon chairs, tables, cabinets, and mirrors. "Sheraton" furniture is at first less classical in shape and style, really Roman only in the brasses upon it, but eventually goes wholeheartedly for the cult and becomes what we know as Regency.

But we must never pretend that a piece was made by Sheraton or Hepplewhite or even directly inspired by those artist-journalists. It is better to realize that the eighteenth and early nineteenth centuries saw a remarkable growth of ingenuity and artistry in the making of furniture based upon ideas brought first from China and second from Pompeii, Herculaneum, and Rome. As many people contributed to what we know as "Sheraton" style as contribute to the making of a Hollywood film, only in the case of the furniture there was never any one producer or director or star performer.

Availability and Price of Good Furniture

There have, probably since earliest times, been two catch phrases about antiques that have been widely accepted by quite knowledgeable people. They are: "The supply of fine antiques is drying up," and "I would like to buy if only I could afford it."

These catch phrases embody popular ideas that are based on misconceptions, especially regarding furniture. There have never been so many antique shops in the world as there are today, and Britain in particular has, it has been said, a new antique shop opening every week. In these shops will be found a remarkable array still of fine old furniture in particular.

Partly this is the product of dishonest fakers and honest reproduction factories, but largely it is the result of the social revolution that has occurred in our times. Britain especially has seen the spectacle of great homes selling their centuries-old contents in order to meet penal

This bow-front Sheraton sideboard is typical of the best English late eighteenth-century mahogany furniture. It is small but very heavy. Reproductions are always light in weight. Collection: Mr. & Mrs. Donald Cowie.

Splendid example of a late eighteenth-century Sheraton-style breakfront bureau bookcase in mahogany. The proportions are such that this large piece of furniture appears small in a room. Collection: Mr. & Mrs. Donald Cowie.

death duties and other taxation, the kindly-cruel chief instrument of the modern, bloodless-revolutionaries. Never before has so much old furniture come on the market as in the last two generations.

Admittedly this sudden availability of goods in our time has been accompanied by a stiff and continual rise in prices. No objects of investment have shown such a satisfactory and constant appreciation in value as antiques and works of art. Land and property values have often been forced back by governmental intervention. The paper values of industrial shares have often fallen as much as they have risen, also under governmental influence but mainly because they have been based on the fluctuating fortunes of individual firms. Gold and diamonds have been rigidly pegged down.

But a good piece of eighteenth-century furniture bought in 1950 is now worth at least twice what was paid for it, and there is no reason why this appreciation in value should not steadily continue.

But what is the price of a good piece of eighteenth-century furniture? It is still less than that of a transient and quick-rusting car, far less than that of a miniature, jerry-built house or flat. While for the price of a refrigerator, a man's suit, a woman's fur coat, a holiday in Spain, or two or three meals at a good restaurant it is still possible to buy a wide variety of articles of old furniture that may not be in the first class but pass as antique and look far more beautiful than modern, mass-produced tables, chairs, and cabinets.

The man who buys such furniture not only enriches his surroundings, his social status, and his mind but acquires an investment that will yield him more in the long run than most of the attractions offered by banks, stockbrokers, and real estate agents.

Among antiques it is furniture that comes first in availability and practicality. But what is this antique furniture? Is it all extremely fine and expensive? Is it mainly reproduction or faked or otherwise of small value? Is it ugly and have all the best-looking specimens gone into museums and transatlantic collections?

For the purpose of answering these very pertinent questions it is only necessary to make a brief visit to the antique shops.

It has been said before that chairs are basic. And it will still be not too difficult to find some very important and valuable chairs indeed. It might be necessary, for example, to pay several hundred dollars for an early Georgian walnut armchair, not only a splendid specimen of its period but covered with contemporary needlework and in perfect condition. Those hundreds of dollars would be easily spent on a second small car for the wife, but within twenty years would be doubled if put into the chair.

Similarly, quite a good Hepplewhite-style chair could still be bought, or a very elegant specimen with those beautifully carved Prince of Wales feathers at the head of the splat.

Tables in period are more difficult to find than chairs. It has always been so. But early oak gatelegs are still quite frequently available, sometimes at lower cost than a washing machine, and late eighteenth- and early nineteenth-century supper tables of the Sheraton and Regency type will be found in the better antique shops and within the purse of a modern young executive, provided he has the right ideas and sense of values.

The same young man could, if he really wanted to, go out and buy, even today, a fine early eighteenth-century walnut cabinet with original Vauxhall plates, or an extremely fine mahogany breakfront bookcase which is fitted with writing drawer, c. 1770. Or a beautifully simple eighteenth-century mahogany bureau bookcase, characterized by the best workmanship, still no more expensive perhaps than a mink coat. Or a rare early eighteenth-century walnut chest-on-chest—or one of the early commodes that are so much in the antiques mode today. French commodes are widely available, if costing as much as a new Rolls Royce or more, but it is possible for the price of a rather dangerous and undeniably perishable sports car to buy excellent commodes of English origin.

Or a rosewood cylinder writing table, or a fine Chippendale-type claw-and-ball stool, or a small piecrust table.

It is still possible to find small Sheraton-style serpentine-front mahogany sideboards, and oak kneehole desks, and many of the card tables that were such an essential item of furniture in the eighteenth century. Then Welsh-type oak dressers are to be had still for less than the price of a color television set; and, more portable, there are mirrors, wine coolers, Canterburys, Chippendale-type mahogany and inlaid bottle stands, library steps, Pembroke tables, teapoys, and tea caddies.

While it is always safer and cheaper in the long run to buy the best that can be found at whatever temporary financial sacrifice, it is also true that a home can be furnished very adequately and yet cheaply if the cruder country furniture and some of the less heavy and repulsive Victorian furniture is bought in junk shops and at local sales. More will be said about this in Chapter 8, (Victoriana), and French and other European furniture will be discussed similarly in its relevant section, as will be "fakes."

IDENTIFICATION OF WOODS

Amboyna: Brown, tinged with yellow, marked with small knots and curls.

Ash: White, veined with streaks in the direction of the growth, most used for chair seats.

Beech: Light brown, tough but easily worked, much used for stained, painted, and gilded furniture because it takes the color well.

Cherry: Reddish color and close, compact grain.

Chestnut: White color and sometimes used as a substitute for satinwood.

Harewood: Sycamore stained with oxide of iron.

Holly: White wood, hard, used in marquetry and inlay.

Kingwood: Rich, violet-brown color shading into black with streaky markings.

Lignum Vitae: Hard, greenish-brown wood.

Limewood: Light straw color and close, compact grain.

Mahogany: The Spanish type of the first half of the eighteenth century was hard and dark red; the "Cuban" used afterwards was often finely figured and marked with a curly or wavy grain; the "Honduras" is inferior in color and figure to the others but lighter in weight and softer in texture.

Oak: Hard and heavy, cigar-brown and even-grained, only very dark when from the bog or grossly stained.

Olivewood: Close-grained, greenish yellow.

Pinewood: Straight-grained, light color, soft, resinous.

Plumwood: Yellow, but red of heart.

Rosewood: There are several kinds, all characterized by blackish brown color and by their fragrance.

Satinwood: Yellow with satiny surface, sometimes plain-grained and sometimes mottled.

Tulipwood: Light-colored with pink stripes.

Walnut: Two kinds, the first pale brown with dark brown and black veining, the second denser and grayish brown with dark markings and veinings.

Yew: Very hard, red-brown, usually in small-diameter pieces.

Zebra Wood: Light brown with prominent dark-brown stripes.

DATES OF ENGLISH FURNITURE PERIODS AND MAKERS

Tudor Period	1485–1558
Elizabethan Period	1558–1603
Jones, Inigo	1572–1652
Jacobean Period	1603–1688
Gibbon, Grinling	1648–1726
Cromwellian Period	1649–1660
Carolean Period	1660–1685
Kent, William	1684–1748
William and Mary Period	1689–1702
Queen Anne Period	1702–1714
Georgian Period	1714–1815
Regency Period	1815–1830
Chippendale, Thomas	1718–1779
Linnell, William	1720–1763
Seddon, George	1727–1801
Adam, J. and R.	1728–1792
Bradshaw, W. and G.	1736–1750
Lock, Matthias	1740–1769
Gillow, R. and R.	1740–1811
Kaufmann, Angelica	1741–1807
Sheraton, Thomas	1751–1806
Ince, W., and Mayhew, J.	1758–1810
Mainwaring, Robert	1765–
Vile, William	–1767
Cobb, John	–1778
Hepplewhite, George	–1786
Shearer, Thomas	c.1788
Linnell, John	–1796
Edwards and Roberts	c.1830

2

Ceramics and Glass

Identification

After furniture the collector turns, or should turn, to porcelain, pottery, and glass. Occasional tables and chests without colorful pieces of old china on their tops are unnaturally austere, while cabinets without contents are bare and strange. Fine porcelain or pottery is required for tableware. Vases are essential. And drinking is as much a heightened pleasure out of old glass as is the still possible collecting thereof.

For the identification and understanding of ceramics the only sure weapon is, again, an innate or long-developed instinct. This is indeed born in some people, but is usually acquired by handling articles and staring at them enviously in museums and the cabinets of more fortunate friends, and, of course, in antique shops and at the antiques fairs and exhibitions.

Then it is necessary to study and learn the various china marks, which will presently be described, and at the same time to appreciate certain rule-of-thumb methods of discrimination.

Thus the chief difference between new and old porcelain is simply that the new always looks younger, brighter, more metallic, more glazed. So far the fakers have found it impossible to counterfeit the mellow appearance that 150 to 200 years give to a baked lump of ceramic material.

But mere crackle or crazing is no guide to age because that *can* be counterfeited easily.

Faked articles deepen in color when left for some months in strong daylight, and they often end with a brownish, singed appearance.

It is easier to judge the age of porcelain than that of pottery (assuming that the collector knows—as he should—how to differentiate between the two, porcelain being fine and translucent, pottery being coarse and opaque).

Porcelains are divided into two main types, hard paste and soft paste. The hard-paste type is cold and can even be repellent to the touch; the soft-paste type is warmer and more sympathetic. But the finest hard paste is always more important than the best soft paste.

CHELSEA porcelain may be identified, early periods, by the fine soft paste and the "moons" or clear spots that may be seen in the body when it is viewed through a strong light, also by the triangle, red anchor, raised anchor, and gold marks (but no "mooning" in the gold anchor period and occasionally not in the red anchor). Indeed, the anchor is most traditionally the Chelsea mark, associated with the Thames, and is more elegantly depicted on Chelsea than on Bow, where also it appears. There are many kinds and colors of anchor. The raised anchor is the earliest type, being used till about 1754. Then came red and gold anchors, the last-named very common after 1760. An underglaze blue anchor is very rare.

But the value of Chelsea porcelain is not to be determined by the color of the anchor alone. Sometimes the best pieces are not marked at all. The triangle mark is found also, and a sort of trident with a "C" across the shaft. One of the earliest Chelsea marks is a triangle with the words "Chelsea 1745." Marks are not to be found under the bases of Chelsea figures but low down and inconspicuously on the backs. Beware of large, fine marks, probably forgeries.

Chelsea is regarded as the most important and finest English porcelain, particularly in figurework, that was strongly influenced by Meissen. The factory was certainly in existence by 1745, and it seems that silversmiths of French descent, notably Nicholas Sprimont, were at first responsible for the enterprise. After a considerable success the factory was sold in 1769, and in the following year it was resold to William Duesbury and John Heath of Derby. (But it seems it did not close finally till 1784.)

BOW porcelain is not as fine as Chelsea, the early paste being thick and heavy, yet soft enough to be too easily scratched. Later pieces were better.

An arrow, a dagger, and an anchor are the marks of Bow, not to mention a bow and arrow, an anchor and dagger, and an arrow stylized almost out of existence and consisting of a circle, a line, and a point. Then the large "B" will sometimes be found, and a small crescent in blue, and the "Tebo" mark, also a large variety of workmen's marks or modeler's initials (among which the most interesting are those "T's" or "T.F.'s," that may perhaps be ascribed to Thomas Frye, one of the founders of the factory). But the anchor, the dagger, and the stylized arrow starting out from the large "O" are the leading marks.

Thomas Frye and one Edward Heylin are generally regarded as the founders of the Bow factory, perhaps in 1744 (although no Bow porcelain has been specifically assigned to this early date). Tableware was the main product of the factory at first, but lively figures were produced later whose very lack of sophistication is their attraction. We know that porcelain with bone ash in the body was produced from about 1749. It was often decorated in relief, with Oriental influences. Bow sometimes gets the credit for the first use of transfer-printed decoration.

From about 1760 the quality of Bow declined greatly. The paste sometimes became quite gray. The figures lost their liveliness. Maybe the ubiquitous William Duesbury took over the factory in 1776 and removed the moulds and models to Derby.

DERBY is chiefly notable for nice use of gilding, vigorous modeling, and unashamed copying of contemporaries, and for marks that were at first variations on the letter "D." This mark was roughly scratched on the paste before 1769 and sometimes continued in the complete word "Derby." Then the "D" developed an arrowhead at the end of its stroke, signifying perhaps Chelsea-Derby after the presumed purchase of the Chelsea factory and its transfer to Derby in 1769, although it should be remembered that this could also apply to Duesbury's similar acquisition of Bow, which has its mark like an arrowhead. Others see the Chelsea-Derby combination as most generally represented by a "D" with an anchor running across it. There is another "D" accompanied by an anchor, the shaft of which is a dagger. Then a crown becomes the favored Derby mark, with various devices underneath: crossed lines, a cross with dots and a "D" (from 1780 to 1830), a cross with dots and a "DK" in monogram, mark of Duesbury and Kean used after 1795—many different variations, culminating in the monogram of two "D's" of modern Royal Crown Derby.

The Meissen mark is sometimes found on Derby; and yet another interesting mark is that of one of the owners, Robert Bloor, a rough crown containing daggers with below it the words "Derby Bloor."

We believe that porcelain was being made at Derby by 1750, although some authorities say 1745. Certainly William Duesbury was mentioned in 1756 as making "English china" at Derby in partnership with John Heath. The last-named went bankrupt about 1780 and Duesbury ran the firm alone till his death in 1786. Duesbury's namesake son William then conducted the enterprise until his own death in 1796, whereupon his partner, Michael Kean, usefully married his widow and continued the business for some years. A third William Duesbury was briefly in charge after that, with a partner, William Sheffield, following which Robert Bloor bought the factory. He went insane in 1827 and a James Thomason took over the management, later with a Thomas Clarke. The factory closed in 1848. It was reopened as the modern Royal Crown Derby Porcelain Company in 1877.

Derby, as we have said, was highly derivative, but there is no doubt that the best Derby figures, in particular, are among the finest ceramic productions of England. Painted decoration was always very good. The figures can be identified often by the fine gilding and by strange patches under the base, due to their having been placed on pads of clay in the kiln.

EARLY WORCESTER up till 1768 shows greenish when held up to the light. It looks somewhat opaque from a distance, not unlike fine pottery.

Marks on Worcester are so widely various that it would be misleading to single out a few as completely typical. But it can be said that the crescent "C," the crossed swords, the words "Flight" or "Flight and Barr" with crown, or stylistic variations on the letter "W" are more common imprints than others that range from Dresden wands of Aesculapius to square seals. Then there are a large number of workmen's marks. Note that the crescent outlined in blue is one of the earliest marks, used frequently down to 1793. The crown appeared after the King's visit in 1788, and was used till 1792.

The factory itself started in 1751 as the "Worcester Tonquin Manufacture," and several locally patriotic people were responsible, notably the famous Dr. Wall of the "period," and Richard and Josiah Holdship. Under Wall and his friends the factory produced its finest work, with underglaze blue, Oriental and Meissen influences, transfer-printing, and painted decoration by such masters as J. H. O'Neale and John Donaldson. In particular the transfer-printing was important, under the Staffordshire man Robert Hancock, who was chief engraver at Worcester for twenty years until 1772.

Dr. Wall himself died in 1776, but his excellent "period" is usually extended till 1783, when the factory was bought by Thomas Flight for his sons, Joseph and John. When Flight died the sons took Barr into partnership in 1792. Various combinations of the names Flight and Barr were used until 1840, when Robert Chamberlain's factory was amalgamated with the older company. The present Royal Worcester Porcelain Company, as such, dates from 1862.

Tableware was always a feature of old Worcester. Figures were rare. Decoration was outstandingly important, with nearly always a strong Oriental influence. "Japan" patterns were an early-nineteenth-century feature. The best of the decoration from the beginning was the figure and topographical painting.

NANTGARW would probably be placed by many people as next in the hierarchy of great British porcelains, not because of the size of the factory, which was very small and exceedingly short-lived, nor because of its antiquity (it was founded in 1813 and ended about 1822), but because it was the creation of a man of enormous talent—William Billingsley, whose life was such a typical and unhappy example of what happens in our society to artists who are first-rate in their work but not in their business affairs.

Billingsley's career as a decorator of porcelain started at the Derby factory. He evolved an exquisite touch as a flower painter, especially of roses. The "Billingsley rose" is almost a trademark for the loveliest in English porcelain. It will be found on the products of many factories, Derby, Pinxton, Worcester, Nantgarw, Swansea. Wherever he went, Billingsley tended to make other people's fortunes but never his own.

His great personal venture was Nantgarw in Glamorganshire, where he was partnered by Samuel Walker. Some superb pieces were made, now of great value, but after a year the partners had to move to Swansea and join forces there with Lewis Dillwyn's Cambrian Pottery Works. Billingsley's secret formula and his beautiful painting were his principal stock in trade, but availed naught to the unfortunate man himself, archetype of the truly great artist. He returned to Nantgarw in 1817 but could not make money, probably because his object was perfection and not the making of money.

Therefore Nantgarw today is greatly sought after for its beauty and inevitable scarcity. It is a glassy yet soft-paste porcelain that contains a large proportion of bone ash. The translucency of Nantgarw surpasses, in the opinion of many, the glassiness of Sèvres because it is more human. Billingsley achieved this extraordinary perfection by such purism that his kiln waste was often ninety per cent.

The glaze of Nantgarw is very thick, in spite of the glassiness, and lines of light appear in the body when it is viewed through strong light. Colors are soft and charming; and the superb rose is a frequent motif.

The leading mark speaks for itself, the rough capitals "NANT GARW," with "C. W." beneath, impressed into the paste. Probably the "C. W." stands for "China Works." There is a rare mark with the "Nantgarw" in longhand. Often the pieces are quite unmarked, but in the case of Nantgarw that does not matter at all, because there is no other porcelain to compare with it exactly.

PLYMOUTH is very similar in the canon of English porcelain to Nantgarw for rarity and desirability, although completely different in substance and appearance. It is the principal English hard paste porcelain, being the first such ever made in England, by William Cookworthy at Coxside, Plymouth, in 1768. The factory, being artistically unique, was financially unsound from the start, and had to move to Bristol in 1770. In 1773 Cookworthy gave up.

Some rare pieces bear the complete name "PLYMOUTH," with coat of arms and date of month and year. One piece actually has the inscription "Mr. W. Cookworthy's Factory Plymouth 1770." That was probably his last fling. But the most common mark on a porcelain that is often unmarked is the characteristic "2/4" sign, as if a 2 and a 4 are joined together, this frequently almost beyond recognition. Then a Bow arrow and circle mark is found, and something almost like a crossed-swords mark, and again a mark consisting of Roman and Arabic numerals.

But Plymouth is best identified by its cold, hard paste and often its resemblance to early white Meissen. Salt cellars and sauce boats ornamented with shells, coral, and seaweed are characteristic. Craftsmanship can be very poor, with some stains of smoke, and firecracks, specks, warping, and running. Yet Plymouth can be strangely attractive, and it is always rare.

China marks

COLEBROOKDALE and COALPORT are synonymous in porcelain, Coalport being in Cole-brookdale, Shropshire; and the most common mark is some monogrammatic combination of the initials "C.B.D." or "C.D." Note that an especially important mark is "C.S.N.," used for a while by Rose after he had acquired the Nantgarw and Swansea enterprises. Also the complete word "Coalport" in longhand has been found. Then an "S" scratched in the body ("Salopian" but not "Caughley") has been taken to apply to porcelain made at Coalport from the Nantgarw body of Billingsley. The marking of Coalport is further complicated by this factory's habit of copying Sèvres and Meissen and using the same Continental marks. Chelsea also was copied, complete with marks.

The factory was founded about 1796 by John Rose, who in 1799 acquired the works at Caughley (which had formerly employed him), and in 1820 secured Billingsley's recipes and molds by taking over Nantgarw. He died in 1841, and his nephew William continued the enterprise till 1862, after which it remained in various hands and was eventually transferred to Stoke-on-Trent.

Early Coalport has an excellent soft-paste body with a good glaze, but has no great individuality. The masterpieces of the factory were its nineteenth-century copies of Sèvres, Meissen, and Chelsea, and in particular some of its superb encrusted wear in the form of vases and inkstands. At one period a French craftsman was employed at Coalport whose floral encrusted wear has few peers in the history of ceramic art.

CAUGHLEY was a very early factory, established in Shropshire in the 1750's, but it did not make porcelain until it was taken over by Thomas Turner in 1772. In 1799 Turner was himself taken over by his former employee John Rose, who used the factory for the making of biscuit porcelain, and gradually ran it down till it was transferred in 1814 to Coalport.

On Caughley porcelain the world "Salopian" is sometimes impressed, but there are inevitably many other marks, such as the letter "S" in blue, the letter "S" with crossed daggers underneath, and a series of elaborate Arabic numerals. Sometimes there is the letter "C" and sometimes a crescent.

The chief claim to fame of Caughley is that it initiated the famous "Willow" and "Blue Dragon" patterns. Apart from that, it is traditionally difficult to distinguish between Caughley and Worcester porcelain in blue (especially where the mark is a Worcester crescent), although true Worcester tends to have a darker blue than Caughley, which is more cobalt. Caughley porcelain is thus mainly blue and white and Oriental.

LONGTON HALL is another strange little collectors' piece among English porcelains. It was very early, started by one William Littler about 1746, and it lasted only until 1760, if then. Its productions fell into two periods, of which the first was characterized by a crude and heavy soft-paste with frequent moons and an uneven surface and a tendency towards the making of dishes in the form of leaves. The second period was altogether finer, with figures that sometimes approached Chelsea in distinction. These, however, are rare; and Longton Hall is usually thought of in terms of leaf dishes and the use of a strong cobalt blue in an uneven underglaze wash.

The principal mark resembles two letters "L," one inverted, the upstrokes crossed. Often there are three dots underneath. Then faked Chelsea marks were used, as well as a large "A" with down-pointing crossbar.

BRISTOL was the second main maker of English hard-paste, even harder than that of Plymouth, but equally distorted and fundamentally ill-made, with the festoon as a much-favored decorative device. Tableware was the speciality, but some figures were made.

The factory started about 1749 for the purpose of making soft-paste porcelain, of which sauceboats with soaprock (steatite) in the paste are the principal survivors. But this was transferred to Worcester in 1752; and Bristol achieved nothing more until the acquisition in 1770 of William Cookworthy's Plymouth enterprise. Cookworthy withdrew in 1772, and Richard Champion continued making the hard-paste until 1782.

A cross in various crude shapes is the leading Bristol mark. Sometimes it is accompanied by a date or a number. Also one finds Meissen-type crossed swords, and a large "B," and the much-discussed "T°" or "Tebo" device, and then there are instances of the word "BRISTOL" in full and also in shadow letters. Pieces of the period when Plymouth was being transferred to Bristol have the rare combination of the Plymouth "2/4" and the Bristol cross mark.

SWANSEA porcelain started in 1814 when Billingsley joined forces with Lewis Dillwyn at the Cambrian Pottery Works. The joint venture failed in the business sense. Billingsley stayed only three years, and the porcelain was made only until 1823. First it was essentially Billingsley's glasslike body, then came a more stable body, the "duck egg" paste, and finally Swansea porcelain was harder and whiter, with more soaprock. Early Swansea is rare and important. The later product is not so favored. Tableware, and particularly plates, was the speciality. The connoisseur looks for the painted decoration of Thomas Baxter, Thomas Pardoe, and William Young. Either a trident or two tridents crossed are the best marks, especially as found on the early glasslike porcelain. But the more common imprints are the words "SWANSEA" with "DILLWYN & CO." or "BEVINGTON & CO." Some specimens of 1814–1816 have the mark "SWANSEA" over "NANTGARW." The general mark "SWANSEA" is either impressed or stenciled in red, blue, gold, black and yellow.

ROCKINGHAM is essentially a nineteenth-century porcelain and does not properly belong to this section. The Rockingham Works were established as early as the 1740's under the patronage of Earl Fitzwilliam, Marquis of Rockingham, but made only pottery until about 1820. Then, under the Bramelds, was begun the manufacture of some of the nicest bone china, which continued until 1842. It was based on a clear white paste with a good glaze, and especially in a very clean green color and a rich plum, both with lavish gilding, looked most attractive as tableware. There was a time, not so long ago, when every ambitious antique dealer of the English provinces had such a table set in his window, and it could be bought for the price of a fur coat. Model cottages and castles (pastille burners) were another Rockingham feature.

The Rockingham mark is usually a Fitzwilliam griffin with the words "Rockingham Works, Brameld." Other marks are "Brameld," alone or in a flowery oval and with an "X" dotted, or the griffin with words such as "Royal Rock Works, Brameld."

NEW HALL is the third of the hard-paste porcelains but not so important as the others. It was about 1781 that some Staffordshire people founded the factory and tried to make hard-paste according to the formula that Champion had got from Cookworthy. After 1810 the product was mainly bone china. The true early New Hall is more a curiosity than anything else, decorated in the Chinese manner with overmuch painting and gilding. The chief mark on this early hard-paste was a cursive capital letter "N" with a number. The later bone china had the words "New Hall" in a double circle.

MINTON, founded by Thomas Minton in 1796, made some unimportant soft-paste porcelain in its early days, but it was not until about 1825 that the factory produced fine porcelain in any quantity, and its greatest products, such as the crusted ware and the famous *pâte-sur-pâte* of Marc-Louis Solon, belong to the Victorian rather than the antique periods. Marks were principally the letter "M," a strange device like that of Sèvres, and the name "Minton."

PINXTON was made at a small factory on the estate of John Coke at Pinxton in Derbyshire from 1796 to 1812. Billingsley was once again the instigator of this enterprise, and while he was there some very choice soft-paste vases and table ware were produced, in the style of Derby with the large-headed arrow as a mark but it is now exceedingly rare. The later products were inferior.

LOWESTOFT was until comparatively recently a strange name applied to porcelain made in China for the European market. Then we learned that there was a porcelain factory at Lowestoft in Suffolk from 1757, and until about 1800 it produced much china that was very similar to Bow, with a paste containing bone ash and much underglaze blue decoration and Oriental influence. The production included small articles and replicas to be sold to visitors as souvenirs with some such inscription as "A Trifle from Lowestoft," and this factory may have the credit for founding that particular industry. So far we have not seen a definite Lowestoft mark as such, but the marks of many other factories were, as usual, quite shamelessly used.

The city of Liverpool has throughout its history had as many small potteries as it has lately had pop groups, and without a doubt much unidentifiable old porcelain originated there. But the only factory so far pinned down is that of Richard Chaffers, which might have operated about 1756 to 1765. His porcelain is like early Worcester. It contains much soaprock and usually has Oriental decorations.

DAVENPORT is the name given to porcelain made by John Davenport at Longport. He started in 1793 but his principal production belongs to the first half of the nineteenth century, what was known as good quality "stone china." The marks were the word "Davenport" with sometimes "Longport," together with an anchor or a crown (after 1830 when many services were made for royalty). The factory lasted till 1822.

Pottery

A vast amount of pottery has been made from the earliest times, and it is the most enduring artefact of man. The two main kinds are earthenware and stoneware. Earthenware is unvitrified pottery, that is to say baked clay that is too porous to use in its biscuit state and requires glaze. There are various names for it according to the type of surface and decoration, names such as slipware, creamware, delft, faience, majolica. Stonewear is pottery that has been fused really hard, almost to the stage of porcelain (indeed the Chinese regard some ringing stoneware as porcelain).

English pottery that is available for collection still and that is worth collecting comes down to us from certain great makers of the eighteenth and nineteenth centuries up till about 1850, and after that the principal interest is in cottage pieces of the fairground variety and in the specialized products of a few rather precious artist-potters.

One of the most important early names is that of RALPH WOOD. He popularized the toby jug, which should have hollow legs and feet to be genuine, and which should not have lost the hat and pipe to be really valuable. Ralph Wood I worked from 1750 to 1770 and made some very fine figures in his time. The business was continued until about 1800 by his son, Ralph II, and his grandson, Ralph III.

THOMAS WHIELDON similarly worked in the eighteenth century to produce excellent figures. He started his factory in 1740 in Staffordshire and retired with a fortune around 1780. His agateware was particularly notable, being pottery in which clays of different colors were kneaded together in imitation of veined agate.

Perhaps the greatest English potters of all were the WEDGWOODS. Their work was always characterized by an individuality that placed it outside many of the classifications. It rarely appears "antique," and many of the eighteenth-century productions of Josiah Wedgwood's great factory at Etruria appear today to be so modern that they do not fit into any category. The family as potters goes back to the early seventeenth century, but Josiah I lived from 1730 to 1795. His first great commercial success was creamware, a beautiful cream-colored earthenware, so well made and cleverly exploited that large quantities were exported, to the great detriment of the European manufacture of faience, which it supplanted.

Wedgwood also achieved fame with, and made money from, his jasperware, cameos, medallions, plaques, and vases in stoneware containing barium sulphate. The body is slightly translucent, and Wedgwood learned how to stain it integrally with colors such as blues and greens, but particularly the impressive black. Note that "dipped" jasperware is less valuable than the "jasper solid" as it is called. "Jasper dip" is colored on the surface only.

WEDGWOOD "basalt" was another great success, and should not be confused with the jasper. It was and is a black stoneware, better than that of Elers (which will be mentioned shortly). Such ware without the Wedgwood mark would have been made by one of the many potters who copied the process.

Wedgwood was the most typical product of the eighteenth-century classical revival. His work was almost entirely pastiche of ancient Greek, Etruscan, and Roman art. His famous jasperware copy of the cameo glass Portland Vase took him three years to perfect. It is a masterpiece of English potting, but is not unique, as many copies were subsequently produced.

Wedgwood's partnership with Thomas Bentley from 1769 to 1780 was the great period of the business. Etruria sadly declined under Josiah Wedgwood II, but was built on such firm foundations that it rose again and again. The Wedgwood pottery today is still among the most important in the world.

The mark is usually "Wedgwood." The period of Wedgwood and Bentley is sometimes indicated by the mark "W. & B." When "Josiah" is added to the "Wedgwood" it indicates that the piece was made in the inferior period of Josiah II.

ELERS, the name already mentioned, applies to the very early work of the Dutch brothers David and John Elers, who came to London and were making red stoneware there by 1690. From 1693 until about 1698 they produced the same kind of rather dull but historically interesting pottery in Staffordshire.

ASTBURY is another name in Staffordshire pottery that has at least academic importance. Modern collectors will be unlikely to acquire attributable examples of Astbury red- and whiteware, but this earthenware with relief decoration in white clay, and the improved Astbury flint whiteware had considerable influence on the eighteenth-century craft. John and Thomas Astbury were brothers who worked together. John died in 1743. His son, Thomas II, established a pottery of his own at Fenton in 1725.

Perhaps the most typical Staffordshire family in the history of English pottery was ADAMS, starting with William Adams I (1746–1805). His jasperware strongly competed with that of Wedgwood, as did his cream earthenware and his blue-printed earthenware. He was at Burslem from about 1770, then transferred to Tunstall in 1780.

WILLIAMS ADAMS II (1748–1831), was at Cobridge and Burslem. He produced a great deal of earthenware and, in his latter days, some porcelain.

William Adams III was initially in partnership with his father-in-law at Burslem, then moved in 1804 to Stoke and set up on his own, making earthenware and stoneware, also PARIAN statuary. Parian is the name given to an unglazed, vitrified porcelain with the superficial appearance of the marble found on Paros. Some bone china was made by William Adams III (1772–1829), whose many sons carried on the pottery till 1864.

PRATT is the name of a Staffordshire family who made much pottery throughout the nineteenth century, but is chiefly associated with the unmistakable work of that Felix Pratt of Lane Delph who made the jugs that were decorated with bearded faces.

Many, many individual names occur in the salty history of English pottery, although few of them have high importance. A name such as that of JAMES NEALE is worth recording mainly for the sake of the toby jugs he made at Hanley from 1776 to 1800 (also cream and other imitations of Wedgwood wares).

JOHN DWIGHT was a seventeenth century London potter who made a translucent stoneware that was near porcelain in appearance. A few surviving busts and figures are so good that it has been wondered if they were made by Grinling Gibbons, the sculptor. Maybe the work of Dwight eventually made possible that of JOHN DOULTON (1793–1872) whose stoneware, particularly relief-decorated and/or salt-glazed, was highly ornamental, and eventually reached the apex of pottery in that characteristic English contribution, the lavatory. An Indian once remarked that in his country the sanitary fittings of English manufacture were regarded as of outstanding aesthetic importance. So it may be that some of the less idiosyncratic potters will not have lived in vain after all.

BOURNE stoneware and brown-salt-glazed ware in particular was first made in Derbyshire about 1812, and again a firm of the name is still in existence.

But the collector of pottery is more likely to go for types than names. He will acquire beautiful English spirit jars without specifically looking for those that were chiefly made by ROCKINGHAM. His principal interest will be the colorful beauty of each individual piece, and the presence if possible of the original tap and cap. His English delftware will not necessarily be identifiable as seventeenth-century Bristol. It will just be nice old tin-enameled earthenware with a similarity in decoration to the genuine Dutch delft. His luster or resist ware will be chosen for its availability rather than its exact source of origin (the silver and gold resist from Wales, the pink from Sunderland, all based on the much more valuable but, to the English mind, less pleasing original Hispano-Moresque ware).

Nor will the collector of those charming old frog mugs, with the once-disturbing model of a frog inside, necessarily ascribe their origin to the potteries at Sunderland that originally made them (or the other frog potters at Leeds and Nottingham); and Leeds creamware, especially with the nice pierced work, will not necessarily be connected with the Green brothers, who started at Leeds about 1760 and their successors Humble, Green & Co., about 1770 to 1800, and Hartley, Greens & Co., about 1800 onwards.

Liverpool pottery was too multifarious to be pinned down as a type; Nottingham was similarly all-embracing, although that center did have the speciality of owl and bear jugs and a brown, salt-glazed stoneware that can be identified because it has an unusual metallic gleam. Similarly, crich or crouch ware is a salt-glazed stoneware that may have been made at Crich in Derbyshire (and salt-glaze is a fine skin or glaze on pottery that is effected by throwing salt into the kiln when the maximum temperature is reached so that one of the component parts, sodium, combines with the silica in the ware to form the glassy protection).

Collectors of "Fair Hebe" jugs should, of course, be aware that they were made by John Voyez, a modeler, who worked from 1767 to 1790 both on his own account and with Ralph Wood and Wedgwood. Similarly the lover of sturdy and colorful ironstone china will know about the Masons of Lane Delph and Ridgway of Hanley in the potteries who chiefly made it, but at the same time might not understand that this opaque stoneware was first developed by Spode at the beginning of the nineteenth century.

And those who collect apothecary jars, chiefly in blue and white, must be content if they are wise with the knowledge that if the articles are squat and tin-enameled they can be important and very early, but otherwise date from the middle of the seventeenth century and are usually much younger than that.

BELLARMINE is the name given to a type of jug with narrow neck bearing a bearded mask, also a large belly, important if made at Fulham in the second half of the seventeenth century, but usually from Germany or Holland.

And blue dash chargers are tin-enameled circular dishes with blue dashes round the rim, dating from about 1650 to 1750.

Staffordshire Figures

So the catalogue could continue, becoming more and more esoteric and less valuable to the person who wants to acquire antiques and not just study them in museums. Perhaps it would be kinder to end this section on ceramics with a brief note about cottage chimney ornaments, and particularly the Staffordshire figures that have become so popular and increasingly valuable in the years since they were made wholesale for the fairground delectation of the "laboring classes."

Chimney ornaments may be recognized by their practical flatness. They had to stand upright on the chimneypiece and could not bulge much. Some of them were made, particularly in Wales, to commemorate marriages, births, and deaths. Some were just flat pieces of pottery with religious or wisecracking inscriptions.

The Staffordshire figures as such were in the round as well as flat, and early examples, of the eighteenth and early nineteenth century, can be fine as well as rare, but Victorian examples are the best target for the modern collector.

These Victorian figures are distinguishable by their whiter clay and glaze. Their parts were molded rather than handmade, and their coloring was rich, particularly the underglaze blues. They started to flood the market during 1840–1845 to take advantage of the public interest in the young Queen Victoria's wedding; and thereafter the manufacturers were most prolific on similar royal occasions, also at the time of wars such as the Crimean. It is thus possible to date figures by historical references, the young Queen to 1840–1845, portraits of such generals as Havelock to the Indian Mutiny of 1857, of famous criminals to the time of their notoriety, such as the Mannings and Rush to 1849. Note that underglaze blue was rarely used after 1870 and that the art began to die out about 1880. Figures made after that, and today, are essentially modern in appearance.

Although dozens of small potteries in Staffordshire and some in Scotland, as at Musselburgh, made these figures it is possible definitely to attribute specific subjects to only two, Sampson Smith and Lancaster. Academic collectors do, however, recognize another two potters without known name who produced some of the best early figures, nearly all with round backs and often near to Rockingham pottery in technical excellence.

Sampson Smith worked at Longton from about 1846 to 1878. In 1948 some sixty of his old press molds were found, definitely identifying as his many popular figures such as those of Wellington, Napoleon, Dick Turpin, Tom King, Moody, and Burns with Highland Mary. To find a marked Sampson Smith or Lancaster figure would be very fortunate, as only a few such are in existence now.

These figures were originally sold for a few shillings. One type was offered wholesale at 7½d each. They have been sold in our time for prices ranging from three dollars upward, and before long they will probably cost from $175 to $250, if not more, for the finer specimens.

Glass

Glass is usually defined as a hard, lustrous but brittle substance, normally transparent, made by fusing sand with soda or potash or both or other similar ingredients. Glassmaking dates back to 2500 B.C. in Egypt and the Middle East. The Romans generally made good glass, and their art was revived in twelfth- and thirteenth-century Venice, from which Giacomo Verzelini and associated craftsmen came to England in 1571 and were granted a license by Queen Elizabeth "to make drinking glasses in the manner of Murano, on the undertaking that he bring up in the said art and knowledge our natural subjects."

For twenty years Verzelini and his friends made their fine glass in London and taught the natives. One of these, Sir Robert Mansell, was a superior businessman, and, acquiring the monopoly in 1618, created a considerable industry, particularly in the making of mirrors and wine bottles. In 1675 the great English glassmaker, George Ravenscroft, developed with the use of lead what became known as "flint glass," more durable than the Venetian type but capable of being blown as thin, also brilliant and rich and, most important of all, sufficiently soft to allow deep cutting. During the seventeenth century, glass houses were established all over the country, particularly in London, Stourbridge, Bristol, Birmingham, and Newcastle upon Tyne.

The finest English glass for collectors was made during the eighteenth century; and in 1784 one John Hill went from Stourbridge with more than fifty craftsmen to Waterford in southern Ireland, where he improved the Penrose Brothers' Glass-house and produced a great deal of excellent, especially cut glassware. The factory continued till 1851.

Venetian glass can be identified by its thin, fragile and almost papery quality, the frequent use of color in it, and the fantastic forms—*cristallo, latticino, aventurine, millefiori.*

A typical Verzelini goblet of the early English period is fragile like Venetian, but sturdy and elegant in shape like a church chalice and decorated with delicate engraving.

The great English drinking glasses of the eighteenth century, and their nineteenth-century copies, may be identified by the lustrous and sturdy yet comparatively soft "flint" body, by the mainly cone-shaped bowls, and by the always self-confident round feet.

The earlier English glasses have capacious bowls and short stems; and the evolution is gradually towards narrower bowls and longer, more complicated stems, with balusters, knops, and enclosed "tears" often from 1680 to 1725, though surviving after, air-twist stems from about 1730, opaque-twist stems during 1730–1740, then color-twist stems. Cut and faceted types continue from around 1745. Hollow diamond patterns were used until around 1770, after which fluted patterns lasted till, in the early nineteenth century, prismatic cutting and raised diamond patterns were developed.

As it may be difficult now to collect the fine early drinking glasses, mirrors, and chandeliers that were formerly so eagerly sought after by connoisseurs, a few words should be said about certain curiosities of early and nineteenth-century glass that can still be found at tolerable prices.

Jelly glasses are not unlike early drinking glasses, often still available in sets of as many as a half dozen. In the seventeenth century they were small and plain with straight-sided, conical bowls, low down on a plain or folded foot. After 1710 or thereabouts the fashion changed and the bowl became bell-shaped, often on domed feet and with double, swan-necked handles on each side. This exuberance was, however, squashed by the Glass Excise Act of 1745, that temporarily enforced a primitive austerity of design again. Later in the eighteenth century came vertical and alternately hollowed fluting on jelly glasses, and the type known as "Hogarth" with the flared mouth.

Then finger bowls can still be collected, and make an interesting subject in themselves.

They were originally called "water glasses," and some authorities maintain that their early use was for rinsing the mouth after a meal. Certainly the earliest sixteenth-century examples are tall and thin like modern tumblers. But by the second half of the eighteenth century these bowls were called "wash-hand," then "finger-glasses." They became broad and shallow, and often had covers known as "plates," these with knop finials. Sets of this period in flint glass, plain but sometimes lightly cut, are often offered still in up to half dozens. The most attractive nineteenth-century specimens are in color, ranging from the blue "Bristol" type to green, ruby, amethyst, and the distinctive *famille-rose* enamel on opaque glass.

"Yards-of-ale" are similarly collectable still—and highly decorative if hung on walls where they can catch the light. They are mentioned by the diarist Evelyn in the seventeenth century as being of flint glass, literally a yard in length, and used for the drinking of very ceremonial toasts on military and royal occasions.

They originally held about a pint of ale and had feet. Sometimes there was a bulb at the end to trick the drinker, who towards the end of his long potation found the rest of the beer to be squirting into his face as a result of a rush of air into the bulb.

Many "Yards-of-ale" were made shorter than a yard. Some of them had two bulbs, while others had fluted or acorn-shaped bulbs.

Towards the end of the seventeenth century East Indian traders brought back the custom of mixing drinks in one big bowl, the monteith, that was usually of silver with a scalloped and removable rim to take the glasses. Thus the punchbowl began. It is not always identified as such or understood, and could still be collected.

Some were made of very fine flint glass, large with short stems, domed feet, and various decoration. Usually the combination of short feet and cut or engraved decorations indicates late eighteenth-century origin.

Then the appurtenances to punchbowls are similarly worth collecting, notably the toddy lifters, or ladles. These were originally genuine ladles in shape and as such are very rare. The term was later applied to a most unusual device from Scotland, the toddy lifter in the form of a miniature decanter. It has a hole in the base, and when it is dipped into a punchbowl liquid rises through the hole. A thumb on the top of the lifter creates a vacuum so that the device can be removed and a glass filled by placing the bottom hole over it and removing thumb from the top. Often a collar encircles the neck of the lifter, to steady the hand.

Or a collection could be made of glass bells, available in many sizes, shapes, and colors. They can be charmingly rung, and vary from toy size to the most favored handbells of the Victorian period. (Once in Sweden a bell was cast in glass seven feet in diameter, and its sound was uniquely pure and sonorous.) Nailsea bells both in plain colors and enameled on an opaque ground may well be regarded as important collectors' pieces in the future.

Nailsea itself was a glass house near Bristol, founded in 1788 by John R. Lucas. At first bottle glass was made, then, from about 1815, various kinds of colored glass and *latticino* or color-twist, a revival of the Venetian process of making a stick of glass look like a piece of variegated sugar candy. Nailsea thus became famous for its "friggers," the popular name given to improbable objects made of colored and *latticino* glass, varying from tobacco pipes to marbles, and from walking sticks to ships, riding crops, bellows, rolling pins. In spite of the popularity of these products the actual process was still expensive and in 1873 the Nailsea Glass-house went bankrupt, so one can certainly expect very high prices for "Nailsea toys" in the not too distant future.

3

Silver and Jewelry

Silver

This is at once the lazy man's subject and the most abstruse. It is the first because the system of marks on silver is such that a knowledge of the system, or access to the tables, enables the collector to identify and appraise pieces without the very specialized knowledge and experience that is required by, say, the collector of old furniture and even the collector of porcelain. Study the marks on a piece of silver and at once not only its exact date may be known but also its place of origin and the importance of its maker. Nothing like that is possible with any other kind of collected article from the past, not even with the nearest best thing, coins.

But the subject is very abstruse just because of that marking system, which contains curious and sometimes fatal snags, and by the complacent frame of mind it induces in the connoisseur, who tends to lean upon the marks and not develop the flair for identification and appreciation that is such a powerful weapon in other fields.

However, in this book it is not necessary to discourse at length upon the various schools and periods of silver as with furniture, ceramics and other departments. The marks will soon lead the collector to a rough acquaintance with the elaborate design of English silver before the eighteenth century—and to the quick discovery that such silver is far beyond his reach now that it has nearly all been locked away save for occasional appearances in the salerooms at millionaire's prices. He will use the marks, moreover, to identify the fine plainness of the eighteenth-century variety that is still available though at prices that mount each day, and then the increasing fussiness of the nineteenth-century tableware, tea sets, cruets, and ornaments that must, probably, be the principal harvest of his searching.

Let us look briefly then at the whole subject of silver marking, which began roughly by statute in 1300, though not enforced until 1363 in the provinces. So the purity of silver exposed for sale has been the concern of the state in England since the thirteenth century, and only a very few pieces survive of the pre-mark period, mostly spoons, understandably of impure metal. Nevertheless the marks were for a long while quite inadequate. Date letters were not used till about 1478. Initials of makers appear before the end of the fifteenth century but not always, and properly not till 1739.

The marks were, of course, initiated to prevent fraud and indicate quality, *not* to provide modern collectors with information. Therefore they can sometimes seem strange and illogical.

The principal marks are the leopard's head, the maker's mark, the date letter, the lion passant, the lion's head erased and Britannia, and the sovereign's head.

The leopard's head is the proper London hallmark, sometimes a lion's head, with crown. But there was no crown until 1719 when the mark was shifted in position to replace the figure of Britannia and at the same time a lion passant appeared in another column. This period is very confusing. In 1821 the crown, mane, and head were omitted altogether to reappear next year and since with an ever increasing resemblance to a cat's head.

The lion passant mark is a guarantee that silver made in England is of stérling standard, 925 parts fine.

The date letter, changed each May, runs in twenty-year cycles, A to U or V, excluding J; and it will soon be noticed that the shape and "case" of the letter (capital or small letter) as well as the shape of the shield in which it and the other marks are enclosed are changed also. As an example, the capital S is 1733–1734 if enclosed in a shield with a point at a foot, but, confusingly, 1814–1815 if rather larger and enclosed in a shield that has a little point at the foot but the top corners beveled off. The earliest known letter in the Goldsmiths' Minutes is the Lombardic "B."

The shape of the shield or "punch" around the lion-passant sign and its periodic changes is a useful way of checking the accuracy or honesty of the date letter. Forgeries may be rare because of the very heavy penalties but naturally do occur throughout the ages. Be especially careful of "Britannia" marked plate with date letter obliterated. The marks of the high "Britannia" standard have indeed tended to erase too easily. The "lion's head erased and Britannia" was used 1696–1697, instead of the "leopard's head and lion," until June 1, 1720.

As the lion passant denotes sterling silver and the leopard's head indicates that the silver was made in London, so the sovereign's head is the "duty mark." This is found on all but very small silver articles made between December 1, 1784, and April 30, 1890, when the duty ceased to be levied. It is a profile of the reigning monarch's head. The head of George II from 1784 until 1786 was intaglio instead of the usual cameo; 1784 plate is found both with and without the sovereign's head according to whether it was made before or after December 1.

The maker's mark was originally the trade emblem of the maker. From 1696 until 1739 it was the first two letters of the maker's surname. Since 1739 it has consisted of the initials of the Christian and surnames.

That is *London* silver.

The provincial marks are different, and first it is necessary to identify the place by the mint mark. We have seen that the leopard's head means London.

An assay office was established at *York* in 1483, but York silver was marked as early as 1411. The first city mark was an involved combination of half a leopard's head and half a fleur de lis. Half a rose was used later. The assay office was close in 1698 for three years, after which we have the modern York mark of a cross containing five lions passant. This is the arms of the city of York. To this were added a lion's head erased and the figure of Britannia for quality. In 1717 the practice of assaying plate at York was discontinued, and it not resumed till some fifty years later, with little more work of importance done by local silversmiths. York is essentially museum and/or millionaire's silver, being fine and important but early. If someone points to a piece of York silver on the sideboard he is most likely mistaken if not an active liar.

The English provincial silver chiefly available to ordinary collectors without benefit of millions is *Sheffield* and *Birmingham*. It is often fine but rarely important. It is the product of the in-

(Courtesy of Asprey & Co., Ltd., Bond St., London, W.1.)
An example of really fine early English silver: a Charles II Tankard made by E. Mangy at Hull about 1685. Weight 23.55 oz., and engraved with contemporary arms and inscription.

dustrial revolution and as such was more or less mass-produced for the popular market in the nineteenth century. The assay offices at Sheffield and Birmingham were both established only in 1773. A crown has always been the Sheffield mark, whereas Birmingham, most unsuitably, is represented by an anchor.

The other English provincial mints are in the history of silver like York in that they made rare objects of beauty and value in the olden days but ceased to be productive in the machine age. *Newcastle* had an important mint as long ago as the thirteenth century, but the assay office there was finally closed in 1884. Great London and mass-producing Sheffield and Birmingham had finally prevailed. The first Newcastle mark was suitably a castle, superseded about 1672 by three castles.

The great period of *Exeter* was the seventeenth century. The first mark was an "X," but the assay office was not opened until 1701, and prior to that the silversmiths struck their own marks in many forms but mostly involving an "X" and a castle. The official mark became a triple-towered castle with the opening of the office, which was closed in 1882.

Norwich silver dates from 1423 approximately until only 1697. The first mark was a tower over a lion passant. From 1624 this was replaced by a crowned rose.

Chester had three wheat sheaves with a sword from 1686 until 1701. Thence till 1780 the mark was a mixture of three lions and three wheat sheaves. After 1780 the original mark was restored, in a plainer shield.

Many other provincial centers made silver, particularly in the early days, and often the local smiths were permitted to use and apply themselves what amounted to a town mark, usually based on the municipal coat-of-arms. *Bristol,* for example, never had an assay office according to the records, but pieces of silver have been found with the town mark of a ship and a castellated tower. *Carlisle* used a cross with a crinkled circle imposed on it. *Gateshead* suitably had a goat's head. *Hull* flaunted a large "H," and also a mark consisting of three crowns. *King's Lynn* had three impaling crosses or daggers. *Leeds* struck between 1650 and 1702 a mark showing a suspended sheep, significant of the wool trade. *Lincoln,* between 1560 and 1706, showed various forms of a fleur de lis. *Taunton* in the fifty years 1640–1690 perpetrated a pun, a large "T" impaling a barrel or tun.

Scottish silver has marks that are essentially different in idea, object, and history from those of England. First, it should be understood that Scottish silversmiths were never subject to the same outside control of their craft as their English colleagues. Second, Scottish silver tends to partake more of Continental than English influence. Third, Edinburgh has the oldest records, dating from medieval times, and has always produced far more than the other centers. Fourth, marks in Scotland were first used to deter goldsmiths from mixing alloy with gold and silver entrusted to them by customers for working. (The original penalty for so defrauding the customer was, fairly enough, death!)

The year 1457 is usually assigned for the first silver marks in Scotland, and they were originally those of the "deacon" or town official and of the working smith. In 1485 the "town mark" or hall mark was adopted, being in the case of *Edinburgh* the triple-towered castle, which, in various forms, has been used down to the present day. In 1681 the date letter was first used, thereafter to be changed annually in September. The deacon's mark was abolished the same year and replaced by the Assay Master's mark, consisting of the initials of the assayer in monogram script at first, then in Roman capitals. This was used until 1759, when a thistle emblem was substituted. In 1784 a duty mark was added, consisting of a sovereign's head (indicating that duty had been paid to the Sassenach), and this was used up to 1890.

The first *Glasgow* mark is usually assigned to 1681, and the town mark used was the burgh arms of "a fish, bell and tree," sometimes including the letter "G." The date letter is used between 1681 and 1710, after which it was not regularly used again till 1819. The letter "S," often used between 1730 and 1800, may possibly stand for "sterling." Complete marks were not used in Glasgow until 1819, when an Assay Office was established there, prescribing use of (1) the lion rampant, (2) the city arms, (3) the maker's mark, (4) the date letter, and (5) the sovereign's head. If the figure of Britannia is added to the above marks it means that the silver is above standard in weight.

The principal Irish silver is *Dublin,* and its tradition goes back a long way, at least till the thirteenth century. But marks cannot be found earlier than 1638 to make an adequate table, although they did begin formally in 1605, when the Dublin City Council decreed that all makers should strike their mark and three others, the lion, harp, and castle. Dublin marks are indeed distinguished by a predictable Irish variability. The harp crowned, in particular, has many shapes, while the date letter is often difficult to follow and sometimes omitted. The figure of Hibernia, starting in 1731, indicates payment of a tillage tax, and itself suffered many changes. The sovereign's head was used from 1807 until 1890.

So Dublin's marks are extremely interesting, and afford considerable scope to the inquiring antiquary, but also, unfortunately, to the designing forger. It should be noted that Irish plate dated prior 1720 is so rare as almost to be nonexistent from the collector's point of view, also that Irish silver can often be recognized by the expert at once, thanks to its Celtic flavor. Spoons and the pouring lips of jugs, for example, tend to be shaped to a point like a bird's beak.

Before completing this section on marks it might be as well to move a little forward from the antique period and say something specifically about the marks on nineteenth-century silver. This is unfortunately the only London silver still available at prices within the purse of the non-rich man.

Note that the crown disappeared from the leopard's head in 1821–1822, and the containing shield was brought to a point at the base. Very slight changes were made in the leopard's head mark thereafter in the century, but in 1896 the shape of the shield was changed at the top; and in 1916—what things England can do during a war!—the whole order of the marks was changed, with the lion passant first, the leopard's head second, and the date letter third.

The date letter from 1816 to 1835 was in Roman small letters; from 1835 to 1855 black-letter capitals; from 1856 to 1875 small black letters; 1876 to 1895 Roman capitals; 1896 to 1915 Roman small; and 1916 black-letter small.

Then the shield of the lion passant becomes smaller and the lion no longer turns its head towards the reader from 1821–1822. In 1896 the shield becomes convected (or fluted) top and bottom. And of the sovereign's head, found on London silver from 1784 to 1890, it should be noted that Victoria's head looks to the left whereas that of previous monarch's looked to the right (politicians please note).

And some words might usefully be said in this section about the identification of coats-of-arms on silver. Often families had their escutcheons stamped on plate (as also on porcelain

OLD SILVER MARKS (LONDON)

Silver marks.

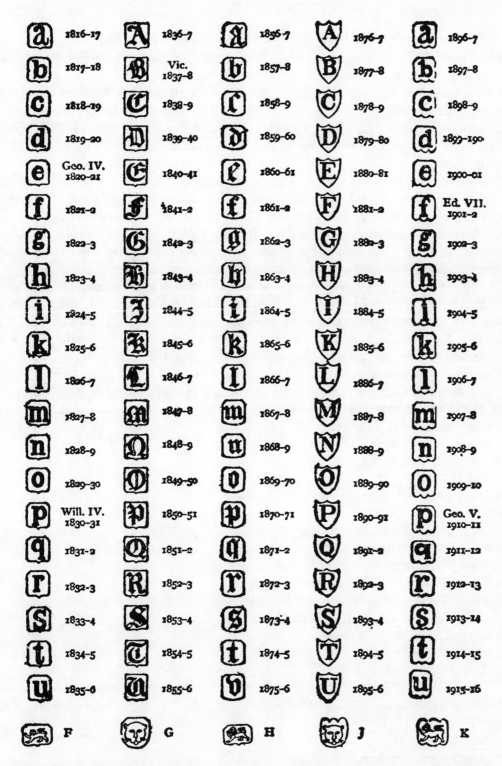

Figs. A and B used 1697 to 1720; Figs C and D used 1720 to 1756;
Figs. E and F used 1756 to 1784; Figs. E and F used 1784 to 1821;
Figs. G and H used 1821 to 1890; Figs. G and H used 1890 to 1896;
Figs J and K used 1896, etc.

and pottery) and if a piece can be identified as originally belong to a certain famous family then it should have enhanced value.

First it should be observed that the shields containing the armorial bearings varied in style during the different periods. From about 1635 until the Cromwellian period the most popular shape was square-topped with laurel wreath surround. Then during the seventeenth century much use was made of helmeted escutcheons, which, towards the end of the century were increasingly ornate.

A feathered ornament on the escutcheons is typical of Charles II silver; and embossed-scroll cartouches appear towards the end of the seventeenth century, leading to the eighteenth-century rococo period of elaborate and beautiful shields in lopsided scrollwork.

Considerable use was made in the eighteenth century of three-pointed tops to Gothic-style, heart-shaped escutcheons; and at the end of that century first appears the shield in square shape with splayed sides. Very florid cartouches after that signify the Victorian period.

So much for the periods. As regards the actual families it is necessary to examine the charges in the coats-of arms. A charge in heraldry is anything capable of being depicted or symbolized in form or tincture. Often families chose their charges from resemblances to their names, i.e., a Ram for Ramsey. It is possible to discover the original ownership of apiece of silver by studying these charges and then doing some inspired deduction. Here are examples:

Three naked men in a wood: Wood, Earl of Halifax.

Three demi-ladies *affronté*: The See of Oxford (although it might be rather difficult or dubious to establish a connection here).

Three human arms: Armstrong.

Two shinbones: Baynes.

A cat: Catt, Catton, Keats, Tibbet.

A lynx: Lynch.

A bear: Beresford, Barnard, Barham, FitzUrse.

An elephant: Elphinston.

A boar: Bacon, Swinhoe, Pig, Hogg, Swineshead.

A wolf: Wolfe, Lupton.

A fox: Fox, Todd.

A horse: Horsby, Coulthurst, Trotter.

Hounds. Talbot, Doggett.

A bull or calf: Butler, Bull, Turnbull, Metcalfe, Laveale.

A ram: Ramsey, Ram, Ramston.

A lamb: Lambert.

A badger: Brock.

A rabbit: Coningsby, Cunliffe.

A hedgehog: Herries, Harries, Harris.

Shells: Shelley, Dacre.

A bee: Beatty.

A grasshopper: Gresham.

A stag-beetle: Dore.

A dragon: in many Welsh coats-of arms, particularly Easton.

A unicorn: Preston.

An enfield: Kelly.

(Courtesy of Asprey & Co., Ltd., Bond St., London, W.1.)
One of a pair of magnificent Charles II English Silver Caskets, by "W.F.," 1683, weight 87 oz. total.

A mermaid: Berkeley (also Sir Walter Scott).
Strawberry flowers: Fraser.
A lemon-tree: Leman.
Hazel leaves: Hazelrigg.
Acorns: Aikenhead.
Apples: Applegarth.
Pears: Perrott.
Bells: Bellchamber, Porter.
A bugle or horn: Forrester.
Cups: Butler.
A spear: Shakespeare.
An eagle: Families that had been embellished with a princedom of the Holy Roman empire.

A pelican: Pelham.
A raven, rook or crow: Corbett.
A cock: Alcock.

The Silversmith

In the eighteenth and nineteenth centuries most of the great silversmiths worked in London, often in the Clerkenwell district (that still has its small family firms and some of its original atmosphere), and many of them were of Huguenot and/or Flemish descent. Several were women. In order to understand how these important craftsmen lived and worked it might be a good idea briefly to survey the career of one of them, the famed Hester Bateman.

Hester was born in Clerkenwell in 1709, and, lived and worked as a silversmith until well over eighty. There is no evidence that she had any formal education at all. All the extant documents relating to her were signed by the illiterate's cross and the annotation in another hand: "Hester Bateman her mark."

She was married at the age of twenty-three to a youth in his teens named John Bateman. So circumscribed were his prospects that the marriage ceremony took place in the Fleet Prison. Needless to say, the couple had already been blessed with issue—a son born out of wedlock two years before.

The young husband was by trade a gold-and-silver wire drawer. This meant making the gold braid for uniforms. We can only believe that the breadwinner neglected his work for more attractive pursuits and that Hester taught herself his trade so as to fulfill contracts and keep herself and children from starving. She continually had these children, of whom six lived and were registered, four sons and two daughters.

This was not necessarily a life of squalor. The records show that the Batemans lived in reasonably good neighborhoods for that time, finally at 107 Bunhill Row, just north of the city boundary and today a drab area of industry, but then upon the edge of green fields and fashionable among tradesmen. Here the Bateman family worked and proliferated for more than a century, during which two adjacent houses were added to the original Number 107 and extensive workshops were built at the back. A neighbor was Samuel Whitbread, another struggling fellow who started his brewery nearby.

Nor was it a particularly difficult age in which to live. Probably it was more rewarding, proportionately, than many subsequent ages. The policies of Walpole and of the elder Pitt had the outstanding aim of promoting the general wealth through trade, and thus the general wealth was indeed promoted. Those struggling and at first illiterate artisans, the Batemans, lived in a house that was typically Georgian, much more substantial than most modern houses. It had some nine rooms, would have been furnished with handmade pieces that would be worth a fortune today, with a servant at four pounds a year and keep from the beginning, and later several maids.

It has been assumed that Hester did not become a silversmith until her husband's death from consumption in 1760. She was then fifty-one, at the age when many women consider themselves to be literally as well as emotionally finished. John Bateman's gold-and-silver wire-drawing trade entailed the use of tools to beat and cut the gold and silver. In his will Bateman left these tools to Hester. She had the will proved with remarkable speed, characteristic of her, on the day of his death.

All work with silver in the eighteenth century was complete handwork; and the tools of his trade were a craftsman's most valuable possession apart from his actual stock of gold and silver, or old gold and silver articles that he could melt down. The finished article was made by hand from a flat piece of silver. It could be that Hester realized that the demand for silver articles exceeded the supply at that particular time, also that she had several potentially good helpers, her son John, her second son Peter, and an apprentice named John Linney.

Nevertheless Hester faced several difficulties, the first being her age and sex and their physical and social effects. Then the demand for silver articles might be great, but locally there were a lot of highly professional silversmiths. Cornelius Bland and James Howell were noted makers who lived in Bunhill Row itself, and many others were nearby. Considerable capital was required for the purchase of raw materials. Finally there was the growing competition of Boulsover's Sheffield Plate, then becoming very popular because cheaper and little different in appearance from silver.

From her husband's death in 1760 until 1774 Hester mainly made or finished work for other silversmiths. Probably her silversmith neighbors helped her by giving her work to finish. Also she doubtless lacked both capital at first and confidence in her own work and mark. Similarly she would have had no sales organization or name in the trade at first.

It is therefore true that much Hester Bateman silver, that made by her prior to 1774, appears under other makers' marks; and there are some experts, those immediately able to detect the style of a silversmith (as some critics can immediately detect the style of a painter without the signature) who have found it possible to identify pieces made by Hester under other marks. Then several pieces exist with two makers' marks, those of Hester and another silversmith stamped somewhat erotically on top of each other.

There are writers who say that Hester Bateman was a disciple of the Adam brothers in design, but this is somewhat far-fetched, especially if it is remembered that the designs of the Adams may be classical but are rarely plain and simple. Surely the true origins of Hester's uniquely simple style are in the good taste of the woman herself allied to the frugality imposed upon her by necessity. She had little capital, and had to keep her costs down by eliminating all frills.

Thus the Hester Bateman style is simple and functional, allied to the early Chinese in those respects, always austere but with the austerity of extreme elegance. It is a style eminently suited to the making of everyday utensils for women and the home, tea and coffee pots, sugar bowls, cream jugs, kettles, urns, trays, salvers, cutlery.

It might be asked if there is any one characteristic of the Bateman style apart from the simplicity and the stamped mark. The answer is that there was, in the form of the tiny bead edge that Hester used so often. Nearly all Bateman silver made prior to 1785 had this decoration; and, after 1785, her sons and others had taken over from her.

Hester Bateman was that rarity among great artists, a financial success. She was as good a businessman as she was craftsman. In due course she and her family became the leading firm of working silversmiths in a London that, at that time, was the most prolific single source of fine silverware that the world had ever known. Bateman silver became so fashionable that few big homes in late eighteenth-century England could be without it, and it was acquired similarly by many livery and city halls and churches.

The Bateman family developed like a family of painters into a veritable dynasty of varied talent. Hester herself formally retired from the business in 1790 at eighty-one. Her sons had been managing it for the previous five years, but now it was entirely in the hands of her two

(Courtesy of Asprey & Company, Bond St., London, W.1.)
Typical Hester Bateman silver: one of a pair of salts, marked 1785, weight 3.50 oz. the pair.

surviving sons, Peter and Jonathan (whose joint mark, PB over IB, is very rare). Jonathan died a few months later, of cancer, and left his share to his wife, Ann. Hester had moved to Holborn, but swiftly aged once she was away from the business and could no longer browse over the bench and counting house. Jonathan's death affected her, and in 1894 she died. She was buried in St. Luke's Churchyard, but there is no trace of her grave or tomb there.

Afterwards Ann Bateman took over, and she became almost, but not quite another Hester, She was the wife of Jonathan, the fourth son, herself the daughter of a Huguenot family and with her own inherited skill as a silversmith, not to mention a useful dowry. Ann undoubtedly made much fine silver herself. She was very similar to her mother-in-law, with no nonsense about herself or her work, and she had a good business sense.

Her son William in due course inherited these qualities from Ann and his grandmother, and became another great silversimth and a wealthy and successful man in early Victorian England.

Sheffield Plate

Mention has been made of the Sheffield Plate that became a competitor to articles of sterling silver in the eighteenth century. It is still a competitor and still for the same reasons: comparative cheapness and availability. The amount made must have been enormous because it is still possible for the modest collector to find nice articles of Sheffield Plate within his means. Meanwhile the material must continue to be regarded as it always has been, as essentially a poor man's substitute for silver and one that must increasingly be handled with the utmost delicacy. Cleaning it in the wrong way quickly removes the thin skin of silver, and the article reverts to its native copper, not, admittedly, without some charm still. The very best Sheffield, as made by Boulton in the second half of the eighteenth century, may be identified, in the case of tray and salvers, by the small circle of lighter-colored silver in the center.

Sheffield is ware made of copper, plated with silver—the sheets of copper being sandwiched between films of silver. The process of welding the sheets together was discovered accidentally in 1742 by Thomas Boulsover, a cutler of Sheffield. It seems, however, that he used the process only for the making of some small articles such as buttons. Probably craftsmen to whom Boulsover confided the secrets of his process made the earliest Sheffield domestic items, mainly coffee pots and candlesticks, from about 1755 onwards. It was at first a rough craft and the surviving specimens have chiefly historic value.

The manufacture of true Sheffield Plate as we know it began in 1762, when a factory was specially established for the purpose by Matthew Boulton of Birmingham, the silversmith and master of ormolu and steel-cut jewelry. Boulton's ormolu has been compared favorably with that of the best French makers. Similarly, his Sheffield Plate was soon a great success, and, as has been said, must have been produced in enormous quantities for so much to survive to this day. It continued to be made by Boulton and by many competitors until about the middle of the nineteenth century, when it was suddenly and then completely superseded by electroplate.

Jewelry

The jeweler rightly regards himself as a member of one of the oldest professions in the world (although not necessarily the oldest). Precious stones have been found in deposits left by ancient cavemen; and a student of classical history knows that the Egyptians, the Assyrians, the Greeks, and the Romans were all fond of gems, and employed artificers to work them into beautiful ornaments, rings, intaglios, cameos, and scarabaeuses.

Most varieties of precious stones were known to the ancients, but they were distinguished only by color, specific gravity, and density, for chemical and other forms of scientific analysis were then unknown. And different people called their gems by different names, so that often it is difficult to distinguish the stones mentioned. However, research work in this field has ever been an absorbing interest to the expert jeweler.

For instance, the inhabitants of ancient Egypt, Greece, and Asia had a stone which they called the achates, because it had been found originally near a Sicilian river of that name. Modern research has established that this was in reality the agate as we know it. According to old writings it was considered a champion against scorpions and spiders, and was greatly prized as a talisman by athletes. Different varieties of the ancient agate were known as the jaspachates and the dendryachates.

Then the opal was known as the paedoros. This jewel came like so much else of beauty from India, and the largest ever seen in the ancient world, the size of a hazelnut, was the lucky treasure of a Roman senator named Nonius, who on one famous occasion refused to sell it to Mark Antony for a great sum. And the topaz has been identified with the ancient topazon, that was first discovered on the island of Cytus in the Arabian Gulf. The stone must have been of enormous size, because when it was sent to Ptolemy in Egypt he had a statute carved out of it and set up in his famous "golden temple."

Probably the largest gem ever discovered was an ancient specimen of the smaragd, or emerald. This was sent by a Babylonian king to the king of Egypt, and, the records say, was four cubits long by three cubits wide—roughly translated into seven feet by five. In those days, however, outsizes in precious stones were greatly favored by wealthy monarchs. There is the story of an obelisk in a certain temple of Jupiter that was sixty-six feet high and consisted of many great emeralds.

Ancient gem engravers used emeralds, suitably cut, as eyes for statues. A great lion in Cyprus, erected to Hermias, winked down at the world through two immense emeralds. The Roman Emperor Nero used a large emerald for a lens when he watched the slaughter in the arena.

A list of curious forgotten gems is given by the historian Pliny, and is so curious that it makes one wonder how he ever got the title of historian. The aspilates, it is alleged, was a fiery stone that burned the hand of the daring mortal who picked it up, and it came from the nest of the Arabian phoenix. Another gem, the aromatites, of Arabia and Egypt, was supposed to have a fragrant odor. And yet another, the alecrorius, was found exclusively in the gizzard of the domestic fowl.

It is believed that the ancient anthrax was the ruby, and the hyacinthus was the blue sapphire. The jasper, most certainly, known in olden days as the iaspis, was a popular stone among the Romans and used often for signet rings. Pliny speaks of a fabulous statuette of Nero, executed in Iaspis, that weighed fifteen ounces. The sardonyx, identified as a variety of the onyx, was also a great favorite of the Romans, and was used for cameos, the light-colored layers being cut down to the darker for a background to the figures. And garnets were known as granatici, jacinths as Lyncurii, and green tourmalines as sandaresesii.

In those times the jewelry trade was almost as well organized as it is today. There were craftsmen for all types of work, artists, engravers, polishers and arrangers. The most common stone used, perhaps, was the diamond, known as the adamas; and the chief engraving instrument was made by splinting these stones and fixing them into metal handles. A drill called the terebra was used extensively for hollowing work, and a kind of emery powder was used for polishing. To aid their vision the artificers used globes filled with water, but it appears that for the most part they trusted to the naked eye.

All the above has been put down not only as a matter of historical but also as a sentimental interest. The account could be continued swiftly through the Dark Ages and then in detail again for the jewelry of the Renaissance and subsequent centuries till the eighteenth. But it would still be sentimental. Sometimes it is possible to find and some women are courageous enough to wear very old jewelry, but the value is so great that well-guarded museums or safe deposits are the best places for it.

The collector today, alas, must concentrate chiefly on nineteenth-century jewelry: but not with quite the same abandonment of aesthetic taste as must accompany similar collecting of furniture or ceramics. Even at the most florid summit of the Victorian period some very fine jewelry was made, for it was still handmade. Simplicity and sentiment were to be found in the style of jewelry as in no other Victorian artistic manifestation. Queen Victoria herself would be resplendent with the jewels of former ages on state occasions, but privately she would wear simple rings and lockets, the last containing a miniature or a lock of hair. An extremity of this sentimental fashion was the bracelet Queen Victoria wore which was set with the first teeth of all her children!

Garrards at the 1851 Exhibition caused quite a sensation with a more elaborate piece of jewelry, that perhaps foreshadowed the increasing elaboration in design that became excessive in the second half of the nineteenth century. It was described as an "elegant gold bracelet of Gothic design, on which are chased out, upon a trelliswork of gold on blue enamel, carved in the style of the fifteenth century, two angels holding a pearl and a ruby, and capable of being detached."

After the death of the Prince Consort jet came into fashion. A considerable manufacture of jewelry fashioned from this substance was based on the jet of Whitby in Yorkshire. Then nature as never before was ransacked for motifs in the manufacture of what we now call costume jewelry, flowers, ears of corn, butterflies, feathers, even lizards, beetles, dragonflies, and snakes. Long earrings accommodated hens and watering cans; and necklaces and bracelets quite shamelessly dangled such Krafft-Ebing emblems as chains and bolts, handcuffs, whips, and spurs. "A very coquettish suite, of dogs' heads cut in colored coral and set in polished jet" was suggested in 1869 as suitable wear for a country house weekend.

Photography made the lockets larger, to contain a quick-fading portrait, and often these were set with turquoises and half pearls. It was indeed a romantic, strange age, the age of the cairgorm, that massive semiprecious stone from Scotland, frequently set in a furry bird's claw, of "tartan" bracelets (from 1850) enameled to appear like plaid and fastened with a diamond buckle.

For some reason or other a favourite design from about 1835 until about 1855 was that of the bird defending its nest against a snake.

Certain brooches were made specifically to fasten the velvet ribbon that was often worn round the throat at a time when any exposure of the feminine flesh was regarded as indecent as it has become obligatory in our own time.

The year 1870 is significant in the history of Victorian jewelry, for it saw the retirement of the Queen to her long widowhood at Osborne, and the appearance on the market of the first South African diamonds. Within two years these diamonds dominated design and the trade and what we know as "modern" jewelry began. It was the beginning of the diamond age, progressively to become less substantial in appearance. The true Victorian age of fantasy was over.

4

Objets D'Art

Enamels

Objets d'art might be defined as small and interesting articles that are collected and kept in cabinets or for ornamental purposes on occasional tables and other flat surfaces of the house—and that do not fall easily into other categories. They need not be antique, but the many examples to be found in the antique shops still give scope to every class of collector: articles such as enamels, paperweights, snuffboxes, tea caddies, chessmen, ivories, treen (wooden objects), card cases—too many to be listed in a single book.

Enamel is a paste of powdered glass fused onto a base of metal (usually gold, copper, or bronze). The traditional methods of application are (1) *cloisonné,* in which the design is divided by metal strips, soldered to the ground, forming small compartments or *cloisons* that are filled with enamel; (2) *champlevé,* in which the small compartments to keep the enamels separate are hollowed out of the ground; (3) *basse taille* or *en plein,* in which the ground is first carved or engraved at a slightly sunken level, and subsequently covered with translucent enamels that reveal the design through their varying depths and strengths of colur; (4) *plique à jour,* in which translucent enamel is strengthened by internal strips of metal, like stained-glass windows; (5) *painted enamels,* in which pictures or designs in contrasting colored enamels are painted upon an undercoat of white enamel. The simple but lovely English contribution belongs characteristically to this fifth group.

The art of the enameler is again one of the oldest in the world, and probably had its modern origins in Greece and/or Etruria between the sixth and third centuries B. C. The classical Greeks and Romans developed the art superbly in most of its forms. After the Dark Ages the late fifteenth century saw the painter disputing with the metalworker for predominance in the craft. Brush-painted enamels were superb in sixteenth-century Limoges. At first treating mainly of religious subjects—the customer is always right—decoration became more and more secular as it was apparent that enamels served so admirably as a substitute for jewels. By the mid-eighteenth century it was found practicable to decorate such bibelots as snuffboxes, *étuis, bonbonnières,* and watch cases with painted enamels; and thus these small objects, formerly confined to a traffic between the jeweler and the very rich, came within reach of a large new public. When this fashion arrived in England it quickly captured the favor of the Georgian gallant—at which the English businessman stepped in.

The development of English painted enamels, as of so many other "antiques," was a commercial and not an aesthetic development. There was, quite suddenly, a demand to be met and, if prices could be brought down, this demand would surely grow. The English are, or used to be, rather good at coping with a situation of that nature. There were technical difficulties to be solved, but with a little bit of luck (or inspiration, such as transfer-printing) the English would soon be exporting enamels to the world.

Battersea, the most important name in English enamels, is the district in which stood York House, former London residence of the Archbishops of York. It was at York House, converted into a factory, that Stephen Theodore Janssen began his enameling venture in late 1753, a venture that was to last less than three years and end in bankruptcy. Janssen, the son of a wealthy merchant, was himself a merchant and stationer. He knew a lot about printing, was a patron of the arts and the friend of many leading artists and engravers. It is not certain that the York House venture actually caused the bankruptcy, that might have proceeded from one of Janssen's other ventures.

It was the application of transfer-printing that made Battersea enamels so quickly notable. Two Irishmen, John Brooks and Henry Delamain, developed the transfer-printing process, and possibly Janssen started the Battersea works specifically to exploit the process, intending to apply it to decorative tiles at first.

The process consisted of the inking of an engraved plate from which a paper print was taken and the inked impression transferred to the ware, the paper being soaked off and the design fixed by firing. The inks used, mainly in soft red, sepia, purple and indigo, were importantly based on metallic oxides, as it was necessary for them at once to give clarity of transferred outline and to be strong enough to withstand the heat of the oven.

Brush-painting was employed at Battersea, and the colors typical of the factory are a deep pink, a bright blue, a light yellow, and a darkish red-brown. They are not subtle colors, but were used with English restraint, and they do show to great advantage on the soft, creamy-white ground of true Battersea enamel, that partakes of the warm brilliancy of soft-paste porcelain.

Since the life of the Batterset factory was less than three years its total output was not large. One authority suggests 20,000 articles, of which perhaps 5,000 could be identified today. Many more than 5,000 Battersea enamels have been sold in the antique shops since. Of course much of the Battersea equipment, including workmen and technique, must have found its way to ever enterprising Staffordshire after the York House closure. Pieces often thought of as typical Battersea were not made there at all, articles such as candlesticks, hot-water jugs, *étuis,* scent bottles, and the small boxes in imitation of Dresden *bonbonnières.* The true Battersea enamels were mainly plaques and medallions, caskets, snuffboxes, watch cases, bottle tickets or wine labels, and, humbler articles such as buttons and cane heads.

The reason why the name Battersea is so important is that the brief products of the factory were finer than those of its successors. Janssen was a purist who made his enamels well and had them decorated with a sureness of artistic touch that was never equalled in the go-getting manufactories of South Staffordshire and Birmingham, where the products might often be more colorful but were never so nice. Janssen employed the best artist-engravers that he could find, notably Robert Hancock and Simon Francois Ravenet (1706–1774), a man who gave Battersea the blandly lovely tone of mid-eighteenth-century France, yet always with an English accent to the French. Favored subjects, many of them taken from prints of the period, were mythological, landscape, celebrities such as royalty, figures, flowers, birds. Note that the pictures on Battersea usually covered the entire surface of the article, whereas the pictures on early Staffordshire work were frequently smaller, with margins.

After Battersea the craft of English enameling was principally transferred to Bilston, Birmingham, and Wednesbury, where it continued to be of a high order, although with the reservations that have already been made. The South Staffordshire enamels were often technically very fine. There was a far greater range of color than at Battersea. Royal blue, turquoise, green, and rose pink were among the outstanding colors used by the Midlands men. The range of their products was much greater than that of Battersea. These included plaques and boxes, tea canisters, caddy sets, candlesticks of several kinds, trays, pots and jugs, salt cellars and mustard pots, standishes, tobacco presses, *bonbonnières,* scent bottles, *étuis,* and many of the small articles known as "toys." But artistic quality was nearly always lower than that of Battersea.

The best period for South Staffordshire enamels was from around 1760 to about 1785. Standards began noticeably to deteriorate from about 1780, with a decline in painting, gilding and transfer-printing. This has been ascribed to mass production, and increased competition at a time when workmen were getting lower rates for piecework so that they could spend less time on each piece; but the real cause was probably the subtle, spiritual "something" that brought the great artistic age of the eighteenth century to a sad if revolutionary end.

Also, the enamel business had to die thanks to its dependence on the Continental market and to the coming of that arch economic dictator Napoleon. In their heyday the South Staffordshire manufacturers sold a large proportion of their wares to Europe, where they could be offered for less than the entirely hand-painted local product. Napoleon, with the same chauvinistic mentality as his spiritual descendant de Gaulle, told the English that they and their products were not wanted, and that was that. The thriving Staffordshire industry was, by 1800, no longer viable.

At its height the town of Bilston alone had some eighteen firms of enamelers. Notable practitioners of the art were the Bickleys. They never used transfer-printing, but often their work is mistaken for Battersea. Another fine craftsman was Henry Beckett, famous for his étuis, and then for what he might have invented, the enameled buckle.

In Birmingham itself enameling of a kind was an art practiced before Janssen started at Battersea, although in that early period the product was of poor quality, being employed on a coarse paste of flint glass that was rendered more or less opaque by an admixture of arsenic. These standards were improved with the help of Battersea experience, and in the 1770s some very fine enamel ware was produced by that Matthew Boulton who similarly made some of the best English ormolu and Sheffield Plate. A very large and fine piece of English enamel was probably made by Boulton, as he produced larger and more elaborate pieces than any other manufacturer.

Samuel Yardley founded the Wednesbury industry in 1776, and it survived the depressions to endure until 1840 under Samuel's grandson John. Wednesbury was never so good as Bilston or Birmingham, although surviving longer as an industry perhaps for that very reason. It can sometimes be recognized by the flamboyant nature of its art work.

South Staffordshire enamels had a dead white ground with brilliant coloring applied to the pictures, but never with the subtlety of Battersea. Effects were achieved by contrasts rather than harmonies. Often colors were applied with such abandon as largely to conceal the transfer beneath, whereas the translucent colors of Battersea always allowed the transfer to be seen. To explain how these English enamels were made it is necessary first to describe the "core," which was a piece of extremely thin copper that had been cut or pressed or hammered into the required shape. This would be coated on both sides with layers of white enamel. Firing fused this enamel to the core. When all was cold, the surface of the enamel was decorated with lines or strokes in colors applied by transfer or brush or both, after which the article was fired again. Then further decoration might be applied, especially gilding, although this was rarely done at Battersea and seldom in the Midlands before 1765. There would be another firing.

The final process was the mounting, necessary because the enamel usually tended to part company and to flake at the edges of the copper. The mounts consisted of frames of copper or ormolu or an alloy such as pinchbeck (five parts copper to one part of zinc). The frame was bound round the exposed and flaking edges of the piece. This would be simple enough with a plaque, but was often a complicated task with a box that might require framing for the rims where box and lid met and also for the vertical and horizontal angles of sides, top, and bottom. This frame-making, also hingeing, and fixing of such items as miniature locks and keys, often cost more in time, money and effort than the enamel itself, but it was a good Birmingham trade.

Needless to say these increasingly valuable and sought-after enamels have been extensively faked. They were never marked in England and there were few great individual artists to impress their personalities on pieces. The famous copier, Samson of Paris, made a great number of "English" enamels, but he was a good boy and always marked them with a cross. The collector should beware of a thin, high glaze, unlike the creaminess of Battersea or the dead whiteness of South Staffordshire. Colors should not be too bright, and hinges should be hand wrought and lack the modern press-tool marks.

Snuffboxes

Let us proceed from the general to the particular, from the whole subject of enamels as objets d'art to the particular instance of snuffboxes. These little articles can still be collected pleasurably and profitably by people who are willing to learn about them and search in antique shops and salerooms. It is possible to find comparatively inexpensive examples still, or important items of considerable and ever mounting value.

They were first made in the seventeenth century, and have been made ever since right up till the present day, in most countries of the world alongside with the use of tobacco and medical snuffs; and a collection could range from Chinese snuff bottles to Scottish horn snuff mulls. Their heyday, as with all objets d'art, was the eighteenth century.

The most important snuffboxes were usually made of gold. During the eighteenth and nineteenth centuries the leading goldsmiths of Britain and Europe lavished all their skill on such. The decorations included engraved or incised designs on the surface, chasing by tapping or pressing, repoussé patterning by beating from inside, enamel fired on the gold, insertions of ivory, porcelain, or glass panels, or of cameos and medallions in mother-of-pearl and other materials, inset of gems singly or in designs (note that a single gem is often used to take thumb pressure at the catch), also employment of different shades of gold.

It must be admitted that the best gold snuffboxes originally came from France, starting in the time of Louis XIII, pausing during the Revolution, picking up again with Napoleon, becoming more ornate and less lovely during the nineteenth century. There are records of several thousand livres being paid in Paris for new little boxes.

But the gold boxes of the Georgian period with London hallmarks are often very good indeed. They are less ornate than the French. Essentially solid in workmanship, they are usually engraved and/or carved rather than enameled. Types have been found in most shapes, oblong, square, oval, round. They were usually made large enough to carry from a quarter to half an ounce of snuff, and they were mostly designed for the pocket, with hinged lids. Table models were larger, and were sometimes given detachable tops. All types often had trick features such as false bottoms or double lids or miniature portraits. Some would contain timepieces or musical-box movements.

Ranking next to the gold boxes are those made of tortoise-shell or ivory. The tortoise-shell types were light to carry and had the reputation of keeping the snuff in particularly good condition. The material ranges in color from cloudy black to transparent gold. Sometimes the boxes are made entirely of tortoise shell except for the metal hinges, snap fasteners and applied decorations; but other times two thin plates of tortoise shell are set in boxes of gold, silver, silver-gilt, Sheffield Plate or even pewter.

A very popular design on eighteenth-century tortoise shell showed features of monarchs. Such lid decorations, notably the work of John Obrisset, showed Queen Anne's head until well on into the nineteenth century.

Ivory was similarly used for all types of snuffboxes, also for pocket snuff rasps or graters. Gold and silver were used for decoration on ivory, as well as many other substances. Outstanding interest attaches to those with miniature paintings on the lid, particularly paintings ascribed to Richard Cosway, who worked during the latter part of the eighteenth and early part of the nineteenth centuries.

In addition to gold, silver, tortoise shell, and ivory, snuffboxes have been made of almost all metals and ceramics and woods. Exquisite examples were constructed with panels of decorated porcelain, often in association with tortoise shell or ivory. These were probably for collection rather than use from the beginning. Then rock crystal, agate, bloodstone and cornelian, smooth-polished or carved, were used in tops and bottoms of boxes, also inserted as individual gems into other materials.

Probably more snuffboxes have been made of silver than of any other substance, and the best silver snuffboxes are of London sterling silver. The majority were simple oblong or oval boxes for everyday use; some were very fine, with *repoussé,* chased and carved decorations, often with engraved coats-of-arms and commemorative inscriptions. There is a very large collection of these in the Victoria and Albert Museum. A particular kind of silver snuffbox was that which incorporated a cowrie shell. It was said that such shells retained the freshness and savor of snuff. Note that silver snuffboxes long enough to take cigarettes are sometimes in particular modern demand.

As regards wood, trashy boxes made of deal were made throughout the eighteenth and nineteenth centuries for the common trade, but some rare wooden boxes are those made in the seventeenth century from carved and often unidentified South American hardwoods. Among wooden boxes are those of the most diverse shape, because the material lent itself to eccentricity: portrait heads, traders' emblems such as boxes made in the form of casks or boots or coffins.

Which leads to a digression. Mr. Edward H. Pinto, the English collector of and expert on treen, relates how he sent an illustration of a coffin snuffbox to a newspaper. He received a letter from America. The writer said he much wanted to buy such a box. Mr. Pinto replied that he was not a dealer, but did possess two of the boxes, and would sell one of them.

The American arranged for a London firm of export packers to receive and ship the snuffbox for him, and a few days later Mrs. Pinto had a telephone call from this firm. They wanted to know if two men would be enough to collect the coffin. It gave Mrs. Pinto much pleasure to reply that she would put it in a ten-cigarette packet and send it to them.

Mr. Pinto further relates how, at the height of the snuff-taking craze, a Mrs. Margaret Thompson, of Boyle Street, off Savile Row, London, stipulated in her will of 1776 that all her unwashed handkerchiefs and enough snuff to cover her body were to be put into her coffin, that six snuff-taking maidens were to be her pall-bearers, and that her servant was to walk ahead of the coffin, scattering snuff over the crowd.

Then there is an extract from *The London Journal,* circa 1830:

> A provincial paper says, that a gentleman in Devonshire has invented what he calls a snuff-pistol: it has two barrels, and being applied to the nose, upon touching a spring under them with the fore-finger, both nostrils are instantly filled, and a sufficient quantity driven up the head to last the whole day.

But to return to wooden snuffboxes as such, a famous type was the Laurencekirk, which probably came originally from that proud small city in Scotland. It had an ingenious hinge of brass pin and wooden rollers to prevent the snuff from escaping, which was a frequent fault of boxes with hinged lids. Most valuable of Laurencekirk boxes are those with decorated lids, especially as painted with miniature scenes after the great sporting painters. Muchlin boxes are those decorated with clan tartans in Victorian times by one Smith of Mauchline. Wooden boxes, although once so prevalent, tend to be rare today, as the wooden rollers in the hinges have snapped with age and the comparatively valueless boxes have been thrown away.

After the invention of papier-mâché in 1772 by Henry Clay of Birmingham, the substance was soon used for snuffboxes, and when papier-mâché became really cheap (following the invention of a new process of manufacture by Richard Brindley of Birmingham in 1836) it tended to supersede wood as a material for the workingman's everyday snuffbox. Unlike wood, they did not require lining. Unlined wood soon ruined the snuff. Note that the really early papier-mâché boxes, made by Clay's process, are lighter, smoother, and tougher than the nineteenth-century boxes made according to the Brindley process, which were brittle—also that the Brindley boxes are the rarer because they did not last so long as the Clay boxes. The papier-mâché type was indeed very common if not vulgar in Victorian England, plain or inlaid with mother-of-pearl or decorated with miniature painting or paper prints stuck not always nicely on the lid. As De Morgan wrote in the seventies: "Fifty years ago a fashionable snuff-taker would be under inducement to have a stock with very objectionable pictures."

Battersea enamel boxes are today of considerable value, but not all Battersea boxes were made for snuff nor were all of them Battersea. Inferior Bilston enameled boxes are more common. Enameled boxes have been faked probably more than any other type.

Pinchbeck, that composite of copper and zinc with the goldlike appearance, makes a very attractive box that is well worth collecting because it has not got the intrinsic value of gold and has rarely been faked. It would not be worthwhile setting up the complicated and old-fashioned process.

Sheffield Plate boxes can be charming. They are among the smallest objects made in Sheffield Plate and some of them date back to very soon after Boulsover's initial development of the process. Most of them, alas, have very little silver left on their flanks. They usually follow the pattern of much earlier silver boxes.

Brass snuffboxes can be very elegant, as the metal polishes so well with the years and suits certain designs admirably. A box in the shape of a boot with steel hobnails has copper toe cap and lace holes. Another wooden box in the shape of a woman's slender boot has the miniature heads of brass nails to form a pattern, and was probably made by a shoemaker at the end of his apprenticeship, as was often the custom. A strange brass box is in bellows shape, with projections to fit the nostrils. Pewter boxes are to be found in almost every shape under the sun, but can be somewhat unattractive to all but the most determined antiquarian.

Horn was one of the earliest substances used in the making of snuffboxes. Early examples have attached or cut rasps. Most designs were used, and a wide variety of decorations. Many came from abroad (particularly the famous *tabatières au petit-chapeau* in the shape of Napoleon's hat). Some early Scottish horn "mulls" consist of an actual small animal hoof, suitably adapted.

Paperweights and Tea Caddies

Now we shall briefly discuss two kinds of objets d'art that illustrate contrasting facets of the modern collecting process. Paperweights have been prime objects of financial speculation in our time; tea caddies, often more beautiful than paperweights and of far greater historical interest, have failed to attract the speculators and have remained within the scope of the ordinary collector.

Various objects have been used to hold down papers on a desk throughout the centuries, but the paperweight as we know it dates only from the first half of the nineteenth century and ceased importantly to be made after 1865. They appeared at a Paris exhibition in 1844 and were described in the following year as "a new item of trade, the round shaped *millefiori* paperweights of transparent glass in which are inserted quantities of small tubes of all colours and forms to look like a multitude of florets."

Three centers in France—St. Louis, Baccarat and Clichy—were chiefly responsible for the paperweights of the "classic" period 1845–1860, a short fifteen years; and types included the "double overlay," the "pastry-mould," the "latticinio," the "carpet-ground," the "millefiori," and the "radiating chequer." Meanwhile in England good copies were made at glassworks in London, Bristol, Stourbridge, and Birmingham. After 1865 the standard of workmanship so declined everywhere that there is no difficulty in determining whether a paperweight belongs to the best period or not.

Paperweights of that period are both lovely and interesting, but not intrinsically worth the money that is now paid for them, unless the purchaser has the same kind of purpose as the man who buys goldmining shares one day in the expectation of selling them next day at a profit. In 1920 a Clichy overlay weight might have been picked up for a few pounds or even for a few dollars. In 1930 it would have been worth perhaps sixty dollars (twenty pounds). In 1970 the dealer-speculators would have been bidding up to 3500 dollars (1500 pounds), maybe more, and, after the sale, would possibly be passing the pretty little object one to the other and taking a substantial profit each time.

By chance the humble paperweight has become an item of international currency, better than diamonds, better than gold, better than rare postage stamps, books, and coins. It is not even a true antique. It just happened that between about 1844 and 1865 a few craftsmen developed a superb process in the making of a completely unimportant objet d'art and then lost the knack as soon as they had found it almost, so that the number of paperweights made to that degree of perfection is strictly limited.

All paperweights cannot be sold for hundreds if not thousands of dollars each, but paperweights that cannot so be sold rarely belong to the all-important "classic" period and so would not be worth holding by the genuine collector.

The financially much more humble tea caddy (also called tea bottle and tea canister) might be described as a receptacle for holding in good condition the dried tea leaves that first came to England in the early eighteenth century from China. Originally they were made of porcelain and pottery, were small and in the shape of bottles or ginger jars, with loose lids and decorated in blue and white. Staffordshire quickly supplied the demand, but coarsely, although some of Wedgwood's products were fine, in jasper and his other specialized wares. Early Liverpool caddies were interesting, often with black transfer pictures of social festivities.

Worcester blue-and-white specimens of ginger-jar shape appeared from 1750 onwards. Bow, Chelsea, and Derby all made caddies; while a great number were imported from China with English heraldic emblazonments.

Meanwhile fine silver caddies were being made, in rectangles, octagons, hexagons, narrownecked, usually to hold five to six ounces of the precious tea, some with sliding lids, others were the characteristic domed tops. Generally speaking the smaller the caddy the earlier it should be, because tea was at first so expensive.

Silver caddies became very complicated and variegated as the eighteenth century came to its end. Sir Joshua Reynolds had a set of three cut-glass silver-mounted caddies in a shagreen case. The great cabinetmakers all made caddies and the Sheraton type of mahogany with harewood (sycamore maple) inlay of a shell design, often made elegantly in diamond shape, has considerable value as well as beauty—also a lock and key to keep the fingers of servants away from the precious tea. Pewter caddies were made for the cottage mantelpiece. The Coromandel caddy was sometimes very nice. Coromandel is the name now usually given to what was also called bantam-work, lacquer into which the colored design was incised, used particularly for screens.

Then the fantastic nineteenth century brought caddies of ivory, mother-of-pearl, tortoise shell, papier-mâché, Tonbridge ware, even beadwork, hairwork, and prisoner-of-war bonework, besides examples from most of the great Victorian potteries. Thereafter the tea caddy declined into a cheap and unregarded colored tin on the kitchen shelf.

Note that the earliest tea caddies were themselves sometimes kept in a "tea chest" that often had two compartments, one for black and one for green tea; and that a teapoy is a small, three-legged table, with collapsing top, on which the caddy was originally kept perhaps, and that would similarly support the teapot at parties.

Chess Sets

Carved ivory figures and "toys" have ever been prominent among objets d'art, but have not captured the imagination of the collector in our time save in certain specialized departments such as chess sets. The collecting of these sets has become very popular, partly because the game has been increasingly played, partly because of the availability of the species, which have always been made in large numbers. The clever carver has throughout the ages found it to be an amusing as well as lucrative spare-time occupation. All he has needed is a piece of ivory or even a piece of wood and a sharp tool (in modern times, alas, only a billiard ball and a sharp tool).

"Chinese" sets are the most common, mainly the red and white type, with or without concentric balls, and with entirely Chinese figures or with a European king (George II or George III) on the white side. In order to determine the quality and value of these sets, pay particular attention to the pawns. Poorly made pawns indicate a largely mass-production set made for the European market.

Some of the finest chess sets in ivory are of French origin. Particularly attractive are those with Roman warriors on the white side and Negroes or Turks on the left. A factory at Dieppe produced notable sets with half-length cuirassiers as pawns on one side, grenadiers on the other, and kings to represent Napoleon and Henry IV. Excellent pottery sets were made at Rouen.

Glass sets are rare and when found are usually of Bristol type. In the nineteenth century the ubiquitous Nailsea Works made some sets of varicolored glass.

The collector will invariably have a set of Indian chessmen, finely carved in white ivory and identifiable by the majestic kings and "prime ministers" and elephants with dignitaries in howdahs and bishops on camels and soldiers on castles. The true Indian set has no queens, because of the purdah system. The collector will, furthermore, recognize juggernaut cars or bullock cars with fakirs for bishops (or even rhinoceroses).

The colored Indian sets are sometimes called "Indo-Persians." They are in green or black and white, rarely red and white, frequently have elephants carrying cannons, and pawns playing the flute, and date from about 1740 to 1850, being made principally in Madras. Then there is an Indo-Portuguese type, with human heads on turned bases. These heads will have a lacquered headdress. The black side will sometimes be made of horn.

Metal chess sets were made largely in Europe and mostly in Germany for popular use. Frederick the Great and Napoleon are the representative kings in the German examples.

Ceramic chess sets often have great value, especially from the best periods of the leading factories such as, on the Continent, Meissen, Fürstenburg, and Sèvres, and, in England, Wedgwood and Minton.

Wedgwood's best-known set was that designed by John Flaxman, offered in various colors. Early examples have sharper lines to the figures than later copies. The style is Gothic; and the kings and queens are said to have originally depicted John Kemble and Mrs. Siddons in their respective roles from *Macbeth*. Great numbers were made for the Russian market. Sets designed for the anticlerical French market had Shakespearean "fools" for bishops.

A most interesting English pottery set is that probably made at Castleford, with kilted soldiers for pawns and mounted light dragoon officers for knights. Queens of this set are sometimes salt-glazed.

Then Minton made about 1850 a set consisting of attractively garbed children in a vivid green and white.

It should be noted that Russian sets can often be identified by bishops depicted as ships, also by their mammoth-tusk ivory and stiff Muscovite figures; while wooden sets are usually of German and Swiss origin, with characters from local history, such as bears from Berne.

Fabergé

Fabergé and associated objets d'art of the nineteenth century *fin de siècle* occupy a special position. They could be defined as not antique but far too fine and important to be anything else.

The Fabergés as a family were forced to flee from France, like so many other Huguenots, when the Edict of Nantes was revoked in 1685. They finally settled in Russia, and Carl Fabergé was born in 1846. As a young man he developed an interest in the mechanical toys and works of art of Peter Hiskias Pendin, so much so that he went to Frankfurt and served his own apprenticeship with the famous goldsmith Friedmann. In 1870, when he was only twenty-four years of age, he took over the family jewelry business in St. Petersburg. Two years later he married Augusta Julia Jacobs. She bore him four children.

But by far the most important action of Fabergé's life was his remembering Pendin and changing the emphasis of the Fabergé family business from the making of conventional jewelry to the hand-fabrication of jeweled and enameled "toys" and other small objets d'art. This work first became prominent at the Pan-Russian Exhibition of 1882 in Moscow, when Fabergé won a gold medal. Two years later Carl and his brother Agathon were commissioned to make an Easter egg for the Tsarina. The giving of these toys was a tradition in the Imperial family. Hitherto they had no particular beauty, only great monetary value as measured by weight of gold and size of jewels. Fabergé's first egg turned out to be something different, an extraordinary little work of art. His craftsmanship and taste were at once seen to be far above those of all other working jewelers, lapidaries, and enamelers.

So successful was that first egg that the Tsar Alexander III gave the firm of Fabergé his royal warrant soon after. The name of Fabergé suddenly acquired that subtle halo which is international fame. Wealthy people all over Europe sent commissions to Fabergé in St. Petersburg; and eventually the firm was employing some five hundred people. Its output was considerable until 1914, when its activities were blighted by the outbreak of war. The Revolution of 1917 forced old Carl to close his doors and flee the country altogether. He died in 1920 at Lausanne in Switzerland.

It should be noted that nothing made by Carl Fabergé was consciously original for its own sake. He had none of the spirit of the modern who believes that if a work of art is different then it is necessarily good. Many of the Imperial Easter eggs reflect the influence of goldsmiths working in Germany and the Low Countries during the sixteenth and seventeenth centuries. Often the snuffboxes and cigarette cases are in the styles of Louis XV and Louis XVI. Other influences are those of ancient Greece and Rome, the Italian Renaissance, and even English pottery, although Fabergé's own mark is always predominant. That mark was supreme *quality*.

Many Fabergé pieces were made in the Chinese style; and wealthy Chinese mandarins were among the important customers of the St. Petersburg firm. On the whole Fabergé avoided excessive decoration, and never produced the more involved kind of "art nouveau" work, although he was subtly a child of the "art nouveau" age. He attained always a lightness of appearance and justness of proportion.

It was Fabergé's custom to summon all his various specialists to a round-table conference when any important piece was being planned. He was a modern craftsman in that he believed in teamwork; and he did not eschew the use of up-to-date machinery; but the most important work was done by hand and it was always based on his own original inspiration.

Fabergé colored his gold in differing shades both by adding metal to it during manufacture and by tinting it when the work was completed. He also made extensive use of oxidised silver, and of platinum, a difficult material to work. He specialized in *en plein* enameling (several smooth coverings of the whole surface). He would achieve an interesting effect by varying the colours of the layers of enamel. Thus the colour seems to alter when the finished article is tilted slightly. Thanks to his having rich customers Fabergé could afford to take his time. Few enamelers before or after him have had the time or money to heat the enamel to the temperature required for really fine work.

The Urals, the Caucasus, and Siberia were rich in minerals; and Fabergé's lapidaries were able to use any stone they wanted in the fabrication of the various works of art that came from those remarkable workshops. Semiprecious stones were used chiefly, such as moonstones, olivines, and cabochon garnets. Fabergé also employed rock crystal and jade, and the deep crimson material known as purpurine. When the objets d'art were finished they were sent to their buyers in attractive wooden cases made from Karelian birch, pailsander, and holly wood.

Fabergé's favorite object was the box, made for many modern purposes, for cigarettes, cigars, stamps, pills, powder compacts. Many were carved in stone, although the celebrated snuffboxes were usually enameled *en plein* on a *guilloche* base of gold or silver. Very few craftsmen can now make the "invisible" hinge that distinguishes so many of Fabergé's cigarette cases. Fabergé also produced clocks; and, although the decoration is often most remarkable (some clocks were made in the form of Easter eggs) the functional purpose of the instrument is never forgotten.

Scientific instruments such as thermometers and barometers were among Fabergé's products, as were desk ornaments like pen trays and paper knives. Even the parasols and walking-sticks of fashionable strollers in the last aristocratic days of St. Petersburg were topped with different kinds of Fabergé work.

Nor did Fabergé neglect the traditional work of his old family jewelers' business. He produced many attractive and original items of fine jewelry. He designed several of the Russian crown jewels, used important diamonds, emeralds, sapphires, and pearls. He was particularly good at the insertion of semiprecious gems in rose-cut diamond settings. Much of this was confiscated by the revolutionaries and has since been allowed to percolate out into the world's markets by various channels in order to earn foreign exchange for communism. Many refugees from that revolution owed their rehabilitation in foreign parts to what they were able to get for Fabergé jewelry and objets d'art they had brought out with them in curious ways.

The Eggs

The custom of presenting elaborately decorated eggs on Easter morning was very popular from the sixteenth century onwards in all European aristocratic circles that owed their cultural allegiance to France. In the eighteenth century artists like Watteau and Boucher painted exquisite designs on fabricated eggs. Fabergé was commissioned by Alexander III to make a surprise Easter egg that he could give to the Tsarina each year. Nicolas II continued the practice after his father's death, and by 1917 some fifty-seven eggs had been made for the tsars alone. Of course Fabergé also made eggs for many other prominent people. A particularly good customer was Fru Emanuel Nobel, whose husband was the fortunate nephew of Alfred Nobel. Thus out of dynamite came literary, scientific and peace prizes, and also exquisite, trivial, but wholly inimitable Fabergé eggs.

Fabergé, like all great artist-craftsmen, was not particularly interested in marking his pieces; and often they have no mark. Objects made in the original St. Petersburg workshops for the Russian market sometimes had the name Fabergé inscribed in Russian, with no initial.

When objects were intended for foreign markets the name can appear as FABERGE, or C. FABERGE in Roman capitals, or just the initials C. F. Then Fabergé opened workshops in Moscow, Odessa, and Kiev; and when Moscow pieces were marked they had the name Fabergé in Russian letters under the Imperial double-headed eagle. Sometimes a workmaster's initials appear on the St. Petersburg pieces, but not on those made at Moscow. Products of Odessa and Kiev can have the mark K. o.

Fabergé's marking was very half-hearted and indistinct, often only half-impressed or faintly painted. Note that forgers—and there have even been forgers with the impudence to attempt the faking of Fabergé—nearly always make clear, strong marks.

Although characteristic items of Fabergé now seldom exchange hands at less than two thousand dollars and usually very much more, it is possible to find what could be Fabergé still unrecognized and not too expensive in the less knowledgeable antique shops and salerooms. Some years ago the author observed an altercation at a provincial antique dealers' fair when a customer bought a strange object from a furniture stand and told the dealer afterwards that he had known all the time it was a Fabergé Easter egg. The dealer wanted the article back. He said he had a right to demand it back. It could have been sold at auction for at least three thousand dollars. The author confesses that he did not remain to see the result of that great argument, in which soon a whole settlement of gesticulating dealers was taking part.

5

Bygones

Copper, Brass, Pewter, and the Fireplace

For want of a better word "bygones" is used to describe everyday articles of the past that do not always possess great artistic importance but that are worth collecting, and, still better, available to collect. Sometimes they are ordinary household or agricultural or military articles. Or they can be curiosities. Or the tools of crafts and professions.

Articles of copper, brass, and pewter were used in the home from early times until replaced by ceramics, iron, tinware and aluminum in the revolutionary nineteenth century. Brass is an alloy of copper with tin, zinc, and other base metals. Pewter is an alloy of tin, lead, or copper and sometimes other metals.

The homely brightness of copper and brass has always much commended itself to those who furnish with antique furniture and who design country antique shops. It goes particularly well with oak and fruitwood furniture. But it has been reproduced so much that much of its value has departed; and the collector should be very careful to look for the lustrous "patina" that can come only with age, for weight and clumsiness of design (the reproduced article is invariably light by comparison and neatly executed), and for original heavy rivets and coarsely soldered repairs. On the whole very old brass and copper was roughly made for everyday use by hand craftsmen who were not good enough for finer work. It is rare to find exquisite craftsmanship in pots and pans and kettles and candlesticks, although fine piercing and chasing and modeling, particularly in brass, will signify that the article was made for some great family and has high value still.

Thus the best warming pans are of brass, beautifully chased and pierced, and should have well-wrought iron handles. The serious collector of that humble article the saucepan would similarly look primarily for "skillets," small metal pots with long handles and sometimes legs. The oldest in his collection would be of bronze, an alloy of about nine parts of copper to one of tin, and the best would be silver examples of the seventeenth century complete with cover.

Candlesticks and rush-holders were originally primitive articles of iron with prickets or spikes for the candles and clips for the oiled rushes. Candlesticks had quite large platforms to catch the grease until about the middle of the seventeenth century; and the removable nozzle dates from about 1760. The last half of the eighteenth century saw the apotheosis of the brass candlestick. Its baluster and classical forms then were never quite equaled again. Authenticity is largely a matter of weight and the presence of deep burning and waxing within the candleholder, plus the presence of the primitive "pusher" below.

Jelly molds of copper with their nice flutings, copper and brass covers for entrée dishes, posting horns of brass banded with copper, coal buckets of both brass and copper (the brass-helmet types tend to be Victorian and those from the early periods are more often copper, plain of shape, with a lip that tends to come to a point), jugs, mugs, ewers and basins, chestnut roasters, skimmers, trivets, handles, escutcheons, and decorations on furniture: there is no end to the catalogue of what can still be collected.

But it must be remembered that in no branch of collecting is there more reliance on sheer instinct. It is difficult to find really important dealers who specialize in brass and copper; and there is no marking system; while the books on the subject either deal with museum items only or are hopelessly inadequate. It is indeed a free-for-all. Even so a good piece of old brass or copper should tend to be heavy, clumsy in execution, and should bear obvious indications of age.

Should brass and copper be cleaned? Most certainly. It was made to shine, and what would the original craftsman feel like if he saw his brilliant workmanship transformed by neglect into the ugliness of dull-brown tarnish? Besides, most articles of copper and brass are chiefly beautiful because of their bright color, and they are bought and included in a furnishing scheme for the specific purpose of reflecting the light and adding cheerfulness to dark corners. With the new long-lasting polishes there is no excuse for the old doctrine of dullness. Lacquering brass and copper is no longer necessary, and it has never been advisable, because the lacquer lasts little longer than good polish and is very difficult to remove (a good substance for removing such lacquer is a mixture of metal polish and nail-polish remover, plus some hours of hard work).

The same does not apply to pewter. It is possible to polish pewter so that it closely resembles silver. Few objects from the past are more beautiful than polished pewter on the shelves of a shining Welsh dresser. But many people are so used to pewter in its dull, sad state that they prefer to keep it so. Some collectors say that pewter is ruined for them when what they call the "patina" is removed by polishing. ("Sad ware" aptly means pewter plates in the plural. A "garnish" is a complete set of a dozen pieces.)

Pewter was made by the Romans most successffully and elegantly. The alloy became the tableware of the medieval mighty, and by the end of the fifteenth century it had descended to the humble dwelling and replaced plates and mugs and jugs of wood and iron. The Pewterers' Guild, first recognized in 1348, was one of the earliest trade unions. The marking of pewter was made compulsory in 1504, and "London quality" became a famous standard, although pewter never had the value of silver and so mismarking or nonmarking did not become such a heinous crime as with silver.

The history of pewter on the Continent ran parallel with that in Britain, but the European product is far more ornate than the British and at the same time tends to be even less attractive in color and substance.

The art of the pewterer began to decline in the middle of the eighteenth century and with it the common use of pewter in the home. Britannia metal was invented about that time, an alloy of 90 per cent tin and 19 per cent antimony that, with its white, silvery appearance, was soon preferred. Note that when Britannia metal is yellowish in appearance it was made from a cheaper alloy of 94 per cent tin, 5 per cent antimony, and a little copper.

Pewter has often been marked, but not with the strictly enforced and generally understood system of silver marks. The collector is better employed at studying the general appearance and in particular the hardness of a piece of pewter than looking for assistance from marks that can be most misleading. These marks are known as "touches." Most important is the crowned rose, signifying that the article was thus stamped by direct permission of the Pewterers' Company, and another valuable mark consists of the words MADE IN LONDON. This last should indicate that the metal is of standard quality or better than most of the metal used in the provinces. If the mark or marks have above separately an "x" surmounted by what could be a miniature crown, then it should be of high quality. This is sometimes called the "quality mark," also the letters I.C.S.

Pewter with a large royal crown in an oval frame can be interesting and valuable. At the coronation banquet of George IV a large quantity of pewter thus marked was stolen, and it still turns up in odd places.

Sometimes pewter has marks copied from those used on silver, but these have no particular interest, except usually to indicate that the pewter is of poor quality and made by a bad maker. Such marks are often found on beer measures, which were rarely made of good pewter and are best avoided by the collector.

The marks that should and can sometimes mean most are those stamped on the pewter by the best makers. Thus the name "R. CHAMBERS," written straight out, refers to an excellent maker of large pewter dishes particularly. The ancient heraldic sign of "a pelican in her piety" is similarly the "touch" mark of Rufus Harrison, and a scallop shell signalizes the work of Henry and Richard Joseph. Henry was Master of the Pewterers' Company in 1771 and Richard in 1805. An early mark is the rose between two twigs of Jonas Sonnan, who joined the Company in 1699. Then the name T. CLOUDSLEY, written straight out, indicates large dishes made by a good pewterer of that name from about 1780. Thomas Burford, Master of the Company in 1779, marked his fine pewter with the names Burford and Green at head and foot of an armorial device.

In Scotland the best quality of pewter was marked with a crown and hammer, but also sometimes with a thistle.

A rose surmounted by a crown can indicate French or German pewter, while it is worth noting that the fleur-de-lis on French pewter dates from about the fourteenth century—and the seeded rose without crown is nearly always a mark of foreign make.

The connoisseur of metal has, however, been primarily interested in the fireplace and its furniture.

From about the twelfth century to the last half of the seventeenth century such equipment was governed by the use of wood and peat as combustibles for heating and cooking. And the original andirons or fire dogs were crude structures of iron, with an iron bar placed horizontally on two legs at the front and one at the back vaguely to resemble that biological rarity, a three-legged dog. One end of the log was placed on this and the other in the fire so that a draught could entice the flames upwards.

Gradually andirons became more and more ornamental. The finest came from the Sussex iron foundries among the forests of the Weald.

Coal began seriously to supplant wood in the second half of the seventeenth century, "sea coal" from Newcastle perhaps, and it was necessary to devise the coal basket, from wrought iron. At first the front bars were vertical. By 1700 this was regarded as a rather stupid arrangement; and the eighteenth-century grate developed with wide-spaced horizontal bars at first, the bars and supports of fine steel, and the baskets, backs, and sometimes legs of crude iron. Really outstanding craftsmen worked on these grates, thanks to the patronage of rich people who were transforming small manor houses everywhere into stately mansions and at the same time developing London homes with similar appurtenances. The design remained basically unchanged until the middle of the century, when the classical influence of the Adam brothers introduced the urn terminal and the patera.

Chippendale and Hepplewhite included grates in their drawing books; and what is called the "Chippendale" fireplace is probably the most desirable of all. The austere basket of three bowed bars of steel with a sometimes ornamented iron back has in front a bowed skirt of brass that has been exquisitely pierced with scroll design, and this skirt has noble supporters at either side with more piercing and decorative finials.

The fireplace then had a unique importance in the decorative scheme. All furniture was turned towards it; and the eighteenth century designers realized that since the fireplace was more looked at than any other object in the room it should engage their supreme artistic attention also. The fireplace then had the same social and artistic significance as the television set today.

The most important eighteenth-century grates often had detachable fronts that could be taken away for cleaning, and this was the origin of the fender. The earliest and most valuable brass fenders consist of a single strip of pierced work similar to what was originally the skirt on the grate. Fenders with sides were developed in the nineteenth century.

The final phase of the portable grate was ormolu-mounted in the Regency as influenced by the French Empire period. Many of this style were imported from France, together with a temporary and anachronistic firedog of flamboyant design—actually two dogs per fireplace with the wrought-iron basket of the grate resting on the back irons of the dogs.

Fire backs, plates, or reredos were originally just cast-iron slabs placed at the back of a fireplace to protect the wall and throw the heat forward. At first they were wide and low, but a tombstone shape was introduced in the late seventeenth century. Many came from Holland; but the finest examples, still to be seen in museums of Sussex, the county where they were traditionally made, are enlivened by designs impressed by wooden stamps into the bed of sand on which the plate was molded. One famous fire plate shows a Sussex ironmaster and his wife being burned at the stake in the reign of Queen Mary. The flames eternally lick around their Protestant steadfastness. Coats-of-arms, Boscobel oaks (after the Restoration), and typical Dutch patterns will be studied by the collector.

Timepieces

Clocks in Europe go back to the thirteenth century, but clocks for modern collectors begin with the lantern type of the seventeenth century. It was made in the shape of a lantern, with frame, dial, and side doors of brass or iron, and a bell on top. The Fromanteels made some still extant specimens in the 1620s, but it should be noted in dating lantern clocks that the type continued to be made until the end of the eighteenth century and has since been reproduced in large numbers. It was also known as the "bird-cage" clock, and its basic principle, with the pendulum hanging beneath, survives in the ubiquitous "cuckoo" clock.

Long-case or grandfather clocks were first developed in the second half of the seventeenth century, and originally had thirty-hour movements. As time passed—no pun intended—the movements became longer and longer, and it is possible to date some old movements in this way. The great makers will be dealt with in a moment, but it should be observed first that veneered oak was first used for the making of cases, up until about 1685. Walnut was used from around 1670 to 1770, and mahogany from about 1760. Floral marquetry was used on fine cases in the second half of the seventeenth century, and the most lovely and valuable of all grandfather clock cases, in seaweed marquetry, belong to the first half of the eighteenth century. Dials were about 8 to 8½ inches square from around 1660 to 1673, 10 inches square from about 1673 to 1695, 12 inches square from about 1685 to 1712, and rectangular from around 1705. It is also worth noting that the hood slides upwards for removal until circa 1710; from about 1700 it slides forward.

Pediments on the top can also be significant—gable pediments from around 1660 to 1675, flat carved pediments from about 1665 to 1730, and arched from circa 1720.

Bracket or mantel clocks had a similar history to the long-case. They originally had verge escapements so that they could be carried from room to room without leveling, but they were very inaccurate. They inaugurated the spring, and had the attention of the greatest makers, and reached their apotheosis in ebonized cases with brass or ormolu mounts and handles and finely chased brass back plates for reflection in the mirrors above the mantelpieces on which they were placed.

Some facts about watches: The best were made on the Continent, at first in sixteenth-century Nuremberg, developing into the "Nuremberg eggs" of about 1600 to 1650. France and Geneva developed the industry, and England came late. It is rare to find an English watch made before 1600. Glasses were not used until about 1600, and watches prior to 1700 had only one hand.

Johannes Fromanteel and his kinsman Ahasueras Fromanteel were among the earliest and most important of English clockmakers although they came from Holland. Johannes probably introduced the pendulum, c. 1658. Fromanteel grandfathers, with crown-wheel escapement and short pendulums, are among the most sought-after primitives of the clock collector.

The most important English clockmaker was Thomas Tompion, 1638–1713, a Quaker from Bedfordshire who, bravely for his trade and sect, achieved the distinction of burial in Westminster Abbey. He established his business at Blackfriars, and was commissioned not only to make timepieces for Charles II and William III, but also for Greenwich Observatory, where his remarkable two-year clocks were used by the Astronomer-Royal for scientific purposes. A genuine Tompion long-case or bracket today is worth many thousand dollars, not only for the name and the technical excellence of the movement but for the fine proportions and general beauty of the piece.

Tompion had as pupil-assistant one George Graham, who was also a Quaker, and marrying the master's niece, succeeded to his business and achieved the double of ending in Westminster Abbey similarly. He lived from 1673 to 1751, came from Scotland, and notably invented the dead-beat escapement and the mercurial compensating pendulum.

Daniel Quare, 1648 to 1724, provides another of the great names of this extraordinary period. It seems that in the last half of the seventeenth and the first half of the eighteenth centuries the minds of small mechanics were turned as if instinctively to the devising of clock

This is the best kind of London basket-top bracket clock. Made by Alexander Hewitt about 1695. The movement has original verge and pull-repeat striking on five bells, also false-pendulum and calendar apertures, pendulum regulator and strikes/silent lever. The case is ebony with superb mountings.

movements as a prelude to the wider engineering discoveries that brought about the Industrial Revolution. The techniques of these nimble-fingered men provided the basis for the work of the machine makers. Quare made clocks for George I, and one of his noble long-cases, constructed to run for a year, is to be seen at Hampton Court Palace. It is said that he was first responsible, in 1687, for placing the minute hand concentric with the hour hand; and Quare was one of the important early makers of barometers (as patented by him in 1695).

We are similarly much impressed today by the clocks of Joseph Knibb and members of his seventeenth-eighteenth-century family. They are very beautiful, very valuable; and Knibb is given special credit for his system of "Roman numeral striking."

Lesser names include John Arnold, important for his work on the marine chronometer and on "repeater" watches; John Barnett, a master of the marquetry long-case; William Bowyer, who made some of the best early lantern clocks; William Clement, a pioneer of the anchor escapement as used in conjunction with the long pendulum; John Ellicott, in business about 1728 at Sweeting's Alley near the Royal Exchange in London, and inventor of a compensating pendulum; Peter Garon, maker of fine watches as well as long-case clocks (specialty of chimes on six or eight bells); John Harrison, 1693–1776, maker of the marine chronometers without which Britain might never have developed her sea power, and also inventor of the grasshopper escapement, the gridiron pendulum, and the going-rachet; Norton Eardley, 1760–1794, specialist in the making of chiming, musical, and astronomical clocks; also Edward Banger, Peter Closon, Nicholas Coxeter, Edward East, John Ebsworth, George Etherington, Christopher Gould, Charles Gretton, Henry Jones, Thomas Lister, Richard Lyons, Thomas Mudge, Thomas Wheeler, Joseph Williamson, and Joseph Windmills.

Barometers were an interesting sideline of these English clock makers of the great period, and the credit for making the first is usually assigned to Henry Jones. He was Master of the Clockmakers' Company in 1691 and developed the primitive mercury tube that the Italian Torricelli had accidentally discovered around about 1643. Several types were made initially by Jones and other horologists such as Tompion and Quare. The cistern, or true Torricellian barometer, had the bottom of the vertical and marked glass tube inserted in a cup or cistern of mercury. The inclined, diagonal or yard-arm type was similar but had a horizontal tube inclined at a sharp angle from the top. Then the siphon barometer had a U-shaped tube at the bottom and made possible the wheel or dial barometer from roughly 1670. The true dial barometer was not generally made till about the middle of the eighteenth century, and the modern aneroid barometer dates from circa 1844.

Early barometers are crude articles of mainly scientific and antiquarian interest. The collector finds greatest pleasure and scope in the eighteenth century dial barometers that were mounted in cases of walnut, mahogany, satinwood, rosewood and Coromandel by the master cabinetmakers and/or by specialist barometer makers in the Clerkenwell district of London and in the provinces.

Musical Boxes

The musical box, and other forms of automata, was another offshoot of seventeenth-century clockmaking. At first chimes were developed in striking clocks, then tunes and moving figures that popped out and performed various evolutions when the hour was struck. But the musical box as such is a typical product of the sentimental and gadget-loving nineteenth century, and most of the great makers, listed here, belong to that period.

Alibert, François: He worked in Paris from 1820 to 1850, or thereabouts. He specialized in small boxes with laminated combs, but also made the larger movements with cylinders 9 inches long or more.

Aubert, A. A.: He was a Swiss maker who came to London and set up business in the Clerkenwell Road in partnership with Louis Jacquard. He died of consumption and Jacquard was burned to death in his workshop.

Bontems, Charles: He made mechanical singing birds particularly, in Paris, and his firm is still in existence.

Bornand, Adrian: He worked at St. Croix and then emigrated to the United States.

Brachhausen, Gustave Adolph: Worked in Leipzig, then went to the United States in 1889 and founded the Regina Musical Box Company. Was the inventor of the self-changing disk machine, and thus the father of the modern record-player.

Breguet and Sons: Specialists in musical watches of the cylinder type.

Chaillet, Octave F.: He transposed the music and pricked the cylinders for several firms in St. Croix, including the makers of the large reed-organ accompaniment musical boxes.

Evans, David: Among the most important of the early English makers of musical boxes and clocks, often made particularly for the Spanish market. Some of his musical clocks are very beautiful in red lacquer with gold ornaments. 1770–1822.

Geater, G.: He imported French and Swiss musical movements into London and had inlaid cases made for them.

Gueissaz-Frères: La Sagne, Switzerland. It was at La Sagne that Jean-Daniel Richard, the founder of modern watchmaking, was born in 1665. The name Gueissaz-Frères is to be found scratched on the bed-plates of many small musical movements made by other firms such as Paillard in the 1890s. It was not unusual for work to be farmed out in this way.

Harris, Heeley and Co.: These were primarily makers of cases for musical boxes, and operated in Birmingham and London from 1810 to 1840. They worked in bronze, ormolu, alabaster, buhl, and coral and lava cameos.

Jacot, Charles Henry and Co.: Founded at Geneva in 1870, this firm invented in 1886 the important Jacot safety check to prevent a musical box from running down, and so spoiling the cylinder and comb if the mainspring went out of control or the escapement broke.

Jaquet-Droz, Pierre: Born in Switzerland, 1721, this very famous maker of mechanical singing birds and other unusual automata also designed organ clocks, musical clocks, and ingenious musical watches that played tunes on bells and combed cylinders.

Lecoultre Frères: Watch and small musical movement makers of Geneva, founded 1810. David Lecoultre probably invented the brass cylinder musical box.

Mermod Frères: Another firm of St. Croix, 1815 to 1889, that made musical boxes and penny-in-slot cylinder machines. Their introduction of the Stella disk-musical box led to their bankruptcy.

Metert, Henri.: A Geneva maker of mechanical singing birds, and of a musical box that used bells for the music.

Mojon, Manger and Co.: Makers of large musical boxes in London, some with dancing dolls and bells and drum. They were also notable for the "Specialite" boxes with double springs that played as long as 150 minutes.

Paillard: This important firm was St. Croix for many years. They became known by the initials "P.V.F." They made fine but also cheap boxes over a long period, certainly from 1814 to 1914.

Ullman, Charles: Maker of excellent musical boxes from 1870 to 1890. His "Excelsior" box was well known, and he was notable for putting the control levers of his boxes outside the cases.

Firearms

Among everyday articles of the past that have become specially important to the modern collector are firearms. The demand owes much to the frontiering tradition and lax gun laws of America, but it is true that early weapons are among the most beautiful objects bequeathed to us by our ancestors. Once again they were made by hand lovingly as if without thought of their ultimate purpose. Their makers wanted them above all to look good.

A case of lovely dueling pistols was on sale in a Somerset antique shop twenty years ago for only thirty pounds. The same set would be worth several hundred pounds today, such has been the appreciation in values and the diminution in supply.

Reproductions have been made in considerable numbers, but without the complicated if crude mechanism of the originals and always lacking the indefinable beauty of age. To make an old weapon completely to deceive the connoisseur would cost even more in work hours than the original and it would be impossible to use wholly authentic materials.

A complete collection of European firearms would contain, first, a matchlock musket of the fifteenth century, extremely rare, clumsy and heavy (14-20 pounds). The name comes from the Italian *moschetto* or sparrow hawk, and the weapon originated in Italy or Spain, whence it was brought by the Spaniards to the Netherlands. Towards the end of the sixteenth century it was introduced into France and England. It was known also as the arquebus, particularly the early German version, and was fired by burning a slow match very awkwardly, after which 9 to 6 bore balls were with any luck propelled from the long barrel.

The firing of these early guns was the difficulty, and the different types that developed are classified by the type of their lock or firing mechanism. Thus the second item in a historical collection would be a flintlock hand gun of the sixteenth century. It might have the Dutch snaphaunce, consisting of a piece of flint held in the jaws of a cock for striking against a piece of steel to cause sparks and ignite powder in a pan below. It would more likely be an English improved flintlock of the important period 1620–1630. The priming pan of these early pieces had a hinged cover from which rose the piece of steel, and the firing action at once forced the flint to strike the steel and threw the powder cover back.

Flintlocks were made and continued to dominate the design of firearms until the nineteenth century, but had the competition, on the Continent especially, of several other devices, such as the wheellock from Nuremburg about 1517, and maybe based on a design of Leonardo da Vinci. A sprung wheel was turned and on release spun round and, with serrated edge, ignited the priming in the pan. Or there was the Miquelet lock, a Spanish invention of about 1587. The feature of this was an L-shaped hinged piece of metal. The lower section was struck by the flint, and the top, hinged section, jumped up and down to make a flashpan cover. Then the "fusil" was a kind of flintlock as used by the North British Fusiliers from 1678; and Nock's patent breech of 1787 had a breech plug wherein a thin gold or platinum touchhole instantly communicated the flash to the powder chamber inside. Flintlocks can be usefully dated by the presence of this breech—not older than 1787.

The great British Army weapon of the eighteenth century, which helped to make it the master of many battlefields, was the famous Brown Bess Musket, so-called because the barrel was browned by pickling to reduce glare and rusting. It was a long-arm, barrel 46 inches long, mounted with brass, and it had a short wooden stock, sharply dropped and with long wrists, with a total weight of about 10 pounds, a burden for the infantryman but not enough to make him mutiny. It had a curious bridle lock, that helped to eliminate misfires, and the weapon could be quite fast and accurate. It would fire six shots a minute and hit anybody at a distance of under 80 yards. Another name for the Brown Bass was the Tower musket.

The British Rifle Brigade in the Napoleonic wars discarded the Brown Bess and used the Baker rifle, an iron-ramrod-and-mallet muzzleloader invented by the gunsmith Ezekiel Baker of London. (Rifling as such goes back to the arquebus in 1460 and many finely rifled weapons were made thereafter.)

The detonating lock of 1807 was the first percussion lock and made possible the firearms of our own era. It was invented by the Reverend Alexander Forsyth of Belhelvie, Aberdeenshire.

Breechloading was attempted in very early days, but did not become practicable until 1776, when a British Army officer named Patrick Ferguson invented his plug-type breechloader, which might well have won the American and several other wars for Britain if only the army had had the sense to adopt it. As it was, they continued to use Brown Bess and the Baker rifle, faithful servants in the eighteenth century but hopelessly inadequate at the time of the Crimean War in 1854.

The Henry rifle introduced lever action in the early 1860s, and Mauser produced the first effective bolt-action rifle in 1898.

Meanwhile many refinements had been introduced in sporting guns, which in the first half of the nineteenth century were infinitely superior to military weapons. The great British gunsmith was that Joseph Manton who improved the flintlock by his elevated rib above the barrel, his gravitating stop, and his recessed double breech. So effective was the work of Manton that many features of the double-barreled shotgun have not changed since his day.

The blunderbuss is the name given to a fowling piece with broad, bell-shaped barrel as first developed in the 1620s, probably in broad-beamed Holland. The idea was *not* to project an assorted charge of nails and old iron, and thus to transfix a whole flock of sparrows to the branches of a tree, but to cause alarm and consternation by extent of noise and flash. If indeed those weapons had been loaded with odd bits and pieces the barrel would have been burst by the irregularity of the charge. They were actually loaded with powder, a wad, a measured quantity of balls or shot, then another wad.

Leaden pellets were used in fowling pieces from the sixteenth century on. A trencher pierced with holes was placed over a bowl of water in order to make this birdshot. Coals were ignited in the trencher and molten lead was poured in. It seeped through the holes and solidified to shot in the water below. In the middle of the eighteenth century it was discovered how to make perfectly rounded pellets by the shot-tower method: dropping the lead through perforations from a great height.

The cartridge as such could be said to date from the fifteenth century and a design of Leonardo da Vinci again. It was originally a paper packet tied at both ends, containing ball and powder, bitten open before loading. The earliest self-igniting metallic cartridge was the Prussian von Dreyse's of 1836, improved upon by Houiller of Paris in 1846. Finally the percussion cap was developed by the Americans Berdan and Morse in the 1850s.

Powder flasks and horns were in use from the sixteenth to the nineteenth centuries. German, Spanish, and French examples of the seventeenth and eighteenth centuries are of special interest as works of art and ingenuity, such as one made from staghorn with silver mountings, showing St. Hubert the patron saint of hunters, and another from Germany combining flask, double-headed spanner, and screwdriver, all finely chased and most ingeniously contrived.

Much of the beauty of early firearms is derived from the quality of the so-called Damascus barrels, made by a process developed by English craftsmen in the eighteenth century. The barrels were made of "skelp," a "rope" of twisted, fused and beaten wire, afterwards acid-treated and covered with artificial rust, which, when polished, revealed the mixed pattern of the twisted and flattened wire. Beware of fakes made by etching the patterns into solid or hastily woven barrels.

Guns were decorated by chasing of brass plates and scroll-inscribing of names. Those of Nicolas Noel, who worked at Versailles in the eighteenth century, are supremely ornate and yet triumphantly beautiful.

The pistol closely followed the military long-arm and the fowling piece in basic design and appearance, although with occasional oddities such as the screw barrel or cannon barrel, invented about 1635 by British gunsmiths. (The barrel was screwed onto a short breech chamber and was unscrewed for loading.)

It is important to be able to distinguish dueling pistols from ordinary twin and/or ornamental sets. They were specially made for dueling, and had the distinctive features of lack of bright or overornate decoration, also of perfect balance so that they would "come up" accurately when fired according to the very strict rules of the duel.

The true ancestor of the modern revolver was the Collier, invented by Elisha Collier of Boston (1814–1815) but developed in England by Evans from 1819 on. This flintlock revolver was both practical and elegant, a most distinguished collector's piece always. After which Samuel Colt of Hartford, Connecticut, more or less took over. He developed and adapted the revolver, after the invention of the percussion cap, for mass production. Most valuable are his earliest "Paterson" models, as made at Paterson, New Jersey, from 1836 to 1842. Then Colt went bankrupt, took up submarine cable-laying—but returned to firearms in 1847 with the Mexican war, which brought him a contract for 1,000 revolvers. Thus began the famous enterprise at Hartford, where all the Colts were made thereafter, except those between 1853 and 1857 from the London factory.

England's real answer to the Colt was the Adams and Adams-Deane revolver patented by Philip Webley and Robert Adams in 1851. It is different from the Colt in being a double-action piece. With the early Colts it is necessary to cock with the thumb before firing. The Adams guns were also stronger and faster and had greater impact stopping power than the Colts, but the parts were not interchangeable, and accuracy was reduced over long ranges. Webley and Scott of Birmingham still make excellent revolvers.

The modern automatic pistol dates from the Spaniard Orbea's invention of 1883 and also from Paulson's British revolver of 1880.

The bayonet started about 1580 as a sword or dagger with wooden handle, stuck into the barrel of a long-arm weapon. At the end of the seventeenth century a Frenchman invented the modern bayonet, that was inserted into a tubular socket above or below the barrel. The earliest bayonets are like broad-bladed daggers with wooden handles.

In 1637 the Gunmakers' Company of London was entrusted with the testing of gun barrels to ensure a standard of safety. This was known as proof-firing. Then barrels were

(Courtesy of Aabenraa Antikvitetshandel, Aabenraa, Denmark.)
Two examples in color of the lovely Danish painted furniture.

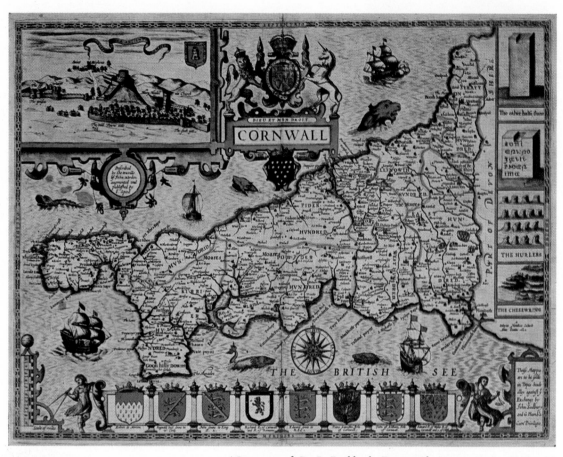

(Courtesy of P. J. Radford, Denmead, Portsmouth, England.)
Two early English maps by the most important names. On the left, a Speed of Cornwall and on the right a Saxton of Hampshire. Genuine examples of this type are undervalued still and will soon be worth much more than their present prices.

(Courtesy of W. H. Patterson, 19 Albemarle St., London, W.1.)
The Dutch romantic school of the nineteenth century is today's best target for the ambitious collector of oil paintings. The above is a superb view of Amsterdam by Kasparus Karssen, 24 by 36 in.

(Courtesy of Sydney L. Moss, Ltd., 51 Brook St., London, W.1.)
This shows in actual color a beautiful tsuba or Japanese sword guard by the celebrated maker Shomin.

stamped according to the rules of the Gunmakers' Company with two kinds of small mark, both headed by a crown. The letter "V" in the first mark meant "viewed after the first test," and the letters "GP" in the second mark meant "gunmakers' proof." Each maker had his individual mark; and the following is a list of the outstanding eighteenth-century gunmakers' initials and emblems:-

Archer	D	
Arden, W.	WA	
Barbar, James	IB	(with star)
Barnes, John	RB	(with black star)
Barnet, Robert	RB	(with white star)
Barnett, Robert	RB	(with coronet)
Barras, Ralph	Fleur-de-lys	
Bennett	IB	(white letters)
Birkett, Wm.	WB	(with black diamond)
Blake, G.	GB	
Bond, P.	PB	
Bower, Richard	RB	(with anchor-head)
Brander, W.	WB	(with black star)
Brander, Wm.	WB	(with thistle)
Brazier, John	IB	(with black crown)
Brazier, Robert	RB	
Brooke, R.	RB	(with trident)
Brookes, Benjamin	BB	(set in diamond)
Buckmaster, Wm.	WB	(with black star)
Buckmaster, J.	IB	(with black star)
Buckmaster, R.	RB	(with white heart)
Bumford	IB	(with crown)
Bumford, John	IB	(with flowery crown)
Bunker, John	IB	(with black cross)
Bunney, J.	IB	(with small crown)
Burchett, Edward	EB	(with dragon's head)
Byrne, Michael	MB	(with three swords)
Chalkley, S.	SC	(with black heart)
Chrystie, J. D.	Bow with arrow facing upwards	
Cole, Elias	EC	
Collumbell	C	(set in circle)
Davis, Thomas	TD	(with crown)
Delaney (?)	G	(with crown)
Dunn, Jeffrey	ID	(with crown)
Dupe	I	(with white eagle)
Delaney (?) Henry	HD	
Egg, Durs	DE	(with crown)
Farmer	Black head with helmet	
Fell, Stephen	SF	(in black heart)
Fort, T.	HT	
Freeman, Isaac	IF	
Gandon, Peter (elder)	PG	(in diamond with white star)
Gandon, Peter	PG	(in black diamond)
Gardner, Charles	CG	
Garrod, Robert	RG	
Gibson, T.	TG	(elided letters)

Gibson, Thomas	TG	
Goff, Daniel	DG	(with star)
Govers	IG	
Green, T.	TG	(with crown)
Grice, W.	WG	(with crown)
Griffin, Joseph	IG	(set in black oblong)
Griffin, Joseph	IG	(set in black circle)
Guy, William	WG	(set in diamond)
Halfhide, George	GH	
Hall, John	IH	(with crown)
Hartwell, Wm.	WH	(white on black)
Harvey	H	
Hawkins	IH	(with crown)
Henshaw, John	JH	(in black diamond)
Henshaw, Thomas	TH	(set in black oblong)
Heriot, Wm.	WH	(black letters)
Heylin, Joseph	IH	(with crown)
Hosey, John	IH	(with sharper crown)
Jeffreys, Thomas	TI	
Johnson, John	II	(with broken black circle)
Joiner, John	II	(with white star on black)
Jones, John	JJ	(stylised letters)
Jones, T.	TI	(with crown)
Kelly, William	WK	(with star)
King, Richard	RK	
Ketland	Crossed lances with crown	
Lamphere, Richard	RL	(with crown)
Leveridge, Benjamin	BL	
Lloyd, Evan	Name set in horseshoe	
Lowe	White cow set in black	
Lowe, J.	V	(with crown)
Loy, Robert	RL	(black letters)
Lugg, Rupert	RL	(white letters)
Manton, Joseph	White Stylised crown	
Marsh, John	IM	(set in diamond)
Maskall, Richard	M	(with dragon's head)
Mayo, John	IM	(set in oblong)
Mead, Thomas	TM	(with crown)
Memory, Michael	MM	(with dragon's head)
Moore, Daniel	DM	(white letters)
Moore, Daniel	DM	(black letters)
Nicholson	IN	(with black star)
North, Edward	EN	(in diamond)
Peele, T.	TP	(white letters)
Pickfatt, Charles	CP	(black or white letters)
Pindar, John	IP	(white letters)
Pratt, Isaac	IP	(black letters)
Probin, J.	IP	(in white surround)
Richards, T.	TR	(white letters)
Richards, W.	R	
Rood, Thomas	TR	(black letters)
Sale, Edwards	ES	
Sandwell, Stephen	SS	

Sinclair, Richard	RS	
Smithett, George	GS	
Stanton, Jonathan	IS	(white letters)
Turvey, W.	WT	
Twigg, J.	IT	(with crown)
Utting, J.	IU	
Vandebaize, Philip	PV	
Walker	Six-point star	
Walker, John	IW	
Wallace, S.	SW	
Wallis, Marmaduke	MW	
Ware, Wm.	W	(set in black heart)
Waters	IW	(in white oblong)
Waters, J.	IW	(crown in beaded circle)
Williams, Thomas	TW	
Wilson, Richard	RW	(with star)
Wilson, Robert	RW	(with diamond)

Apart from the dates given in this section already there are others that should be of use to the collector, such as:

Touch-hole: Probably first used at Ghent 1274.

First Hand Gun in England: Perhaps around 1386.

Matchlock: 1509–1547.

Wheel-lock: Invented by Johann Kiefuss, Nuremburg, 1515–1517.

Rifled Barrel: One made by Augustus Kutter, Nuremburg, 1520. And probably first used in England about 1635.

Flintlock: Probably first used about 1600.

Snaphaunce: Imported from Holland to Massachusetts 1628–1629.

Percussion Lock: 1807–1845.

Pin Fire: By Lefauchaux of Paris, 1845.

Rim Fire: By Frobert of Paris, 1847. Then by Smith and Wesson, who made the first .22 in 1855.

Central Fire: 1855.

In order to complete this section the author paid a visit to a London dealer in old firearms, and what he had to offer was so interesting that it should be briefly surveyed here. These items will have been sold long before this book is printed and read, but they indicate what can still be available.

First: a pepper-box revolver af around 1845, which, made according to the patent of J. R. Cooper, had horizontal nipples with partitions between each. The hammer, partly enclosed in the weapon, struck the lowest nipple. Price would now be between $85 and $135.

The first percussion revolving pistols were called pepper boxes, and another, of about 1840, was self-cocking and had six barrels, checkered butt cheeks, and the breech end of the cylinder chambered and turned down to a small diameter to make for compactness. Present value between $70 and $85.

Then there was a cannon barrel flintlock pistol by King of London, made between 1770 and 1790. It had a silver butt cap and silver wire inlay. The box-lock sides, sliding safety catch and other parts were finely engraved. The pan with a raised lip fitting into a matching depression in the cover indicated an early rain-proof type. Nearly a foot long, this fine piece would now be worth perhaps $220.

Earlier still was a flintlock holster pistol of Italian manufacture, circa 1740, with brass butt cap, trigger guard, side plate, finely engraved, and stock and fore end carved in the Oriental manner. This would now be worth about $150.

A rare pair of "under-and-over" tap action flintlock pistols in almost mint condition, flat-sided with perfectly plain burr-walnut stocks, made by Ryan and Watson of London about 1800, would today be worth perhaps $325.

Even more notable was a cased pair of percussion pistols, double-barreled (side by side), converted from flintlocks by H. Nock, London, about 1800. They had walnut stocks with checkered butts, and engraved lock plates, hammers, trigger guards, finials, and sliding safety catches. The case also contained a nipple key, a bullet mould, a cleaning rod, a tin for percussion caps and bullets, and a powder flask with powder, balls and linen patches. Inside the case was a label describing the maker's method of converting the weapons from flintlock to percussion cap. This very interesting collector's item would probably be worth over $450 now.

A cheaper pair of target-dueling percussion pistols, by Westley Richards of London, about 1835, had octagonal barrels and fore and back sights, was finely engraved, and would be worth about $265.

Another revolver was of the percussion transition type and had Liège proof marks. The design was unusual in that the hammer was hidden and struck the horizontal, partitioned nipples through the body of the gun. The hammer was cocked by means of a thumbpiece on the right, and there was an unusual loader in the butt. The weapon was over a foot long, was made by Devisme Bte. around 1830, and would now be worth some $135.

This dealer also had several interesting long-arms, such as a Moorish flintlock with Miguelet lock, the butt inlaid with metal and ivory, worth about $85, an eighteenth-century Japanese matchlock, of which the octagonal barrel was inlaid with silver, about $65, a "Paget" carbine, for cavalry use, the first military weapon with a stirrup ramrod and the first carbine with a short barrel, London circa 1800, about $125, and a flintlock blunderbuss of about 1700 with steel barrel, brass butt plate, trigger guard, ramrod pipe and side nail cups, worth about $130.

Swords, daggers and spears are equally available in considerable quantities to the collector still, also suits of armor, but are not so much "in fashion" as firearms. They belong to a different era of collecting, when large houses afforded suitable space for display.

Locks

The modern collector with his mechanical turn of mind is often attracted to old locks and keys, which can be interesting as well as strangely beautiful. The lock is a very ancient invention, going back more than 4,000 years to the Egyptians. Warded locks, with a fixed obstruction to prevent the wrong key from being used, date from medieval times. The tumbler lock came next. It contains an obstruction that moves when the right key is inserted, and may have been invented by the Chinese.

The lock protected by a metal case first appeared in the early sixteenth century in England. It is still possible to find examples of late seventeenth-century cased locks that are finely decorated with engraved or pierced work.

In the middle of the eighteenth century the mortise lock was invented, and it was soon accompanied by the exquisite door furniture, handles and plates, key escutcheons and the like that in itself is a fascinating subject for the collector.

A connoisseur of old locks would want to possess items such as a wooden Egyptian type, a fine steel piece of the sixteenth century from Germany, a Banbury lock of wood and metal made some 400 years ago, a German jewel casket of the seventeenth century with elaborate lock on underside of lid, two spring bolts at the front and one fixed dog bolt at the back, or an enormous chest lock, measuring 18 inches by 7 inches, and, of course, a perfect brass-cased rim lock of the eighteenth century.

These locks were handmade, and their keys alone are objects of beauty and historical interest that can be found and collected quite inexpensively still.

Dental Antiques

As an example of how everyday and technical objects of the past can still be acquired and assembled in a valuable collection there is the remarkable dental museum created by Dr. J. Menzies Campbell of Glasgow. Over a long period of years this well-known practitioner acquired early books on dentistry, early instruments employed by dentists, early toothbrushes, advertisements, artificial dentures.

Dr. Campbell's books included:

A Short Philosophical Essay . . . (London, 1715). *Anon.* This claimed to explain many prevailing superstitions regarding the teeth scientifically. For example, there was much about the wearing of an anodyne necklace (often pulverized roots of henbane and peony) to prevent fits and convulsions during dentition, besides being efficacious for "Toothaches, Headaches, Red sore and weak Eyes, Vapours, Hardness of hearing and Sore Throats."

A Practical Treatise upon Dentition . . . (London, 1742), by Joseph Hurlock, a London surgeon, who advocated lancing the gums to stem the prevailing high mortality from convulsions arising from dentition.

The Harangues, or Speeches of Several Quack Doctors . . . (London, c. 1745). A most interesting collection of speeches delivered in the market places by itinerant empirics. Included were the songs of the accompanying jesters, whose duty was to attract the crowd. There were many references to the serious results of neglecting the teeth, and unfailing remedies for their cure. However, the compiler, in his notes of *The Character of a Quack,* remarked ". . . no man in his perfect wits would have anything to do with him . . ."

A Treatise on the Teeth . . . (London, 1752). By A. Tolver, surgeon, who was convinced that sensible living and diet were important factors for ensuring healthy teeth. He condemned confections and sugars, which, in his opinion, contributed towards the destruction of the teeth.

A Treatise on the Teeth, their Disorders and Cure . . . (London, 1753). By Frederick Hoffman, M.D., who adhered to the medieval belief that worms caused dental caries, and recommended that they should be dislodged by a decoction of coloquintida, pills of aloes and myrrh, and the "smoak" of henbane. In other cases he advised the application of a red-hot wire to the exposed nerve prior to filling the cavity with lead. (An explanation of why so many people had convulsions when they visited the dentist in those days?)

A Treatise on the Tooth-ache . . . (London, 1768). This anonymous writer recognized two kinds of toothache—in a sound tooth and in a carious one. For the last he advised inserting cotton-wool saturated with laudanum. Should the pain persist, his remedy was to "burn the nerve with a red hot wire," and, if this failed, to extract the tooth.

A Practical Essay on the Human Teeth . . . (London, 1781). By P. E. Jullion. For an annual payment of four guineas this author was prepared to undertake "the care and treatment requisite for preserving the teeth and vigour of the teeth and gums." His fee for a set of human teeth with "gold springs" was £73.10s.

Dr. Campbell's collection contained no fewer than 37 curious forceps. The earliest was an excellent example of Italian craftsmanship, of the period 1600 to 1650, with a box joint and ornamented brass rivet recessed to represent the spokes of a wheel, and ends of the blades embellished by an entablature. The baroque pattern of another, c. 1675-1725, was reminiscent of Spain; circular ends with seals were added, around 1812, to convert the forceps into a holder for tapers or wax for impressing documents. Then there were superb examples of French and Arabian workmanship. Three (one c. 1786) bore a crown surmounted by a star, indicating "Maker to Royalty." Two, c. 1815 and 1840, were designed for the vertical extraction of teeth. Others included Savigny's work; the favorite French parrot-beak pattern, c. 1815; Shepherd's "Safety" forceps, c. 1834, with gouge-shaped blades tapered to a cutting edge to free the gum; John Gray's design, c. 1840; Hullihen's "Compound Screw Forceps," c. 1850, with an ingenious device for extracting roots; and Physick's pattern, c. 1840, with excising beaks for molar teeth.

Then there were thirty artificial dentures, the most outstanding being two complete sets (upper and lower), one of them with springs, constructed entirely of de Chemant's "mineral paste," and a four-page illustrated handbill, c. 1797, advertising them. There were bone, elephant and hippopotamus ivory dentures, some with human teeth most adroitly fitted, others beautifully colored with dyes; early tube teeth fitted to gold and dental alloy bases; several porcelain gum teeth, 1845-1855, some plain, others colored by the dentist; examples of human teeth sold to dentists; and an ivory splint, c. 1830, constructed by Mallan and Sons.

There were five exquisite silver toothbrush sets, comprising toothbrush, container (with two compartments) for toothpowder and tonguescraper, in original cases and hallmarked 1794, 1795, 1799, and 1827—matched by a pewter holder for double-ended toothbrush, c. 1800, and several toothpick sets, the earliest from around 1800.

Horse Brasses

Horse brasses have been derided, thanks to their humble origin, low price, and lavish reproduction, but genuine examples are exceedingly interesting as well as decorative, and could eventually be important.

They originated in the primitive belief that darkness was evil and light was good. At the same time horses were valuable and could perhaps be protected if decorated with emblems of light, such as the sun, moon, and stars. Such amulets for horses are mentioned in the Old Testament, Homer's *Iliad,* and other ancient writings. The Crusaders brought back Saracen specimens; but the heyday of the horse brass was the Nineteenth century when the horse population was at its height and it was necessary to decorate the animals for special occasions.

The earliest types were plain, circular, or crescent in shape, but a wide variety of patterns were used in the Nineteenth century. Similarly bronze was the first material, followed by lead coated with brass or other metals, then brass hammered or cut by hand, and finally cast or stamped brass. No brass examples were made in England before the reign of Queen Elizabeth I. Brass casting as such was first developed in the Seventeenth century. In our time a great number of brasses have been made by the machine-stamping process at Walsall and district. By comparison with the genuine article they are light and meretricious. Weight, as ever, is nearly all.

It is a curious fact that horses liked to be decked with martingales and sidepieces with the dangling brasses. Sometimes they would not work until provided with their finery. One of the strongest animal instincts is the instinct for display, which, indeed, is primarily responsible for this present book and its subject.

6

European

French

The intelligent collector of antiques will have observed three main geographical sources, England, the Continent of Europe, and the Orient. And for many the Continent of Europe will primarily mean France, although, as will be seen in this chapter, other European countries have made contributions that are almost as important as those of France, notably Italy (without whose classical and Renaissance artists and craftsmen Paris might never have existed).

The four main French styles are known as Louis XIV, Louis XV, Louis XVI, and Empire, with the Régence as an interregnum style between Louis XIV and Louis XV.

The period of Louis XIV between 1660 and 1715, also known as the *Grand Siècle,* is characterized by heaviness and squareness, but a great sumptuousness in design. There is an almost mechanical formality about the period that derived partly from State control of the means of aesthetic production. Louis XIV formalized his era by direct governmental intervention in the lives and work of cabinetmakers, ceramic artists, and makers of tapestries and carpets. Stucco and gilt metal ornaments and marble were much used on furniture and in the decoration of rooms. The brass and tortoise-shell marquetry of Charles André Boulle (1642-1732) was a symbol of the era. It was ingenious and, when new or restored, not without nobility and charm, but age would reveal its tawdry and unaesthetic quality. The decorative motifs of this period belong to what is known as the baroque, an essentially involved, grotesque, and "overdone" conglomerate of applied or carved ornament, which is chiefly effective when overwhelmingly rich. Then there is nothing like it, as at Versailles and in the finer churches of southern Germany, Austria, and parts of Italy and Spain.

The Régence period was from 1715 to 1723 only, the Regency of the Duke of Orleans; and it is interesting to see how in this short time the designers were able to throw off the heavy incubus of the past. Articles became lighter and nicer; baroque ornamentation gave way to the rococo.

The style of Louis XV (1723-1774) is without doubt the summit of French achievement in the household arts. The chairs and tables and cabinets sloughed off the overbearing weight of the *Grand siècle,* and became curved and fragile in appearance but not in basic strength. Small items of furniture were designed in great numbers. Decoration was reduced to a discreet minimum in the new rococo forms, based on the shell and asymmetrical by comparison with the heavy

(Courtesy of Nystad Antiquairs, Lochem, Holland.)
French Louis Quatorze: Signed by the master cabinetmaker Migeon.

The finest Louis Quinze commodes have never been surpassed in beauty, exactness of cabinetmaking and richness of mounts. This example was made in Paris by Macret about 1760.

baroque of the preceding period. The purist could admittedly complain that the Louis XV style would have been perfect but for the perversion of the rococo; and the severe judgment of Fowler is always worth remembering. He said that "rococo is regarded as a form taken by the baroque when it aimed no longer at astounding the spectator with the marvellous, but rather at amusing him with the ingenious."

During the reign of Louis XVI, 1754-1793, the straight line was gradually restored to French design. The classical rediscoveries of the second half of the eighteenth century were largely responsible for this change. The Louis XVI style could be described as a tactful marriage of the best in the two preceding styles with a Graeco-Roman gloss.

The Empire period is usually assigned to 1794-1830. It breaks almost entirely with the traditions of the past except in actual excellence of cabinetmaking, and is characterized by an essential awkward unloveliness yet by such a curious flavor that it has great interest. Briefly they tried to re-enact not only the ancient Greek and Roman but also the Egyptian and Assyrian scenes. The furniture particularly of the period is a bad pastiche of ancient museum pieces, chairs with arms ending in lions' heads and sphinxes and bearded deities, also with gilded feet of mythological animals, tables resting on dolphins, cabinets and bureaus of rosewood with gilded animal feet again, and winged figures everywhere, and wreaths, pateras, urns.

In ceramics the principal French contributions, from the viewpoint of the foreign collector, are faience pottery and Sèvres porcelain.

Faience is a pottery of pale red hue, covered with a white glaze made usually from tin, lead, alkali and fine sand. The discovery of the method is usually assigned to Bernard Palissy (1510-1589) but his efforts as a potter were directed towards glazing earthenware in the same way as pieces he had seen from Italy, Spain, and the East, notably the pottery of Faenza in Italy. He experimented for some sixteen years, completely denuding his finances and the patience of his

(Courtesy of Nystad Antiquairs, Lochem, Holland.)
Typically fine French commode of the Louis Seize period, made by Lebesque.

(Courtesy of Nystad Antiquairs, Lochem, Holland.)
Very important example of the best French furniture, Louis Seize period, made by the master cabinet-maker Oeben about 1775.

wife and children. Towards the end he was unable to pay the wages of his assistant and had to tear the clothes off his own back to raise a few sous. All the furniture in his squalid dwelling was burned to provide fuel for the potter's oven.

It was at the very end, and when the last chair leg was being burned, that Palissy achieved success and took from his oven what was for him a perfectly glazed plate. Henry III was the king, and had sufficient education and taste to recognize the glazed pottery of Palissy as an unusual achievement. He established him in the Tuileries with a small workshop, and there Palissy would have lived happily ever after if his parents had not been so cruel as to instill in him the tenets of the Protestant creed.

When Henry promulgated his edict of 1559 against the Protestants several chances were given to Palissy to recant, but he refused to do so and was dragged off to the Bastille. The King visited him there and begged him to be sensible and free. Palissy characteristically replied that he was already free. It was the King who was in the chains of his Catholic faith. Palissy was left to molder, and did so for thirty years. He had such character that they could not kill him even with the most horrible privations. Eventually he had to die, in that same Bastille.

Faience of the best period was made from 1700 to about 1775 in Lyons, Marseilles, Montpellier, Aprey, Nevers, Rouen, Sceaux, Moustiers, and Strasbourg (although also in Italy, Holland, and Germany). Often the true French can be recognized by a fleur de lis in the decoration. Some of the most interesting pottery in this genre was made at Strasbourg by Charles François Hannong and his son Joseph, from about 1720 to 1760. After 1760 a decline set in and the factory was closed in 1780. The best Strasbourg is in the form of pottery models of armoires and sedan chairs and the like, and sometimes has the blue "H" mark.

Faience of the more ordinary type was made principally as tableware for middle-class families, especially during wartime when it was necessary to hide or melt down the plate. Then it was used for stove tiles, basins, bidets, cisterns, ewers, and even for garden pots.

Early faience was in sober shades of green, yellow, orange-red, purple and blue, formed from metallic oxides. After 1750 brighter colors such as pink, crimson, and vermilion were introduced. *Faience Japonais* was painted in these more striking hues, and in the style of Oriental porcelain. *Faience Parlante* was decorated with popular proverbs or songs. *Faience Porcelaine* was an attempt to imitate genuine porcelain, by decorating richly with enamel colors on glaze. *Faience Anglais* was similarly an effort to copy English creamware—and it should be noted that by far the main output of the trade was undecorated white or cream faience.

And it was because of the superior quality and lower price of Wedgwood and other English creamware that the making of faience in France eventually came to an end. At the close of the Eighteenth century nearly all the great kilns were cold.

Soft-paste porcelain was being made at St. Cloud in France prior to 1700, and there followed the enterprises of Chantilly, Menneçy, Vincennes, Sèvres.

Sèvres started at Vincennes in 1738. Orry de Fulvi was the founder, with two workmen from Chantilly. The enterprise did not succeed, and in 1745 a new company was formed by Charles Adam. He used influence at Court to obtain a thirty-year monopoly from Louis XV, proved successful at engaging good workmen, and moved the factory in 1756 to Sèvres where it has been ever since.

Soft-paste porcelain was made at first under the name *Porcelaine de France,* and the products of the soft-paste period 1756-1786 are the most desirable from this factory, inimitable, lovely and

(Courtesy of Dr. H. G. Bunke, Maximilianstrasse 15, München, Germany.)
Fine French porcelain: A white Chantilly cachepot with fleurs de Vincenne, mid-eighteenth century.

in the modern taste. A hard paste was introduced in 1769 and gradually ousted the soft. It was called *Porcelaine Royale,* and eventually achieved such a glasslike consistency and perfection of finish that it became almost repellent in its exact beauty.

The colors of Sèvres have a mechanical richness and depth that no other porcelain can show, the famous pink or *rose Pompadour,* the strong rich blue or *bleu de Roi,* the dark blue or *gros bleu* and the turquoise or *bleu celeste.* The most characteristic subjects in decoration are cherubs and roses with rococo borders of gold. A double "L" crossed is the principal mark, based on the royal monogram. A letter of the alphabet at the center of this indicates the year of manufacture, starting with "A" for 1753. The first series ended in 1777, and the "double letter" series began in 1778. The monogram varies in shape, and often has additions such as initials and symbols adopted by painters and gilders. During the republican period of 1792-1804, the monogram "R.F." for République Française was used, together with the word "Sèvres." A complicated mark including the letters "Imp" was used during the first Imperial period 1804-1890, and an elaborate revival of the early double "L" mark with a fleur de lis in the middle was used from 1814 to 1824 during the reign of Louis XVIII. Most other marks on Sèvres indicate a later date than 1824—and it should be understood that Sèvres of the unique soft-paste period is very rare, extremely valuable. Nearly all extant pieces are known and should not be purchased without authentication.

Certain terms used in the French school should be understood. Thus *barbeau* is the cornflower often found as a motif in the great porcelains, and a *bergère* is a type of armchair first made in France around 1725, with padded arms and upholstered sides and back, gilded or painted wood.

Bombé furniture swells outwards with an appearance of pregnancy; a *chiffonier* is a narrow piece with drawers like an English tall-boy; *Chinoiserie* is a design based on the Chinese; and an *ébéniste,* originally a worker in ebony, is a cabinetmaker. The maître ébénistes, as famous in their day as artists today, stamped their names usefully, if sometimes fraudulently, on the backs of pieces.

A *guéridon* is a slender piece of furniture used for supporting a light originally, and, as the name first came from a Moorish galley slave, so the piece will often be supported on a Negro figure. The *torchière* is similar piece of furniture but taller.

The term *mille fleurs* derives from medieval tapestries with floral backgrounds; *pâte tendre* means soft-paste porcelain; and *vernis Martin* is generically a name used to describe French lacquer work but specifically refers to the mid-eighteenth-century lacquer of the brothers Simon-Etienne, Julien and Robert Martin, who developed a process which involved the admixture of gold with the lac paste plus elegant painting in bright colors.

An outstanding French contribution in furniture was the development of metal mounts. These were first used for the practical purpose of protecting feet, edges, corners, and keyholes. Charles André Boulle was the first famously to develop their decorative possibilities; and a special guild of craftsmen, the *fondeurs-doreurs,* obtained the monopoly to make the mounts on all furniture. Cabinetmakers who dared to make their own were prosecuted. The supreme craftsman was Pierre Gouthière of the Louis XVI period. His cutting was superbly sharp, and his gilt bronze work in particular was notable for contrasting effects, partly burnished and partly matt.

These mounts were made by what was known as the *cire perdue* method. First a wood model had delicate details applied in wax. Then the master mount was expensively cast in ormolu, brass of high purity containing an admixture of zinc, or bronze (alloy of copper or tin). But note that the process was so expensive that recasting from original master mounts was extensively the method employed in later days, a reason why the designs of mounts changed little through the successive periods. And that the attachment of the mount to the furniture was an important part of the art, helping us to determine today whether pieces and their mounts are original. The good cabinetmakers designed their marquetry, for instance, so that spaces were left for the mounts to be applied without overlapping the marquetry. Screws, often with unconcealed heads, were used, and sometimes pins, but the great craftsmen liked to employ screws with a head concealed by the decoration in a permanent hole with nut at the back. Therefore the collector should look for mounts that do not fit, or overlap, or have beneath them old screw or pin holes that have been plugged. The "carving" of the ormolu should be sharp and confident, and inferior mounts of base metal with gold thinly applied are quickly revealed by rubbing.

German

The principal German contribution is the hard-paste porcelain of the Meissen and other great factories. True porcelain had long been made in China, but the secret of its manufacture was not mastered by Europeans till Johann Friedrich Böttger (1682-1719), working as a court alchemist for Augustus the Strong of Saxony, realized that he would never be able to make gold and might lose the patronage of his master if he did not produce something of commercial value and aesthetic interest. He turned to the porcelain problem, and by 1708 had succeeded in making the first European hard-paste, albeit white and unglazed. The next year he discovered how to glaze the substance satisfactorily (and at the same time invented a very hard red stoneware). The year after that Augustus financed the establishment, twelve miles from Dresden, of the Royal Saxon Porcelain Manufacture, in the small cathedral town of Meissen.

Unfortunately Böttger died in 1719 just as the factory was getting into commercial production, but happily Augustus was a determined man. He set up a commission to enlarge the factory; and from 1720 till 1756 Meissen produced the finest of our European porcelain, at first according to the designs of baroque silver, then distinguished by the painted decorations that were applied under the direction of Johann Gregor Herold, an enameler and miniaturist who liked brilliant colors, yellows, blues, greens, lilacs, grays, crimson-purples as applied particularly to landscape and Oriental designs.

Then a superb modeler, Johann Joachim Kändler, came to Meissen, and, completing the trilogy of talent, gave the factory its figurative fame. Kändler did not invent the porcelain figure, but the porcelain figure as we know it would never have existed but for the artistic skill and inventive genius of Kändler. Nearly all the motifs of European porcelain derive from this Meissen period, the modeled gallants and their ladies with the most intricate sculpture in the finest hard-paste, the shepherds and shepherdesses, the street traders, the monkey bands, the gods and goddesses, and also the molded flowers and vegetables, the encrusted ware, the great table services with richly painted scenes of the Watteau school.

All this temporarily came to an end in 1756 with the outbreak of the Seven Years' War, but in 1763 and until 1774 Meissen entered a new period of accomplishment. This is known as the Academic Period. Michel-Victor Acier was appointed as chief modeler jointly with an aging Kändler, and designs became classical and stiff. A notable innovation was lace decoration (dating from about 1770).

The appointment of Count Camillo Marcolini in 1774 led to a decline in standards. This period lasted till 1814; and thereafter Meissen produced only what we now know as "Dresden," a cheap copy of its old self. During the nineteenth century "Dresden" figures and other porcelain

(Courtesy of Dr. H. G. Bunke, Maximilianstrasse 15, München, Germany.)
The finest German porcelain was that of Meissen in the Herold Period. This beaker and cover was painted with harbor scenes by Herold around 1738.

articles were almost mass-produced for the undiscriminating nouveaus riches of England and America.

The first Meissen mark was the monogram "A.R.," signifying "Augustus Rex," but this is found on only a few very important pieces. Then the famous crossed swords appear, together with the monogram and with the letters "K.H.C.W.," also the letter "G." The initials stand for the words *Konigl. Hof. Conditorei Warschau.* There are numerous other marks, such as swords crossed on the top of a cross, the wand of Aesculapius, crossed swords with date, the letter "W," the letters "G.L.," and "B.P.T." During the Marcolini period, 1774–1814, the crossed swords had a star between the handles. Since Meissen was subsequently copied by other factories and by near-forgers, it is worth noting that the Wolfssohn imitations at first bore the royal monogram, sometimes surmounted by a crown, then had the mark "Dresden" with a crown. Meyer und Sohn used crossed rapiers with an "M" between the hilts. Samson of Paris used crossed rapiers with sometimes an honest "S," sometimes a large star alone. A cross line on the swords of genuine Meissen indicate that the piece was sold white out of the factory. Several cross lines indicate defective porcelain.

Fürstenberg was porcelain made from 1753 at a factory established by Duke Karl I of Brunswick in 1747. Excellent hard-paste came from Fürstenberg during the years 1770–1800, with an "F" as the usual mark, sometimes accompanied by the date or by the depiction of a strange animal. Höchst was porcelain made at Höchst-am-Main under the patronage of the Elector of Mainz, from about 1750 to 1798, with a wheel as the principal mark.

The first Berlin factory ran from 1752 to 1757, making hard-paste of the Meissen type with "W" as the principal mark. Frederick the Great was the patron, and in 1763 he acquired another Berlin pottery and made of it the large *Konigliche Porzellanmanufaktur,* that, under the marks "G," a scepter, and the letters "KPM" with an orb or Prussian eagle continued to make porcelain of average interest until our own time.

Nymphenburg derived from the factory established in 1753 by J. J. Ringler at Neudeck. This enterprise was transferred in 1761 to the grounds of the Nymphenburg Palace, where, under the patronage of the Bavarian Prince and of a Count Sigismund von Haimhausen, it employed the modeler Franz Anton Bustelli, and produced many fine rococo figures, services, and other articles under the shield mark. The great period ended in about 1770.

Vienna porcelain dates from 1719 and, until 1744, under Claudius Innocentius Du Paquier, a court official, it closely resembles early Meissen and is usually decorated in the Chinese manner. From 1744 to 1784 the factory was run by the state and produced a great number of figures, groups, and other articles, often in the Sèvres manner. Konrad von Sorgenthal took over the factory from the state in 1784 and, until his death in 1805, much fine tableware particularly was produced in the neoclassical style. Vienna marks are variations on a barred shield.

This is, of course, only an outline of German porcelain production. Many factories have not been mentioned. But attention has been paid to what the reader of this book is likely to find and may want to know. Similarly, much could be said about other articles produced in Germany that have antique interest, but they would not come within the scope of the English and American collector.

It is necessary, however, to explain the name "Biedermeier," which applies to a German style of decoration dating roughly from 1815 till 1848, that primarily meant curved legs and backs for furniture, then, more pejoratively, large and heavy and overornamented pieces, the German nineteenth-century Empire style whose dead hand still uglifies so many of the lesser antique shops of the Continent.

It is almost presumptuous to speak of "Italian antiques," as the word "antiques" is itself an Italian derivative; and the modern social custom of collecting and furnishing with elderly articles began when eighteenth-century aristocrats went to Italy during their "Grand Tours" and returned with Roman and Graeco-Roman relics they had been eagerly sold there.

Such relics are still collected, but the few genuine articles available are so expensive as to be beyond the reach of all but millionaires and museums endowed by very wealthy patrons. Classical busts and columns and figurines that cost less than a small fortune are products of the great industry that developed in Italy during the eighteenth century to supply those aristocratic travelers with pieces of Greece and Rome to take home. This industry still tends to thrive.

The "modern" Italian period begins with early Gothic-style furniture mitigated by Lombard, Tuscan, and Byzantine-Romanesque influences. The chief items, *cassone* or coffers, chairs, benches, stools, cupboards, and tables had horizontal as opposed to the vertical northern Gothic lines. Decorations included colorful *intarsia* (inlays), gilding, painting and carving, with scrolled brass bands often round the *cassone,* and the Florentine lily as a favored motif.

Two outstanding types of Gothic chair were the *dantesca,* that had two front and two rear supports of X-form with seat and back panel of leather, and the *savonarola,* that could have as many as seven X-shaped supports, and a narrow seat of slats and cushion.

Table were at first long boards laid on trestles.

By far the most important item of furniture was that *cassone,* or chest. Many types of table and chair and armoire developed from it, and it was in itself not only a receptacle but also a seat and even a bed. The decorations for that reason are rarely on the top but usually on the front and sides. The earliest and best *cassone* are those with *pastiglia* decoration, a plaster worked in low relief and gilded or painted, often with mythological figures. Those that are elaborately carved with Gothic tracery came originally from northern Italy thanks to trans-Alpine influence.

When the Italians rediscovered their classical past, in the late fourteenth century, the period known as the early Renaissance, these Gothic types of furniture had superimposed upon them the classic Roman orders, the Graeco-Roman human figures, and other ancient motifs such as the egg and dart, or guilloche, the acanthus leaf, and the urn. Furniture became more stately, but still had the characteristic horizontal lines of old Tuscany, and was still inlaid frenetically, as in the fifteenth-century *certosina* of Venice with its elaborate *intarsia* of ivory or bone.

During the high Renaissance period of the rich Italian sixteenth century, the sumptuous furniture was at first a marriage of the classical and the Gothic that gradually became the wholly elaborate baroque, which assumed subtly different forms in each main center of the country.

Thus Florence made the most purely classical and restrained pieces, wonderful craftsmanship but always less fantastic than those of Venice. Already Venice was making much painted and gilded furniture, but with fanciful designs in low relief at this period. Sienese high Renaissance art was simple and severe; that of Piedmont and Savoy remained the most Gothic in style. Roman craftsmanship was influenced by the classical discoveries, strong, imposing, bronzed, decorated often with human figures, and pervaded by the shape of the oft-disinterred ancient sarcophagus.

The late Renaissance was the period of artistic and political decline, and yet of much new development in design. Michelangelo's larger than life figures and his heroic style generally led both to the fantastic climax of the baroque and to much heavy furniture. At the same time the architect Palladio did influence the craftsmen to strive for stateliness, fine proportions, and classical lines.

Certain marks of Italian high Renaissance furniture are carvings of figures, banderoles and cartouches, heraldic devices. An exotic form of inlay, characteristic of the essential decadence of the time, was *pietra dura* work, cut and polished semi-precious stones set in ebony, or other very dark woods, especially on tall cabinets and tables.

A very popular article of furniture in the late Renaissance period was the *sgabello* or stool chair, usually walnut, often with *intarsia* work, the seat a narrow, boxlike structure, and the back tall and narrow, often fan-shaped. Our late Victorian hall chairs are direct descendants of this form. The *panchetto* was a cruder, sometimes chip-carved version of the *sgabello*. Meanwhile a favorite larger chair was the plain square type with upright square back and upholstered velvet seat and back, ancestor of the English wainscot and Jacobean chair.

The *cassapanca,* originating in Florence, was the progenitor of the modern couch or settee. It was an elaborately carved and inlaid chest with back and arms.

Tables that were originally developed in Italy at this time included the refectory, the three-piece draw-top, and the center table in various shapes.

The *bancone* was a flat-top writing table of which the top extended well over the bottom. This bottom section had side drawers.

The design was essentially architectural of all this furniture, particularly of large walnut writing cabinets with much picture *intarsia* work as well as elaborate carving.

The ubiquitous *cassone* continued to be the most important article of domestic furniture until towards the end of the late Renaissance, with flat, shaped or arched lids, sometimes rectangular, sometimes boat, sometimes sarcophagus-shaped. The *cassette* was a small chest.

The *credenza,* or domestic cupboard, was another great, architectural piece, superbly proportioned, similar to the writing cabinet only with cupboards instead of bureau interiors. Smaller, homelier versions were the *credenzina,* the *madia* (for storing bread), and the *armadio* (often a wardrobe in function).

Baroque is a term from the Italian, and originally meant misshapen pearl. The Venetians took over this involved and superluxurious mode from the Romans and made some of the finest pieces. They similarly exalted the Rococo, and by the middle of the eighteenth-century Venetian painted furniture in this form included some of the loveliest domestic pieces ever made, light and harmonious in line, delicately tinted, smooth-surfaced. The method of painting was watercolor on a gesso undercoat, finally varnished.

Then the excavations at Pompeii and Herculaneum provoked the Neo-Classical Revival, or Second Renaissance. The Venetian, Giovanni Piranesi, published his *Diverse Maniere* in 1769, an important pattern book that strongly influenced not only Italian but also French and English design. Rococo scrollwork and ornament were replaced by classic architectural detail. The severe rectilinear form was revived, together with pilasters and columns. Marquetry was a feature.

The French Directoire, merging into the Empire style, influenced Italian late eighteenth-century and early nineteenth-century furniture, of which characteristic forms were the Greek-inspired *klismos* type of chair with rolled-over and concave crest rails, and the Grecian settees for reclining and other less graceful activities.

White and gold was the predominating Italian color scheme in the southern version of the Empire style. Console tables and curule-type chairs were outstandingly well designed.

In ceramics the most important Italian contributions are majolica pottery and Capo-di-Monte porcelain. Majolica is an earthenware with tin-enamel glaze. The name derives from Majorca, whence Spanish lustreware was exported to Italy. The great age for Italian majolica was the sixteenth century; and the main centers were Faenza, Forli, Siena, Orvieto, Florence, Ravenna, Deruta, Urbino, and Castel Durante. Brilliant colors and classical designs and luster effects and basically clumsy potting are main characteristics, plus the *istoriato* painting, a method that ignored the purpose of the pot and treated it as a canvas for display of the painter's art.

Capo-di-Monte porcelain dates from 1743 when Charles, King of Naples, set up the factory at Capo-di-Monte near that city. It was originally soft-paste, and some of the early figures and jewel boxes were superb in decoration if often crudely shaped and fired. An outstanding method of decoration was relief molding of classical scenes wherein the figures were beautifully hand-colored and then surrounded by lavish gilt margin lines. Early, genuine Capo-di-Monte is rare. The enterprise was moved to Buen Retiro near Madrid in 1759 when Charles became King of Spain. Many of the Capo-di-Monte molds were acquired in the nineteenth century, after the closure of Buen Retiro in 1808, by the Doccia porcelain factory near Florence; and most Capo-di-Monte now on offer originated in that factory. It can be identified by its crude hard-paste, very white, as against the crude soft-paste of the original. Early nineteenth-century Doccia reproduction Capo-di-Monte has considerable beauty and value, but as the molds wore out and the nineteenth century developed along its characteristic slapdash and mass-production lines, so the pieces became less sharp in outline and badly colored.

Dutch

Dutch and Flemish furniture in its best early periods so closely followed the French and Italian that it does not require separate treatment. The readers of this book will principally need to recognize the solid architectural and bulbous-footed quality of Dutch seventeenth-century cabinets, tables, and chairs in oak and walnut, also the more intricately carved appearance of the highly polished and rich-colored Flemish versions, after which it is sufficient to understand that Dutch marquetry is, for some, charmingly clumsy compared with French and English, and makes considerable use of the tulip, other flowers, and birds as motifs. This marquetry is of colored woods inlaid in Dutch walnut, which can be a lovely golden with age but in youth is a less pleasing and more garish color.

Undoubtedly Dutch antique silver is the most important contribution of the Low Countries apart from the superb work of the great painters. It can be second only to London of the best periods in importance, and is often more interesting than London, but more ornate and therefore not invariably so popular in our time. It has been widely collected outside Holland without full knowledge of its characteristics and grades. Today, with the sudden steep increase in values, it requires more careful study.

The earliest period generally examined is the Late Gothic, 1500-1530. This is of academic interest only; and collectors cannot hope to acquire the few examples remaining of flamboyant ecclesiastical monstrances and ostensories in the elaborate pinnacle style of Gothic architecture.

The next period is that of the Northern Renaissance, 1530-1590, again not for ordinary collectors and dealers. The silver was part Gothic and part Renaissance or "classical-exuberant" in style, with rolling cartouches, pilasters, satyrs, cherubs, and foliage.

Then came the mingled periods of mannerism and proto-baroque, about 1560-1650. Interest in natural history led to the mounting in silver of such objects as the coconut and the nautilus shell, and to the silver-modeling of birds and animals. The baluster stem was often replaced by the human figure. Then a remarkable style was evolved of working the silver by blobs and folds into fantastic masks and faces, notable in the products of the van Vianens, first of the great names in a list of Dutch silversmiths.

Paul van Vianen's brother Adam developed his ideas and imposed them firmly on Holland during the Rembrandt period. The silver of Adam van Vianen was often pure sculpture. Adam's son Christian continued the work and spread its influence to England. Then Johannes Lutma was even more monumental in his style. The influence of this school has been potent in Holland ever since; and offshoots were fancies such as windmill cups, "Johnnies in the Cellar," marriage caskets, and richly engraved alms dishes.

There was a brief mid-seventeenth-century period during which the taste for the fantastic seemed temporarily to die, and silversmiths such as Johannes Lutma the younger and Gilliam Bossche of The Hague returned to classical clarity and proportion. Then the full influence of the baroque (1650-1690) encouraged Nicholas Lookemans, Claes Baerdt, Johannes Bogaerdt, and others to produce the fantastically beautiful silver of what is possibly the best Dutch period.

This was ornate to a degree, with a multitude of floral and other shapes hammered out or engraved on still half-flowing forms. It was the pinnacle of achievement.

Hard upon this period came the first stirrings of the modern revolution. Huguenot refugees and the William of Orange link with England introduced a more sober taste; the demands of the growing middle class for domestic silver resulted increasingly in a supply of "sensible," small, everyday pieces.

But the eighteenth century brought many, often conflicting styles, notably those influenced by the various Louis periods of France. Thus the years 1710-1745 are assigned by Dutch silver experts to a "Louis XIV" period, with the *leitmotif* of the Borghese urn, forming the shapes of coffee, tea and mustard pots, also the knops of balusters.

Johannes and Gabynus van der Lely in Friesland (great makers of brandy bowls and brandy spoons with S-handles, bird-terminated), and silversmiths such as Jan Pondt of Amsterdam, Esaias Engouw and François van Stapele of The Hague, also Nicolas Verhaar of Utrecht made fine, solid articles in the plain styles of France and England but beautified by the Dutch traditional artistry and always superb in sheer craftsmanship.

The next period, roughly 1750-1770, partly follows the rococo style of Louis XV, returning for a while to graceful curves and concave, natural surfaces, but along characteristically Dutch lines. French immigrants such as the brothers Metayer introduced very acceptable silver and gold boxes and toys.

Other makers of the period, such as Van Stapele and Joosten of The Hague, Reynier Brandt, "W. W." of Amsterdam, Rudolf Sondagh of Rotterdam and Thomas van Meervoort of Bois-le-Duc made lovely, lacy, always beautifully curved silver.

The influence of the succeeding Louis XVI period was largely classical and architectural; and Engelbart Joosten, Johannes Siotteling and Frederick Manicus were among silversmiths who in the last part of the eighteenth century developed the Dutch style broadly along what we call Adam lines.

From 1770 to 1813 Dutch makers continued to follow English and French trends. They produced much imposing silver of the Empire style while dominated by Napoleon. Immediately afterwards they reverted to the broad shapes of their basic national taste; and fine developments from this might have enriched the nineteenth century had it not been for the coincident maladies of uncultured demand and mass-production philosophy.

Dutch silvermarks date from at least the fourteenth century, when the guilds insisted that every object must have a maker's mark, a town mark, and a date mark.

Generally the town mark is the town arms, with exceptions such as the Dordrecht rose and the Gröningen numbered and lettered shield.

Sometimes shopkeepers' marks were added, usually a name written in full, such as that of the famous Diemont.

An additional complication in Dutch silver is the "duty mark," too involved for explanation here.

The Dutch date letter can be confusing because the style of typeface was not always changed at the beginning of a new series.

Hallmarks are *not* protected by law in Holland, and wrongly marked or forged pieces are not destroyed there as officially they are in England. This has resulted in the survival of doubtful silver, but also in the survival of much lovely silver that would have been destroyed in London.

This would be particularly interesting if it were not for the coincident fact that other enemies have depleted the Dutch stock of antique silver, notably in times of war. Until quite recently it could be said that more Dutch silver was to be found in safer England than in Holland (and of course much early Dutch silver was actually made for the English market). But Dutch prosperity in recent years has attracted back to Holland a great deal of important plate; and the general lack of confidence in currencies has increased demand for old silver and hugely enhanced market values.

It was once the fashion to associate Holland with delft, a tin-enameled and blue-decorated earthenware made at the small city of that name. It is still true that old delft has great interest and value, but its popularity with English and American collectors has been perhaps fatally assailed by modern manufacture of the pottery in Holland and its association with tourist souvenirs. Early marks on delft were associated with the signs of the breweries that first housed the potteries, such as De Blompot (the Flower Pot) and De Vergulde Boot (the Golden Boot). Another class of marks features initials of the potter. Most clearly marked pieces are, however, modern reproductions. The many-colored "delft" of Friesland is very attractive to the modern eye, but has been forged and reproduced so much that it is scarcely worth attention.

Scandinavian

There are two kinds of Swedish antique furniture, that based on French models, and that made for farm and peasant. The first is the more important, consisting of finely constructed strong commodes, bureaus, chairs in the Louis styles, heavier than the true French but not clumsily so, as the Dutch, or ornately so, as the Italian, nor over-Anglicized, as the English. Swedish aristocratic furniture could be French and yet it is at once less feminine and more "domestic" than the French. Often it is usefully signed and nearly always it is valuable.

The farm and cottage furniture is completely different, true folk art, clumsily made and often painted in what were originally bright colors, with designs of primitive Celtic and Russian origin. It is not so plentiful or so (comparatively) inexpensive as its Norwegian, nor so lovely as its Danish counterparts.

Not only is Swedish silver very important and valuable, but Sweden has such a strong feeling for silver and other forms of metalwork that she has for years been a leading buyer of English silver, of which large quantities now exist in an essentially wealthy country.

The design of Swedish silver is basically similar to that of French and English, but more substantial and with a trace of Norse primitivism in its whorls and tracings.

Fortunately there is no need to be an art expert to identify Swedish silver, as it is well marked, with ordinary letters of the alphabet for dates from 1689 to 1758 (properly Stock-

(Courtesy of H. Bukowskis Konsthandel, Stockholm, Sweden.)
Typical piece of fine old Swedish Silver: Funeral Beaker for the Swedish King Fredrik I, Made by Gustaf Stafhall, Stockholm 1751.

holm), and a combination of letters and numerals from 1759 onwards (the national mark). The standard work on the subject is *Svensk Silversmide,* three volumes, by Olle Kallstrom and Carl Hernmarck. Gustav Munthe's catalogue of the Falk Simons Collection is also useful.

Then there is much Swedish glass of great interest and value, but this country's supreme contributions in glass are chandeliers, surprisingly light and delicate in design and of what is called the waterfall type mainly. They are closely allied to the Russian variety, but are probably unequaled for quality of construction, fineness of crystal, and that overall effect of delicacy.

The most popular Swedish coins are recent issues, from 1873 onwards. Earlier issues in FDC condition are very scarce. The most desirable of all Swedish coins are the gold issues, especially the de Ducat and Carolin series, but a completely Swedish curiosity is "plate money," the largest item of currency ever made, sometimes 40 pounds in weight (the copper equivalent of what was the silver value).

In ceramics the outstanding contribution is Marieberg porcelain, started by Sten in the second half of the eighteenth century. It is rare and valuable, and similar to Menneçy. Particularly choice are the little, well-modeled cream pots with covers, fluted spirals and delicately painted bouquets of flowers, also the statuettes and rococo candelabra with the mark MB.

There are three kinds of Danish antique furniture: the painted, the Holstein, and the Danish adaptation of the French modes.

Danish painted furniture is among the loveliest and most desirable in the world, comparable only with Venetian, that it closely resembles. The elegant, slim lines, and the delightful faded colors of the originally bright paint make these Danish colored pieces eminently suitable for inclusion in modern schemes of interior decoration.

Holstein furniture is quite different. It is similar to the best Bernese, only with a higher gloss and lovelier brown color allied to great ingenuity of cabinetmaking. It is plain and light brown and brightly polished.

Danish versions of Louis-style furniture are sometimes painted, sometimes plain as Holstein, sometimes direct copies.

Then Denmark is essentially a land of neat farmhouses, and can accordingly offer considerable quantities of country bygones, ranging from Norse-style brass utensils to peasant ceramics and ironwork and implements and treen.

But one of Denmark's most important contributions is porcelain. The modern, remarkably fine products of the Royal Copenhagen Porcelain Factory tend to obscure the fact that such fine porcelain has been made in Denmark since 1772 (soft-paste was made in 1760). The characteristics of the Danish ware are high glaze, subdued colors with pearly tints, and superb modeling of figures, particularly animals. Three wavy lines are the famous old mark.

Norwegian painted furniture is really delightful, like the Danish only more rural and with the attraction sometimes of Bruegel style paintings and its typical feature of "rosemaling" or "rose painting." This is a decoration where flowers such as roses and tulips, and different kinds of leaves, have been used as a main symbol, together with scrolls and the acanthus in various lovely tonings of color.

The more valuable pieces of Norwegian painted furniture can include charmingly primitive figures of soldiers, trees, churches, and houses, decorating particularly the panels of cupboards, bureaus and bridal chests.

Norwegian glass is both primitive and extremely delicate in design, characterized by applied strips of glass "beading" often, and with a faintly nautical appearance. Pewter from this country

The beauty of the best old Danish furniture is always revealed at the famous Antikvitetshandel at Aaben-raa in Denmark.

also has a distinctive appearance, essentially Norse and delightful in a full range of kitchen utensils, always the color of German and Flemish rather than English pewter. Country items generally include a great variety of treen, articles of wood usually made by the farmers themselves with a single knife as tool in the dark winter months. Characteristic decorations of Norwegian treen beer mugs, barrels and utensils for making cheese and bread and butter are principally rosemaling and "poker-work" consisting of brown and black dots burned into the wood with red-hot iron needles to make primitive patterns. Often the date of making or giving and the initials of the maker or recipient were incorporated.

Swiss

Heraldry has remained alive in Switzerland as in no other country save England, but, while in England it has been confined to royalty and aristocracy, in Switzerland it has been largely a bourgeois and popular art. Heraldic devices are found above the doors of householders, on mullions and oriels, and applied in relief on wood or plaster ceilings. It was a custom in the Switzerland of former days for friends and relatives to present each other on certain occasions with heraldic window panes and small hanging devices in stained glass. The most humble families had their coats-of-arms. These panes have attracted the attention of connoisseurs, and there are several collections in England and America.

Then Switzerland has throughout the ages produced furniture in the popular European styles of each day. There are Swiss antique pieces in the Gothic oak, the French seventeenth and eighteenth century, the German, the Italian, and even the English styles. Switzerland can be prouder, however, of her true native styles, of which there are several, each the product of a separate state or canton. The furniture of Berne, in particular, is immediately recognizable, walnut, severely utilitarian and unpolished, yet undeniably elegant and increasingly valuable.

Pictorial and graphic artists are not being dealt with in these national surveys, but the landscape prints of Switzerland are so important that they must be mentioned as general collectors' pieces. They probably evolved to satisfy the demand of visitors in the eighteenth and early nineteenth centuries. The Swiss artist Aberli invented the "vedute" method of etching on copper plates and tinting by hand. Two artists, François Diday (1802-1877) and Alexandre Calame (1810-1864) especially catered for the early tourists with pictures of mountains and waterfalls that were continually reproduced. J. H. Füssli or Fuseli (1741-1825), was the only European name that emerged from the school; but the work of Segantini and Hodler, Gessner and Topffer in the form of delicate, accurate, and unerringly beautiful prints will always be worth collecting.

Swiss pottery and porcelain, relatively unknown outside Switzerland, is colorful and often very good, beginning with the seventeenth century faience of Winterthur, of which lovely, clean tiles for the great domestic stoves, and plates decorated with family coats-of-arms are the outstanding features. Then pottery from various villages in the Simmental near Berne included, during the eighteenth century, the ivory, blue, green, brown and yellow bird- and flower-decorated plates and bowls of Langnau, the white and polychrome pots of Blankenburg, and the darker wares of Heimberg.

Boccalini is the name given to small jars with a white ground from which red wine was drunk, a characteristic product of the Ticino, but also of the Grisons.

Two faience factories were established at Berne in the middle of the eighteenth century, both notable for fine painting on the clean background of scallop-edged plates. The bailiff Willading's was one, from 1758 to 1763; the other was Colonel Frisching's, 1760-1777, famous for tiles with floral decorations in glowing, assured colors. Large chrysanthemums were frequently depicted, and "B" was a mark.

Then a life of only four years sufficed to make lasting fame for the pottery of Hunerwadel and Klug at Lenzburg. Plates and dishes, bowls and jugs, candlesticks and centerpieces were invariably painted with green-clad huntsmen in pursuit of game. Producing so much beauty, the factory naturally failed. Mark: sometimes "LB."

And the pottery of Beromunster was started in 1770 by Andreas Dolder at the age of only twenty-six. Dolder produced very beautiful rococo coffeepots and the like with white, fluted backgrounds, charming floral decorations with much rose-red, as well as tiles. Mark: "M."

With Zurich the era of Swiss porcelain is approached. The original faience pottery of

Zurich at Schooren, started in 1763 by a syndicate of members of the local Natural Science Society, was among the most interesting in eighteenth century Europe, in that it gradually produced everything from pipe clay to *pâte tendre,* from earthenware to true porcelain. Adam Spengler was the manager, previously at Frisching's in Berne, and from the beginning a highly commercial and proper attitude was adopted: with a shop at the Munsterhof in Zurich.

The Zurich faience was similar to the white-grounded and rococo-shaped pieces with brilliant floral and biological decoration that characterized the best from other Swiss factories in the eighteenth century. Mark: a "Z" in blue under the glaze.

The Zurich porcelain painters were wholly admirable, nearly as good as those of Meissen and Sèvres, so much so that in 1790 the whole enterprise collapsed. The porcelain had a fine body of quartz, kaolin and felspar fused at high temperature.

Finally a painter named Ferdinand Muller started rather unusually to make porcelain at Nyon on the shores of Lake Léman near Geneva. This was in 1781. And Muller had the assistance of one J. J. Dortu, who had worked at Berlin.

Nyon porcelain is quite unlike Zurich and departs almost entirely from the homely designs of Swiss faience. It is nearer to Sèvres, nicely delicate and translucent, symmetrical, blue or rose overall backgrounds with much gold-rimming and knops, or white background with finely painted pastoral scenes and more gold-rimming. No great Swiss family was without its Nyon tea, coffee, and table services. Mark: a blue fish. In 1811: out of business.

7

Oriental

Chinese

Chinese antiquities are chiefly ceramics, jades, and metalwares. Furniture has always been collected but is nearly always of comparatively recent origin, and those who make it in China tend to suit the taste of each European age. Thus collectors in the nineteenth century would import fussy, lacquered pieces, while what reaches us from China today is mainly plain and simple and just low enough to make perfect coffee tables and not obscure the view of the TV set.

The history of China is so long and the names of the emperors and periods and places are so involved that it is necessary for the collector to adopt an arbitrary scheme of historical identification. It will not be completely accurate, but it will serve, roughly as follows:

1. *Prehistoric wares.*
2. *Early historic wares.* From the twelfth century B.C. to the tenth century A.D.
3. *Sung wares.* From the tenth century to the thirteenth.
4. *Ming and Ch'ing wares.* From the fourteenth century to the present.

The prehistoric wares are of academic interest only, comprising mainly painted mortuary pottery of the late neolithic period as well as ritual bronzes.

A gray, unglazed pottery is the first manifestation of the early historic period. Known as Chou pottery, it is primitive in form, and decoration consists of simple hatched designs or impressed basket patterns.

Next come the jars and tripods, olive in color and lead-glazed with molded ornaments, known as Han pottery, and a gray pottery with decorations of red, white, black, and green sometimes known as Wei.

This was succeeded by the really important productions of the early historic period, that are often known as T'ang (618-907), the figures of horses and other animals and human beings in pottery, green, blue, yellow, brown, with its fine crackle, and the first true porcelain, surviving mainly in small white bowls. This was one of the greatest ages in the history of mankind. Our own ancestors were grimly surviving the collapse of Roman civilization, but the Chinese were enjoying and exploiting all that we now most admire, exquisite manners, poetry, beauty of house and garden. It was at this time that they invented printing, paper money, gunpowder, many devices of architecture, some remarkable tortures, and, for our particular interest at present, the ceramic material that we know as porcelain and that we were unable to make ourselves until the eighteenth century.

(Courtesy of Bluett & Sons, 48 Davies St., London, W.1.)
Typical pottery of the Chinese T'ang Dynasty A.D. 618–907. Jar with cream glaze, height 6⅝ inches.

The succeeding Sung period, from 960 to 1279, tended to consolidate and refine the discoveries of the previous period. This is an era that has been carefully studied by Chinese scholars; and it is notable for the fine ivory-white porcelain with impressed or incised designs and "teardrops" known as Ting yao, for Ju yao porcelain with its opaque lavender glaze, for the flowerpots and bulb bowls, lavender inside and crimson outside, which we call Chun yao, for the black or dark brown small tea bowls known as Temmoku, and for the renowned celadons.

Celadon means a glaze in various shades of green. It was evolved by the Chinese potters in an effort to simulate jade, and the color of this austere, lovely pottery varies from the bright "onion shoot" green of Lung Chu'an in Chekiang Province, to the deep brownish and olive green of north China.

The Ming and Ch'ing period are best studied in terms of the *style* of decoration, starting with blue and white, an exquisite white porcelain decorated under the glaze with cobalt blue, then the Tou-Ts'ai of the Ch'eng Hua period, a more complicated porcelain with the design outlined in underglaze blue on the white body and painted over the glaze with delicate enamel colors.

Polychrome Ming is a term used to describe most of the other enameled porcelains of the Ming era, except for Wu-t'sai, a style of five-color decoration over underglaze blue from which the renowned *famille vert* was a development, that beautiful ware with the overglaze blue and green enamel painting. Then there were *famille noire* and *famille jaune,* and greatly improved celadon wares. Much of the manufacture of this porcelain and pottery was concentrated in a single great city, Ching-te-chen, that was surrounded by quarries of china stone and clay, a city of potters who could rejoice in their production of a pure "heavenly-white" translucent porcelain, and of artists who could paint scenes and designs with a dexterity that has never been known since.

During the final Ch'ing or Manchu period, 1644 to 1912, the imperial factories at Ching-te-chen were completely rebuilt and began to cater to an entirely new trade, that inaugurated by territorial expansion to Tibet, Nepal, Korea, Mongolia, Manchuria, and Turkestan, and by intercourse with European travelers. Eventually the Chinese craftsmen had the European market almost entirely in view when they designed their products, and everything European was copied. It was the end of a long tradition.

But certain products of this *fin de siècle* period have their interest and are widely collected. The famous ruby-back eggshell plates were made, as fine technically as anything in the history of ceramics; and at the other end of the scale came the ubiquitous blue and white ginger jars and tea caddies. The invention of a rose-pink enamel made possible the almost too-popular *famille rose.* In fact the products of the Chinese seventeenth and eighteenth centuries were regarded by our fathers as supremely worth collecting; and it is only since comparatively recent antiquarian and archaeological discoveries that we have come to appreciate the infinitely more honest work, in the aesthetic sense, of the great Ming and Sung potters.

Jade is a subject by itself. It was so important as long ago as 700 B.C. that Pein Ho, a minor official of the Duke of Ch'u, could have his feet cut off for offering his master a piece of sacrificial jade that his friends demonstrated to be a forgery. Subsequently Pein Ho was found to be innocent, and was doubtless grateful still to be able to hop about on his stumps, but the jade had established its supreme importance in a collectors' world.

The original Chinese jade was of nephrite or jadeite, not to be confused (as it usually is) with the emerald-green jadeite often imported into China from Burma. The true material ranges

MING DYNASTY

年製 洪武
Hung Wu
(1368–1398)

年製 永樂
Yung Lo
(1403–1424)

德年製 大明宣
Hsüan Tê
(1426–1435)

化年製 大明成
Ch'êng Hua
(1465–1487)

治年製 大明弘
Hung Chih
(1488–1505)

德年製 大明正
Chêng Tê
(1506–1521)

靖年製 大明嘉
Chia Ching
(1522–1566)

慶年製 大明隆
Lung Ching
(1567–1572)

曆年製 大明萬
Wan Li
(1573–1619)

啟年製 大明天
T'ien Ch'i
(1621–1627)

年製 崇禎
Ch'ung Chên
(1628–1643)

CH'ING DYNASTY

治年製 大清順
Shun Chih
(1644–1661)

年製 大清康熙
K'ang Hsi
(1662–1722)

正年製 大清雍
Yung Chêng
(1723–1735)

隆年製 大清乾
Ch'ien Lung
(1736–1795)

年製 嘉慶
Chia Ch'ing
(1796–1820)

光年製 大清道
Tao Kuang
(1821–1850)

豐年製 大清咸
Hsien Fêng
(1851–1861)

治年製 大清同
T'ung Chih
(1862–1873)

緒年製 大清光
Kuang Hsü
(1874–1907)

年製 宣統
Hsüan T'ung
(1908–1912)

年製 洪憲
Hung Hsien
Name adopted by
Yüan Shih-k'ai in 1916

Reign marks on Chinese porcelain.

Superb Example of Chinese seventeenth-century porcelain: A blanc de chine seated figure of a dignitary, height 16 inches.

in color from green, white, and brown to yellow, red, and black, and can offer combinations of these colors. The earliest examples, of amulets and ritual articles from the Shang, Chou, and Han periods, are mostly light green, brownish red, or black. In the final Ch'ing period of Chinese art the jade is at first simple and restrained in decoration, evincing many tones of green as well as the famous "mutton-fat" yellow, but towards the end it becomes what we so often see now, overcarved, flawed, and fussy. The early workers used a drill driven by clumsy foot treadle, and they took months to carve a small piece. The final, nineteenth century work was done in mass-production sweat shops with impersonal machinery.

Japanese

China has always tended to overshadow Japan in artistic achievement. Yet the Japanese have been making objects of beauty with often uniquely indigenous qualities for almost as long as the Chinese.

The first recorded period of Japanese art is the Asuka, dating from A.D. 552 to about 710. Buddhism at that period strongly influenced the artists, and the bronzes that survive are mainly sacerdotal in function.

The succeeding Nara period (A.D. 710-784) is named after the capital city of that time, called Nara. This was an era of strong Buddhist influence, but also of graceful beauty particularly in sculpture, primitive but T'ang like in simple subjects and uninhibited treatment. This was followed by the Early Heian period of 784-897, when Japanese objects of art began to assume the "frightening" appearance that has been one of their characteristics ever since. Possibly the priests and the overbearing warlords were responsible. The people were constantly terrified and their art reflected this fear. During this period the capital city moved to Heian Kyo (Kyoto).

The Middle or Late Heian period of 897 to 1185 is also known as the Fujiwara period because the Fujiwara family secured a dominating position in the country and countered the influence of the priests and warriors with examples of refinement in living and cultured behaviour generally. The Fujiwaras encouraged the endeavors of artists and craftsmen, who produced the first narrative scroll painting without religious influence in what is known as the Yamato-e style. Lacquerwork was developed to a high degree of technical excellence.

Next came the Kamakura period of 1185 to 1392. The Fujiwara influence waned. The country again became the warring province of several military men and their wild families, mitigated only by the efforts of the priests to continue beautifying their temples, particularly with sculpture. Swordsmiths plied a lively trade, and were sometimes artist-craftsmen of great importance such as the legendary Masamune. In ceramics one of the most interesting Japanese marks is Seto, and it was during the Kamakura period that the first Seto porcelain was made. This Stoke-on-Trent of Japan continued to produce pottery and porcelain throughout the ages, and was responsible in the nineteenth century for the outsize vases that were mass-produced for export to Europe and America.

Seto pottery became increasingly important in the succeeding Muromachi period (1392-1568), when Japan continued to suffer from the warring of rival clans. Many fine swordguards or *tsuba* were made and are collected all over the world today. The author once found a dealer's collection of these beautifully fashioned articles in a side street of remote Stockholm. Austere simplicity was the mark of the Muromachi (or Ashikaga) period. The central government of

Courtesy of Sydney L. Moss, Ltd., 51 Brook St., London, W.1.)

A selection of Japanese tsuba or ornamental sword guards made in iron.

Hokusai (1760–1849) was the supreme master of the Japanese color print. The above example, from his famous "Waterfall" series, perfectly illustrates his strange mixture of realism and formal fantasy.

the Shogun established an official school, known as the Kano, for the development of arts and crafts, and encouraged the Goto family as goldsmiths and Kaneiye and Nobuiye as ironworkers. The soft earthenware known as Raku became prominent, and a school of painting called Suibo-kuga was fostered by the Zen Buddhists.

There followed, strangely, a period of peace, the Momoyama (1568-1615). During this time the simple demands of the warlords were succeeded by the self-indulgence of an Oriental people with plenty of money to spend. The arts and crafts became florid and ostentatious. Furniture was lavishly lacquered and decorated with gold and silver. Flamboyant colors were used in pictures and ceramics. Koyetsu's pottery and lacquer were famous, and the swords and guards of Mioju. Arita porcelain began.

The final Japanese period, if we ignore modern industrialism, was from 1615 to 1867, known as Edo or Tokugawa. This was the era roughly corresponding to the European eighteenth century, when the arts and crafts reached their heights of achievement, and most of the articles were produced that are now collected. Japanese print-making became an industry and a science as well as an art. Carving of netsuke, as will shortly be described, became almost a religion to its practitioners.

The true Arita porcelain manufacture was established about 1615, and became one of Japan's most important marks. There were two main kinds, based on the styles of decoration called Imari and Kakiemon. Imari decoration is like brocade, very involved. The port of Imari is a few miles from Arita, and through that port vast quantities of the ware were shipped to Europe in the eighteenth century, and strongly influenced European and British ceramic decoration, even more than the true Chinese. Chinoiserie was often Imari. This export trade continued right through the nineteenth century.

Equally important but much healthier in its influence on factories such as Meissen and Sèvres, Chelsea and Worcester, was the Arita porcelain called Kakiemon (after a family of potters who worked at Arita). Kakiemon had designs of flowers and animals in bright colors, and was first imported into Europe during the seventeenth century by the Dutch, whose delftware often closely followed its style. Square, octagonal, and hexagonal vases were typical.

During about two hundred years, 1660-1860, carved woodblocks were used in Japan for a great output of hand color printing aimed at a popular market of merchants, artisans and visitors. The favorite subjects were folklore stories and actors and wrestlers and courtesans and Fujiyama. These prints were worth little at their time of original sale, and represented a popular art like that of the modern pictorial postcard or tourist poster, but towards the end of the nineteenth century their very artlessness as well as their clean designs, lines and colors had a strong influence on Western artists. Since then the main Japanese masters of the color print have been carefully studied and their products widely collected.

Today it is uncommon to find examples of the work of such as Hokusai, Hiroshige, Koryusai, and Shesho in the shops and galleries where they were once prolific at very low prices. They rest as valuable investments in collectors' portfolios, and, when they come on the market are often worth ten times as much as they were a few years ago.

Netsuke

The word "netsuke" literally means "a root to fasten." The primitive Japanese would tie a cord or cords to a piece of gnarled root and fix it under his girdle, then suspended from the cord or cords another object or objects for everyday use such as a key or a small tinder or tobacco box or purse. The root became in more sophisticated times a small piece of carved or otherwise decorated ivory or other substance.

Thus the netsuke has been from time immemorial in Japan a very humble object indeed. It has been rather like a button or buckle or chatelaine, useful but aesthetically unimportant, although, being Japanese, it has probably always been beautiful. The Japanese, unlike some other peoples, find it difficult to make anything small without embellishing it.

The collector of netsuke usually starts with the end of the sixteenth century, when the fashion began among the Japanese aristocracy of carrying small cases called *inro*. These contained seals, and were fastened to the netsuke.

The use of netsuke declined with the introduction of Western dress in the late nineteenth century, because Western dress had pockets. The netsuke had been necessary on pocketless gowns to control the objects that Westerners kept in their pockets. By now, however, the world had started to collect netsuke, so their manufacture continued, but more elaborately, and it is roughly true that very elaborate netsuke are comparatively modern as they would have been

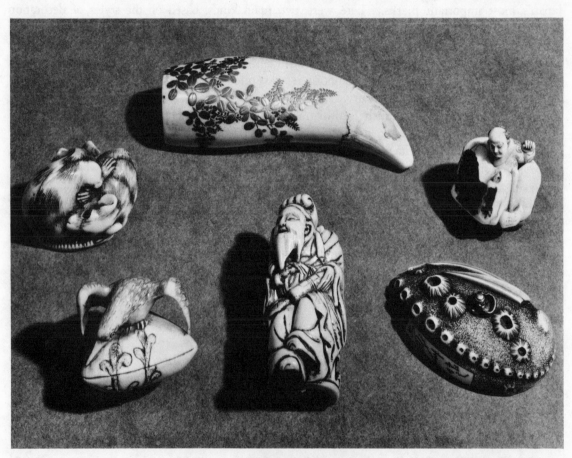

(Courtesy of Sydney L. Moss, Ltd., 51 Brook St., London, W.1.)
A selection of lovely Japanese netsuke by such artists as Rensai, Kokusai, Hidemasa, and Kajikawa.

impracticable to wear. The latterday netsuke, more suitable for the showcase or mantelpiece than the girdle, are called by the Japanese *okimono* or "place things."

Wood was the most common material used in the making of old netsuke; and the woods included the rarest of fragrant kinoki or Japanese cypress, the tsuge or boxwood, then cherry, bamboo, ebony, persimmon, camphor. Often the wood was colored, or lacquered, or gilded, or inlaid with various materials. Then netsuke were made of ivory, and indeed of practically all workable and available substances, but especially horn, bone, fruit stones, nuts, and amber. When two materials are used in a netsuke it is usually of later rather than earlier date. Any sophistication is suspect, as always.

The principal shapes of netsuke have been roughly codified by the experts, and first we recognize the manju type, just a plain round button, one to three inches in diameter, with holes through it to take the cords. Then the mirror-lid type is a manju with piece of high-polished metal set as a lid over a depression on one side. The statuette netsuke, as the word implies, incorporates a carved figure or group of figures, and the seal variety has a figure on a base like a Chinese seal.

The clam-shell netsuke is clam-shaped with mouth wide open and carving within, usually ivory; and the mask was derived from the popular Japanese dramatic device. Makers of masks for actors — hideous, frightening masks usually — would sometimes make a netsuke in the same shape as a sample. The greatest maker of mask netsuke was one Deme Uman of the eighteenth century, who boasted that he was the "first under heaven." It certainly paid him, because he is still remembered when so many better men are forgotten.

The sashi was a form made up of a rod with hole at upper end; the gourd or hyotan was a genuine dried gourd or copy of a gourd in some other material; the saishiki were netsuke in the form of highly colored figurines of wood, mainly made during the early nineteenth century in Nara; the ichiraku were made of woven materials; the trick and toy netsuke consisted of novelties like faces with movable tongues; and the suigara ake or ashtray netsuke was a little cup of metal or wood in which the smoker emptied his diminutive pipe before refilling and relighting from the same economical dottle.

Owing to the complicated character of Japanese calligraphy it is impossible to read signatures on netsuke without a really expert knowledge of the language, but it is possible to memorize some of the famous signatures, such as those mentioned in Inaba Kichitatsu's great book *Soken Kisho* (Osaka, 1781).

As said before, netsuke makers were rarely more important than European makers of small domestic brooches, tie pins or buttons, but some names are regarded as important, as follows:

Tosa Mitsuoki or *Shuzan* (d. 1691). He worked chiefly in hinoki or cypress, and was renowned for his brilliant coloring. He did not sign his work, and it is unlikely that the many signed examples in existence are his.

Miwa was a renowned carver in wood of netsuke in the form of grotesque figures with his signature on the soles of their feet.

Masanao was noted particularly for his wood and ivory carvings in the form of animals and toy sparrows, greatly prized.

Tomotada mostly carved in ivory the figures of animals, but especially recumbent figures of oxen.

Ryusa had great skill at the making of turned or round netsuke, and invented the deeply undercut type, to which his name is given.

Onagi Senzo similarly invented the method of inlaying wood carving with shell and other material, known as Shibayama ware.

Ogasawara Issai did his best work in ivory, and is regarded as one of the finest netsuke makers, belonging as do most of these famed ones to the second half of the eighteenth century.

Ikkwan, however, worked in the middle of the nineteenth century, mostly on models of drunken sprites and of rats.

Kwaigyoku Masatsugu (1812-1892) was the most important nineteenth-century name, whose signature was undoubtedly used by his inferior pupils on account of his popularity. A genuine Masatsugu must be really good.

The Japanese are so skilled as craftsmen still that it is important to be able to recognize fakes and forgeries in netsuke. Conventional tests are looking for signs of wear from rubbing against the clothes or from the cord in the hole, or looking for signs of bleaching on the parts exposed to the light, but all these signs can be and are faked, whereas often genuine netsuke show no indications of that kind for the simple reason that they have been stored away carefully for years.

It is, however, possible to say that a netsuke with many projections on it is not old because it would not have been practicable for wearing, and it is known that rats, snakes, snails, and frogs were chiefly popular during the years 1800-1850. Similarly seals and grotesque monsters were liked during the eighteenth century.

Above all great beauty and superlative skill in the carving or modeling are the qualities that make a netsuke worthwhile to the collector. Fakes and forgeries in this as in other articles rarely have the beauty and charm of the genuine.

To clean netsuke, use turpentine and a soft camel-hair brush—on the wooden and lacquer types. The brush soaked in alcohol will clean elaborately carved ivories, of which the smooth surfaces may be cleaned and burnished with an indiarubber. Liquid ammonia will brighten tarnished metalwork, but must not be used on ivory or lacquer.

8

Victoriana

General

We are still too close to the nineteenth century to be able to study its works with unprejudiced minds. At least two hundred years are required for historical perspective. The habits and surroundings of our immediate ancestors are always distasteful. It has been said frequently in this book that the most desirable objects for collection ceased to be made when Queen Victoria came to the English throne and the world began on a mass-production scale to use machines instead of hands.

If the collector of "antiques" is to judge the objects of his collection by their handmade quality and craggy individuality, and if he is to prefer simple, clean designs to involved ornamentation that is imposed for its own sake, then he will most definitely eschew Victoriana.

But the facts must be faced that we are indeed still too close to the nineteenth century to be able to study its works with unprejudiced minds—and that already a large number of people do collect nineteenth century articles with pleasure and profit.

The antiques trade has been forced to encourage such collectors in order to maintain a livelihood. It is no use setting up as a specialist dealer in eighteenth-century furniture or porcelain when stocks cannot be replaced save at such cost that customers cannot afford to buy. So the term "late Regency" is coined to describe early Victorian furniture, and cameo glass is offered without mention of the fact that it is not properly an antique. A constant effort is made to create the impression that a collection of waxed fruits or Goss seaside porcelain is "fun," and that it is fashionable again to sleep in brass-knobbed bedsteads and hang samplers on the wall and encircle the feminine breasts with fichus of beadwork or darkest jet.

All this may be inevitable, and it may be deplored, but it must be studied and can sometimes lead to interesting and remunerative acquisitions. Thus the Victorian era was overwhelmingly the age of what is rather pejoratively known as bric-à-brac. The furniture, the decorative schemes were alike designed to support such a weight as the world had never known before of small articles of often smaller value but undeniable sentimental interest, that were hoarded and displayed both to give the neighbors something to think about and to collect the dust.

Victorian bric-à-brac ranges from cabochon-decorated inkstands to ivory chessmen, from glove caskets to card cases, from chatelaines (or devices for carrying keys, watch, pencils, and the like at a woman's belt) to fans. It includes hand-coolers (that were more often used for

Two very typical chairs of the English Victorian period.

(Courtesy of Quality Wood, Cropley Grove, Ousden, Newmarket, England.)
One of the most remarkable bedroom suites ever made: Victorian papier-mâché throughout. (Discovered by Mrs. Violet Wood, author of the book *Victoriana*.)

darning socks), and posy-holders of various kinds, and scent bottles, snuffboxes, vinaigrettes, fitted workcases and boxes, pot lids, Tonbridge ware, witch balls, and, of course, Billies and Charlies.

The last-named were lead figures and other objects made by two Londoners at the end of the nineteenth century, used as door-stoppers and sometimes vividly painted. When first made they were offered as antiques, but today there is a lively industry in reproducing these fakes.

That is the trouble with so much Victoriana. It was not very beautiful or well made in the first place, and the molds and machinery that made it are often still in existence. China dogs, usually poodles, for use originally as door-stoppers—they were very badly hung apparently, those Victorian doors, or the houses were very draughty—have been reproduced in some cases by the thousand to meet overseas orders.

We can indeed be thankful to economic law in this matter, which has recently ordained most ironically that the fakes sometimes cost more to make thanks to higher wages and shorter hours of work than the genuine originals still cost to buy. Goss seaside china is being offered new by commercial travelers to shopkeepers at twice and three times the prices, the utmost prices that can still be obtained for the old.

Victorian furniture was of two kinds, the large, heavy pieces that have given the period such a bad name aesthetically, and a great variety of smaller pieces of a daintier kind, such as davenports, whatnots, work tables, etagères and bonheurs-du-jour.

The heavy items are usually quite inadmissible, but the antiques trade has already had a way with them also, cutting them down to size and converting them into two or three separate pieces. It can at least be said that the wood is usually good and old; and sometimes the modern young cabinetmaker, employed at the back of the antique dealer's shop, is a craftsman in his own right with the skill of his ancestors in his fingertips.

By davenport we are referring to a small writing desk (not an overstuffed sofa) intended for feminine use primarily, and comprises a carcass of side and dummy drawers and a sloping

(Courtesy of Quality Wood, Cropley Grove, Ousden, Newmarket, England.)
The finest Victorian furniture, of which the above is an example, was made in the French style about the middle of the nineteenth century.

This is a genuine period photograph showing an actual Victorian interior in the 1860s: The home of the great-grandfather of Mrs. Violet Wood, author of *Victoriana* and Antique Dealer at Cropley Grove, Ousden, England.

raise-top mounting to a gallery of wood or brass. The remarkable aspect of davenports is that two of them are seldom alike, and a very interesting collection of these pieces could still be made.

The whatnot is a series of shelves, mounted in various ways, and in the purer kinds open at all sides, that was intended for the accommodation of bric-à-brac. Much fretwork can disfigure the ideal Victorian type.

An interesting study is the Victorian chair, that blossomed or luxuriated, according to taste, in the widest variety ever known to man in any one epoch. There are the Abbotsfords, or Scottish Baronials, a Victorian elaboration of the Jacobean type. There are the Balloon Back, the Bentwood, the Camel Back, the Cameo Back, the Cane Back, the Corset Back, the Eaton Hall, the Hall, the Grandfather, the Nursing, the Prie-Dieu, the Sewing, the Slipper Back— and an extraordinary variety of music stools.

The chaise longue is one of the few items of furniture that was not elaborated by the Victorians, for the very good reason, as Mrs. Violet Wood has pointed out, that it was "considered indelicate for a lady to receive guests with her feet up."

Military and seamen's chests were made in great numbers during the nineteenth century, and may possibly be regarded as the most elegant furniture of the period. Made usually of light Honduras mahogany, in two sections, perfectly rectangular and without any kind of decoration save sunken brass handles at the sides and on the drawers, they were regulation equipment to serving officers until about 1870, and have simple lines and a beautiful color that appeal to the modern taste. Unfortunately, their very simplicity makes them easy to reproduce, and the buyer's chief protection is an eye for proportions and for patination and for interior age.

On the whole Victorian furniture is best when it is of the strictly functional type that was not regarded of importance in its own day and age. A great Victorian would have scorned the idea of putting a military chest in the living room, and he used his collectors' cabinets strictly for the coins or birds' eggs or butterflies which it was their original purpose to guard from the prying fingers of the children or the staff. Today such specimen cabinets can be regarded as very fine pieces of simple cabinetmaking for their own sake.

Large Victorian tables have mostly disappeared (many of them to be cut up into small Victorian tables) but certain kinds of small occasional tables were well made and not without charm, notably some Sutherland tables—a dwarf type with wide flap leaves and pull-out leg supports—and a few of the round pedestal tables with inlaid marble or slate tops. A vast number of worktables were made, to accommodate the sewing materials and wools of the females who in those days were sometimes wisely confined to the drawing room for the term of their unnatural life, but very few of these can satisfy the collector who has handled similar slender items of the late eighteenth century and the Regency. The Victorian variety have heavy legs and feet, tops like slabs of solid rosewood, and a general ugliness of conception that cannot be endured by the eye that has been accustomed to the products of finer ages. It must be remembered, however, that the Victorians themselves found this ugliness to be beautiful and thought that the eighteenth century was an unpleasantly bare and crude period. The possessor of Chelsea and Bow porcelain in the high Victorian period kept it out of sight lest he might be considered out of fashion.

Of all Victorian crafts that of glassmaking may well prove to be the most enduring. A fiscal restriction removed about halfway through the century encouraged glassmakers to experiment and to expand. In the period 1850-1890 so-called Bristol (mostly Stourbridge) in the types known as Amberina, Burmese, Mary Gregory, Satin, Opaline, Cobalt Blue, Purple Marble, Spangled, Vaseline, and the ubiquitous Cameo were made in vast quantities but with extraordinary precision and a beauty all of their own, if the collector can get used to the essential gaudiness of the genre. American glassmakers invented and developed many of the forms, but the English output was enormous, often under American license. Collectors in the United States have similarly been foremost in the field.

The English collector is best advised to specialize in a single type of Victorian glass that is not too gaudy for his taste, as, for example glass hats. These were originally holders for toothpicks and are to be found in every kind of substance and color and shape. Or miniature glass swans, hands, items of footwear, bells, eggs, ships.

Victorian textiles and needlework were similarly characteristic of the age and unique. No previous age had used so much cloth and upholstery for decorative purposes in the home. Hundreds of thousands of intelligent and skilled women, being restricted by social convention to this genteel occupation, lavished care on the production of bedspreads, tapestries, pictures,

Courtesy of Quality Wood, Cropley Grove, Ousden, Newmarket, England.)
Superb example of the finest late Victorian glass: A dolphin epargne or branched center dish for holding sweetmeats on table.

napery, in chenille work, crewel work, crochet work, cut work, beading, knitting, embroidery, patchwork, quilting, tatting, woolwork, and human hair. Victorian laces from Honiton, Buckingham, Bedford, Limerick, and Carrickmacross to the humble product of the nearsighted spinster are infinitely various, often lovely, and another distinct collector's subject.

The ornamental metalwork of the Victorian age ranges from domestic copper and brass to iron garden seats and tables, railings, gates, and the knobbed bedsteads that in our youth were demoted to gates on squalid farms and have since been restored to sophisticated night use all over the world.

Collections could similarly be made of Victorian featherwork, garden vases and ornaments, miniature scale models, native and Oriental work, shellwork, valentines and scrapbooks, waxwork. Throughout the emphasis is not on art, nor even on craft, but on "work." The Victorian was a serious age. Virtue proceeded from application to a job, not from the job itself. Thus no other age was so productive as the Victorian, and if some of us do not as yet like all the products they at least existed.

Ceramics

The taste of the eighteenth century and Regency survived for some years of the true Victorian period, then became characteristically florid and heavy, and finally entered the strange asymmetry of what is known as Art Nouveau.

The Coalport factory produced some of the finest Victorian porcelain of the early period, the famous encrusted ware of the Roses, uncle and nephew, then the Sèvres copies with Randall's lovely painting. Coalport was almost alone among the nineteenth-century factories in confining their production to porcelain alone. Most factories mixed it, perhaps fatally.

The outstandingly widespread Victorian names were those of Copeland and Copeland and Garrett, successors to Spode, and principal makers of the fine bone china that was the chief ceramic contribution of the age. Bone china is a hard porcelain rendered half soft by an admixture of bone ash. Copelands produced ceramics on a very large scale, even specializing in "slabs" for door furniture and fireplaces and table tops, and in services sold and exported by the thousand in crates. But many famous artists worked for this firm, and lovely articles were produced, while the porcelain and glaze were always excellent. This glaze has endured wonderfully well, and is still free from crazing or hair cracks, while the delicate ground colors endure perfectly, together with the gold and jeweled enrichments.

Robert Bloor took over the Derby factory in 1811 and virtually ruined it by debasing the standards of production. Nevertheless many good artists were employed on interesting work, among them John Haslam (whose contemporary account of the factory provides some useful historical material). The works were closed in 1848, but the Derby tradition, and often the old crossed baton marks, were continued by the Stevensons and others at King Street, Derby. In subsequent years the old molds were used to turn out many of the original Derby-type figures such as the Four Seasons. Towards the end of the Victorian period new men had reconstructed the old firm, and the Royal Crown Derby Factory, royal-appointed, was large and prosperous again.

In the 1840s the bisque figures of Minton were famous; at the time of the Great Exhibition this factory was regarded as the most important in the country. It employed the most and the best artists, and its methods were impeccable. Indeed Minton porcelain and pottery tended to become too perfect mechanically and strangely soulless as a result, the chief Victorian fault, although we should not complain who in our own age have become both soulless and imperfect mechanically. There was a brief period when splendid floral encrusted ware was produced, and the celebrated *pâte-sur-pâte* of Marc-Louis Solon was a speciality of the factory from 1870. In the dark Potteries district of Staffordshire it is still the custom for experts to regard Minton porcelain as the finest ever made, and pieces of Minton are treasured above all in china cabinets there.

The former Worcester works of Flight, Barr and Barr was taken over in 1840 by Chamberlain and Company. They produced some fine Victorian porcelain, notably the eggshell china that was first made about 1850, but on the whole they tended to pander to the commercial demands of the age, and most of their output was devoted to true Victoriana.

The Martin brothers started to produce brown stoneware at Fulham in 1873 and continued until 1914. Their work took the forms especially of grotesque figures and heads, and of jugs with strange, ugly heads. It was sincere and untouched by the cheap and mass-production spirit of the age and as such will endure, but not magnificently.

A less pretentious but perhaps in the long run far more important modeler of pottery was Walton of Burslem, some of whose lovely little rural figures with their well-chosen colors have a homely charm that is completely English, and, for some patriots, more attractive than the most valuable Meissen and Sèvres.

Two Victorian potters who may similarly have an important future when collectors realize their interest are Moorcroft and W. H. Goss. Already the larger figures of the last-named are rare and quite expensive. The vast quantity of seaside commemorative china produced by Goss is of such a high standard technically and covers such a range of subjects that it is bound to be sought after in the future.

Belleek is a village on the western side of Ireland, in Co. Fermanagh, near Ballyshannon. Here, in about 1856, on the estate of John Caldwell Bloomfield, clays were found that were suitable for the making of fine pottery or stoneware or porcelain. An advertisement to let the bed of clay appeared in *The Times* of April 1856, and subsequently, in 1857, after a series of experiments, the company of D. McBirney and Co. was formed between R. W. Armstrong of London and D. McBirney, a merchant of Dublin.

Armstrong himself supervised the factory; and principal products for the forty years of its existence were useful china wares such as table and toilet services, also tourist souvenirs. Large quantities were exported to the United States of America.

But it so happened that genius touched Belleek in those years. Sometimes the china produced was extraordinarily thin and translucent, with a glittering, iridescent glaze like mother of pearl, only comparable with that of Brianchon of Paris. And the modelers of Belleek acquired a remarkable facility in what amounted virtually to basketwork weaving with their white porcelain. The finest Belleek, with these characteristics, is a ware of importance that will be increasingly rare and valuable.

Leading characteristics of Belleek design are marine: dolphins, sea horses, tritons, nereids, aquatic plants, shells, coral, and rockwork. The three-legged cauldron was a favorite form. Some services have raised patterns round the edges, of shamrock and grasses in green and orange. The mark—representing an Irish round tower, the harp, the greyhound, the three-leaved shamrock and the name BELLEEK—is printed on to the ware in red, brown or green.

Art Nouveau

The heavy and meretricious quality of late nineteenth-century arts and crafts was arrested at the end by a development that is generically described as Art Nouveau. This represented the beginning of an era when artists would increasingly try to defeat the machine by originality, and when craftsmen would seek an uneasy compromise with the machine by using its cement, steel and other new materials. Art Nouveau as such dates from approximately 1890 to 1911. Perhaps William Morris in England was the chief progenitor. But the movement was universal, expressing itself not only in the furniture of Guimard, the glass of Lalique and the vases of Tiffany, but also in some of Fabergé's enamels and in the painting styles of Gauguin, Picasso, and Kandinsky, a link between the work of the Post-Impressionists and the Fauvists and Cubists.

Although the essence of the Art Nouveau movement was a break with accepted tradition, it had its roots in Celtic art, even in Gothic, rococo, Japanese and Chinese art, and the work of William Blake. It was wavy, asymmetric, slightly decadent and sexy, always hopelessly involved, exciting at the time but correspondingly ugly afterwards; and it left behind very little that we would yet care to collect. It ranged from the beautiful, sick drawings of Aubrey Beardsley to furniture made in the shape of animals with lopsided lines. It was important only because it dealt high Victorian endeavour a body blow that eventually killed it as stone dead as the flower of Europe's youth and indeed all European culture were killed by the First World War.

Pot Lids

The true collector would always be more at home with pot lids than with Art Nouveau, for the simple reason that the first can be collected and codified and are concrete, whereas the second is largely an idea and it is impossible to make a good display of a case filled with abstractions.

What is a pot lid? The dictionary says coldly, "Lid of pot, jar or box originally made to contain pomade and (later) foodstuffs, the decoration being polychrome color printing under the glaze by means of a mechanical process; nineteenth century." But the story of the humble pot lid is much more interesting than that.

Though men began to relinquish the wearing of wigs towards the end of the eighteenth century, they were not immediately willing to show their hair, dandruff and all, in public. At first the fashion was to coat the hair with a white powder, thus achieving some of the effects of the wig. But then came "pomatum," grease for the hair, bear's grease. The container of this pomade had a colored picture of a bear on the lid, and the pictures became popular and helped sales. Other manufacturers were soon making use of this form of packaging, notably the concoctors of potted meats and shrimp and fish pastes. A new method was used for printing pictures on the pottery lids.

The period of the collector's pot lid dates from approximately 1846 to 1880, but printing on pottery as such was a development of the eighteenth century. The method first evolved, transfer-printing over the glaze, was quickly adopted in London (Battersea Enamel Works), Liverpool and Worcester, but did not reach Staffordshire until about 1775. William Adams, Josiah Spode, Thomas Minton, all experimented with transfer-printing, over and under the glaze, but using *one* color only until well into the nineteenth century.

In 1835 George Baxter took out his patent for color printing in oil colors. Baxter prints are a small collecting subject in themselves, and undoubtedly they must have given at least an idea to Jesse Austin (1806–1879) who, in 1846, perfected a technique for the production of underglaze color picture prints on earthenware. With Baxter the outline printing came first; with Austin it came last. Baxter first engraved the complete outline of his picture on a copper or steel plate, which he printed in the tint that was to predominate in the completed picture. Then by means of as many as fifteen wood or steel blocks, each a separate color, each printing in turn on top of the initial outline tint engraving, he built up his picture. Whereas Austin arranged his picture in three tints only, with sometimes a fourth tint plate for brown or black. These tints were printed on a transfer paper known as pottery tissue, and then each was transferred to the surface of the lid. Only afterwards was a completely engraved outline of the work superimposed.

The firm that pioneered underglaze color picture transfer printing was that of F. and R. Pratt and Co. of Fenton near Stoke-on-Trent. Felix Edwards Pratt (1813–1894) was head of the firm when, somewhere between 1843 and 1845, he took into his employ the copperplate engraver Jesse Austin, who had for a time been in business on his own account. Austin stayed with Pratt for the rest of his life, save for a year with the firm of Brown, Westhead, Moore and Co. of Stoke.

The first firing of the pots and their lids was from fifty to seventy hours at a temperature of about 1,100 degrees C. The next stage was the printing, by means of transferring the colors in a manner shortly to be described. The lids were then glazed, by being dipped in a liquid consisting of flint, whiting, feldspar, china clay, borax, and white or red lead. Then came the second firing, of about thirty hours at a temperature appreciably less than the first. If this firing were successful it would be seen afterwards that the colors were bright and fixed, the glaze was fused with the ware, and the surface was smooth and glossy. If gilding were to be applied a third firing was necessary, more of a difficult operation, in a kiln rather than an oven, for about twelve hours at a temperature of approximately 740 degrees C.

First Austin would take a water-color drawing of the intended picture, and then he would engrave his plates from this. An engraved plate would afterwards be charged with color mixed with oil, and a sheet of pottery tissue, soaked with soap and water, would be placed upon it. Pressure would be applied, and when the tissue was removed from the plate it should carry with it the colored picture. This would be impressed on the pot and rubbed with soaped and then rolled flannel. Each color would be similarly applied, and finally the brown outline color. The paper would be washed off in water and the colors, with any luck, would adhere to the pottery. It can be seen that this was handwork of a high order, and it might be wondered if it was worth the trouble. Would not a tame artist to paint all the pots separately have been infinitely cheaper and more efficient?

But the process was used for some thirty-four years on thousands of pot lids and other articles, which are now worth collecting just because they vary so much in handmade quality.

As said the bear was the most popular early subject for the pictures, to be followed by scenes of Pegwell Bay in Kent, home of the shrimps. Further important subjects for the collector are "The Bride," "The Wooer," "Lady Brushing Hair," "In Pensive Mood," and "Lady with Guitar," also portraits such as those of Wellington and Shakespeare that bring high prices always, and those of Dr. Johnson and Garibaldi that do not. There is a Crimean War series; and among sports and pastimes the rarest lids are those depicting "The Buffalo Hunt," "The Bull Fight," "The Master of Hounds," and "The Boar Hunt." It may in some way be significant that the less favored lids are those that depict such innocent diversions as "Blind Man's Buff," "Hide and Seek," and "Skating." The pictures cover so many aspects of nineteenth-century life that a collection of pot lids is in itself a pictorial history of the period.

Fortunately it is not necessary to worry too much about faked pot lids, for the simple reason that, although the original copper plates are often still in existence, it is at once too expensive to use them today and, if they are used, the old skill has been lost. Fake pot lids are badly printed and the colors are not firm and strong, while there is an absence of fine crackle and the body rings when struck due to the different, recent potting. A collector very quickly recognizes the inferior lids that were faked during the period 1880-1924. They are just wishy-washy, and not the same.

A few years ago it was possible to buy good genuine pot lids for a few dollars. Such specimens can now be worth 100 dollars or more, and may soon be in the paperweight class of speculators' currency. They are nearly as good as paperweights for that purpose.

Marking & Dating of Nineteenth-Century China

The whole subject of marks on nineteenth-century porcelain and pottery will increasingly command the attention of collectors, and it is a much more satisfying subject than that of eighteenth-century marks. Often the factories used cyphers and letters, and for a period there was a public registration mark that enables pieces to be identified and dated precisely.

This registration mark was diamond-shaped. It was frequently used from 1842 till 1883, and indicated that the piece had been registered at the Patent Office in London. There was a different letter for each year, "X" for 1842, "H" for 1843, "C" for 1844, and so on, as will be seen from the table at the end of this section. Small letters were used to denote the months of the years. Thus it can be determined that a piece was not made before the date of the stamp, although it might have been made much later, as a popular pattern would continue to be used for years. In 1884 the system was changed to marking by numerals, and the complication soon becomes such that it is difficult to tell the year any longer except by search at the Patent Office.

There were also *pattern numbers,* that help to determine the factory of origin. They were of two kinds, a number with a letter prefix, and a number in fractions. Certain factories, such as Copelands and Mintons, used only the first kind (so that if a piece of "Minton" is offered to a collector with a fraction mark on it then he knows that it is definitely not Minton). The purpose of this pattern number was to help in re-ordering or matching.

After 1891 it was necessary to mark porcelain for export with the word "England" or "Made in England." It could be said that most porcelain marked "Made in England" was made after 1900. The mark was made necessary by American tariff regulations.

Then we have the individual factory date marks. Certain great manufacturers, such as Wedgwood and Minton, had their own exact scheme of date lettering during the Victorian period. The year marks on Wedgwood, for example, started with the letter "O" in 1860 and continued till "Z" for 1871. "A" began again in 1872, and the series concluded with "Z" in 1897, thereafter beginning the alphabet again. Wedgwood also used letters of the alphabet to indicate the month of making, and the series on a piece runs as follows: the month letter; a workman's letter; the year letter. The final letter of the series indicates the exact year when the piece was made.

After 1852 Worcester incorporated "51" in their mark. This refers to the foundation of the factory in 1751. A crown was added in 1862. Such facts can be very useful.

Similarly the date 1750 on some late Coalport refers to the date of the factory's foundation and has naught to do with date of manufacture, save that it indicates it is not early.

Then Masons Ironstone added after 1859 the name "Ashworths" to their mark, a useful aid in dating.

REGISTRY MARKS ON ENGLISH CHINA

Years		Years		Months	
1842	X	1855	E	January	c
1843	H	1856	L	February	g
1844	C	1857	K	March 1845	w
1845	A	1858	B	April	h
1846	I	1859	M	May	e
1847	F	1860	Z	June	m
1848	U	1861	R	July	i
1849	S	1862	O	August	r
1850	V	1863	G	September	d
1851	P	1864	N	October	b
1852	D	1865	W	November	k
1853	Y	1866	Q	December	a
1854	J	1867	T		

System changed from 1868 to 1883 as follows:

Years		Years		Months		Months	
1868	X	1876	V	January	c	July	i
1869	H	1877	P	February	g	August	r
1870	C	1878	D	March	w	September	d
1871	A	1879	Y	April	h	October	b
1872	I	1880	J	May	e	November	k
1873	F	1881	E	June	m	December	a
1874	U	1882	L				
1875	S	1883	K				

9

Carpets and Textiles

Carpets

Threads from carpets made in ancient Egypt have been found intact in tombs after four thousand years. The skills of Egypt, Babylon and Assyria eventually condensed in Persia, and the Persians have for hundreds of years been the carpetmakers of the world. Neighboring regions such as Asia Minor and the Caucasus have learnt from them. The Chinese, the French and the English have evolved native styles and methods, but it is to Persia that the collector must look for his inspiration, a country where long tradition has taught the carpetmakers how to rear and choose the best wool, how to concoct vegetable dyes, and how any work of art is principally a product of long and ill-paid labor with the naked hands.

The best Persian carpets were originally made for princes after years of work with wool from sheep that had a more careful upbringing than the local children, mixed with the finest silk, so minutely knotted as almost to defy counting, colored with dyes that never fade in schemes that cannot jar according to designs of deep religious significance that yield a maximum of aesthetic pleasure. Cheaper copies were made for the middle class eventually, and, in our own time, still cheaper copies have been made in large numbers for sale to undiscriminating buyers in the West.

Persians come first for the collector, and, after them, carpets and rugs from Asia Minor, the Caucasus, Turkmen, and Uzbek. Chinese are beautiful, and early English have historical interest, while French of the best periods and factories have enormous but mainly museum value. Let us examine the types in detail, noting that they are usually named after places, with, of course, Persians first. It will be easier to discuss these in alphabetical order.

The carpets and rugs known as Bakhtiyari may be recognized by the amount of yellow and rich wine red in the coloring, also by their irregular shape. They are not so important as the larger Bijar group, which combine wool and camel hair in a coarse weave for hard wearing, colors of deep red, blue, green, yellow, ivory, and chocolate brown in floral designs with a three-stripe border.

The Feraghan is another large Persian group, with short wool pile, that can often be recognized by the typical turtle design in the main stripe of the three-stripe border. A characteristic pistachio green is sometimes used in the border. The field is soft red or dark blue with an all-over floral or leaf design. The weave can be coarse.

Then Hamadans are Persians of very coarse weave, and the best old pieces have pile of camel hair with some wool. Colors are soft reds, yellows and blues on a natural camel background, and designs tend to incorporate medallions. Another similar group is the Heriz, coarse again, floral-patterned with angular designs in light blue, brown, yellow, green, and ivory, wool and cotton and very important when in silk.

Perhaps the finest Persians of all are the Ispahans, not so much a geographical as an historical term, covering all Persians of the sixteenth and seventeenth centuries. They are classified in eight groups, the Garden, the Floral, the Animal, the Vase, the Medallion, the Compartment, the Silk and the Tapestry weave. Ground is usually a dull wine red and colors are beautifully blended, with red and blue predominant. The best are the early examples with splendid workmanship and rather clumsy designs. Towards the end of the period the drawing became more formal and the workmanship less fine.

Then the Joshanghan type has a soft, lustrous, short woolen pile with very rich coloring in red, blue, yellow, brown, green, and ivory, with the characteristic designs of vases and diapers.

The Karaja is a Persian group of coarse weave with small, regular floral patterns in dark blue or plum color and red; and the Kashan is a finely woven group that feels strangely stiff when handled, is frequently of silk with borders of seven stripes and graceful designs employing curved medallions and clean-cut floral borders in dark blue, red, and light brown.

The well-known Kirmans are finely woven carpets that have floral and bird patterns in soft and delicate shades, with white, gray and pale rose predominating. Roses in the border can be a feature; and a similar group is the Kermanshah, large carpets of light rose, ivory, buff, blue, and green.

Then Kurdistans are Persians of medium texture, with numerous patterns in, notably, blue-greens; whereas the Mesheds are mainly in rose, blue, and white, floral designs with large central medallion; and the Polonaise group, as the name suggests, have designs that suggest Western influence, exceptionally fine silk carpets with a great deal of gold and silver thread, colors exquisitely blended with a multitude of shades that contrast with small areas of deep, rich coloring.

The Sarabends can be recognized by their pattern of small cone devices on a red, blue or white ground, and their five- to seven-stripe borders with more small cones; and the Sarouk group is mainly in dark blue and red, designs like the Kashans showing curved medallions, very finely woven.

Asia Minor carpets and rugs are chiefly different from the Persian in their less subtle colors and their more geometric and Occidental designs. The Anatolian group can often be identified by designs that incorporate eight-pointed stars and hooks. Colors are mainly red, blue, green, brown, white, pink, and bright yellow. Then Bergamas (from Pergamus whence parchment originally came) are nearly square in shape, patterned usually with a large central medallion surrounded by small geometric figures or flowers, dark blue and white on red ground.

The famous Gheordiz group originally came from the city of the Gordian knot and Midas's ancient capital. The colors are mainly red, blue, yellow and white, and valuable old pieces are characterized by richer coloring and better designs than the more modern. Colors are mainly red, blue, yellow, and white, and the prayer rugs are important.

The Kouba group of Asia Minor have bold designs of large, irregular octagons, with serrated edges, softly colored in reds, blues, and browns with some greens and yellows, whereas the Koulas may be identified by their characteristic borders of five to ten stripes that contain minute floral forms, and by the use of a stylized vine in the secondary border: colors mainly red, brownish yellow and blue, green, dark brown, white.

Once all the world knew Laodicea. Now it is the village of Ladik, that has given its name to a group that is characterized by hexagonal medallions and vandyke end panels in red, blue, and supporting colors, also four borders consisting of stripes separated by dotted lines, the main stripe usually with Rhodian lilies and rosettes.

Then the Melas group usually has a narrow field containing prominent designs, frequently in the form of angular, serrated leaves, mainly red, with blue, yellow, white and mauve; and finally the Ouchak is an Asian Minor carpet or rug from the great weaving center of Ouchak, perhaps four hundred years old if very important and valuable, with a bold design, well balanced with graceful arabesques and small floral motifs, colors chiefly red, blue and green.

So we proceed to the Caucasians, and firstly the Baku group, that has geometrical patterns, usually with a fringed, diamond-shaped medallion in the center, with much use of cone shapes, eight-pointed stars and S forms, rather coarse weave and colors of blue, tan, yellow and black. The area of the Caucasus, centering around Mount Ararat of the Ark, took in the civilizations of the Persians, Turks, and Russians, so that the carpets are Persian as regards weaving and dyeing methods, often geometrically Mahommedan in design yet with a primitive northern flavor.

Thus the Chichi group of Caucasians has varied, delicately drawn geometric or cone designs in ivory, blue, and red, with brown and green. The geometric designs of the Daghestan group have an almost mosaic appearance, light and dark blue, red, yellow, ivory and green, rich colors that with the short, clipped pile give a very clean effect. Derbends have bold designs and colors and can be crude. A few very fine old pieces exist with diamond lattice pattern containing geometrical or stylized floral forms. Then Kabistans have a silky woolen pile and usually geometrical or cone designs in rich tones of blue and red, with ivory, brown and green, whereas Karabaghs, especially the older specimens, are very Persian in appearance. Later Karabaghs are poor by comparison.

Kazaks have bold and primitive patterns with a lot of green, as befits their being made by the Kazak or Cossack tribes living in the northernmost part of Caucasia. These patterns incorporate various nomadic devices such as S forms and eight-pointed stars.

Good Shirvans are rare. The Shirvan type can be identified by large figures on the field that are joined to form a pole medallion, the remaining space being covered with small geometric devices in blue, red, green, ivory and a brown-purple. Soumaks are from the hill districts surrounding the capital of the Shirvan area. They are pileless, a flat stitch being used; fields are mostly composed of three or more large, diamond-shaped medallions; and colors are mostly red and blue, with brown, white, and yellow, and occasionally a rich green.

The Turcoman group comprises principally the various Bokharas, frequently of goat's hair, usually dark red that dominates other colors, and essentially primitive in patterns; while the Beshirs may be identified by their three-stripe geometric borders, their coarse weave, their reds, browns, blues, yellows, and white, and their wide end webs bearing several colored stripes.

Chinese carpets are usually divided into three groups, covering the sixteenth, seventeenth, and early eighteenth centuries. Into the first come the Ming carpets of three colors, with designs consisting of dragons and birds in the center and corners, carried out in deep blue on an old goal field, with outer border of brown.

The second Chinese period, from 1645 to about 1727, is known as the Kang Shi to carpet fanciers. Rich, lustrous wools were used, and simple designs on old gold or deep blue fields.

The Kien Lung period of approximately 1726 til 1795 was especially important for rugs, and for the introduction of peach bloom and apricot colors. Designs were based on the Kang Shi style, but with greater ornamentation, and employing four or five colors.

The two main French groups are Aubusson and Savonnerie. The first is a woven type, of wool, lacking pile and characterized by large areas of pale coloring in the early days, then by bottle green, dark red and gold in the Empire period. Typical Louis XV designs are found on the earlier types, while the later Aubussons have multi-colored floral wreaths, with the speciality of the daisy. Savonneries, named after a former establishment where there had been a soap factory, are like Aubussons save that they are hand-tufted and consequently show a good woolen pile.

Early English carpets similarly have hand-tufted pile of wool, and may be identified specifically by their warp of hemp or linen. Axminsters were started at the town of that name by Thomas Whitley, a weaver, in 1755. By 1779 the industry was booming, but the factory closed in 1835, when the looms were taken to Wilton, where a factory was established in 1740 thanks to the efforts of the Earl of Pembroke, whose original idea was to make carpets in the velvet style of Brussels. After the acquisition of the Axminster looms knotted pile carpets were made.

This has been a swift survey of a specialized subject. Much could be said about Indian carpets, of which the Agra type is the most important (large, heavy, in delicate shades of blue, green and fawn), about Brussels cut-looped-thread carpets, or the North Africans and their offshoot the Spanish (knotted on a single thread of warp, with many shoots of weft, Moorish designs modified by European makers).

Rugs

Rugs are especially interesting because they can be hung on walls (although it is not true that early rugs suffer from the usage of feet: on the contrary they acquire their natural silk sheen and richness of color tone from the polishing of those who walk on them). Moreover a large part of the weavings of Asia Minor in particular has always come in rug sizes, particularly the namazliks or prayer rugs. Then there are the odjaliks or hearth rugs, so important in the Mohammedan household, and the sedjadehs, that are long, narrow rugs for placing on the seats of couches.

It should be noted that odjaliks can be distinguished from prayer rugs by the fact that both ends of the field come to a pointed arch. The Bergama types with their square shapes and strong characteristic patterns in dark blue and white on a red madder ground, are especially worthy of study and collection, as are the Broussas of silk with their Turkish designs and full-bodied colors and their characteristic that they always lie flat and do not curl at the sides thanks to very well-balanced weaving.

Rugs of various kinds were also the best productions of the Ghiordiz industry. A Kiz-Ghiordiz is particularly nice, being a rug woven by a maiden for a bridal gift to her husband both as a sign of devotion and a proof of her skill as a weaver, so essential to a good wife.

The silk Herekes with Persian patterns were made at the Sultan of Hereke's private

An important Isfahan prayer rug of the Sefavi period (seventeenth century). Size: 5 feet 3 inches by 3 feet 5 inches.

factory on the shore of the Sea of Marmora, and they usually bear the name Hereke in Turkish Arabic characters in one corner of the outer border stripe.

Mudjars are extremely colorful; Kulahs are floral; Makris with their paneled fields and eight-pointed stars, are valuably rare; Melas have very narrow fields and extra wide main border stripes; and it is still possible to acquire sixteenth- and seventeenth-century Ouchaks in fine condition—early Ouchaks with their typical Turkish traceries, or the seventeenth-century "white" type, also known as Tamerlanes from the three-disk badge of Tamerlane in the design.

Keshir prayer rugs are characterized by the mihrab or series of steps that rises from the sides of the panel. These steps in the Keshir are carried out in several parallel lines of different colors.

Care of Carpets and Rugs

On the whole, old carpets and rugs last indefinitely, barring accidents, and this is due partly to chemical changes brought about in the fibers by actual use, a kind of pounding that continually toughens them, and partly to the original toughness of wool from sheep that grew the wool to meet the exigencies of life at over 7,000 feet above sea level. Even accidents need not be too serious with these carpets and rugs. A cigarette may be dropped and a great hole burned, yet native restorers can pick up the threads and replace and re-dye them so cleverly that nothing may be seen. This is done by the reknotting process. There are two kinds of knot in Oriental carpets and rugs, the Ghiordiz or Turkish, that makes the pile lie along the length of the piece, and the Sehna or Persian, that makes the pile lie across the rug. If a piece is damaged the restorer will replace the warp threads with authentic wools or cottons, analyze the design and find what parts have to be replaced, and then rework the design knot by knot. The result is trimmed with a pair of curved scissors to the exact height of the surrounding pile, and afterwards only an expert can detect the repair.

Most old rugs and carpets are finished with edges that can be frayed or otherwise worn, whether with pile right to the edges, or sides overcast with wool, or completed with selvages. At the first signs of such wear the owner should have the piece repaired, as otherwise the damage can quickly run into the body. Such initial repairs are cheap by comparison with the larger restorations that might otherwise be necessary. The same applies to fringes, that should always be kept in good condition. If part of a fringe frays out it should be stopped immediately, to prevent what could be a disaster: and the work should of course be handed only to an important specialist dealer in Orientals who has the craftsmen as well as a reputation to protect.

Similarly Oriental rugs and carpets should never be cleaned either at home with soap or detergents or at ordinary dry cleaners who would use detergents that dry the natural oils in the piece and leave them brittle and short-lived thereafter. Much of the life in Orientals comes from the natural oil in them. After handling good rugs there should be grease and dirt on the hands.

Once again, therefore, entrust cleaning only to specialist dealers of the first rank, who know exactly how to do it.

Perhaps the worst enemies of carpets are the clothes moths, although even these eat only at the pile and rarely touch the warp and weft, so that repairing of such damage is a comparatively inexpensive matter of expert repiling. The best way to avoid moth damage is to make sure that rugs and carpets are frequently moved away from their underfelts, and that pieces of furniture are not allowed to stand on them for long. The moth likes undisturbed, dark places.

Carpets and rugs should never, of course, be beaten or vacuum-cleaned with appliances that beat too heavily. They are best shaken lightly and carefully brushed.

Textiles and Lace

Tapestry is a heavy, woven fabric in which the weft is supplied with spindle instead of shuttle, and a design is formed by stitches across the warp. Tapestries were primarily intended for the covering of walls, and those of Arras in the Pas de Calais from the fourteenth to the sixteenth centuries were so famous that the name Arras became English for the sort of wall covering behind which a rat might hide.

There are two main kinds of tapestry, the *haute lisse,* made on an upright loom with leashes or weaving cords worked by hand, and *basse lisse,* made on a horizontal loom with leashes operated by treadles.

As said, Arras was the great center of tapestry weaving in the Middle Ages. Aesthetically the heights were reached by the factory started in Paris during the fifteenth century by the Gobelins, a family of dyers. Louis XIV, the great father of state control and centralized patronage, took over the establishment in 1662. His minister Jean-Baptiste Colbert was placed in control of this and other Parisian workshops. Gobelin had already developed a superb technique in silk and wool, as well as silk and cotton. The new organization engaged the artist Charles Le Brun to design cartoons; and Gobelins of the great seventeenth-century and early eighteenth-century periods are distinguished by beautiful, typically French and aristocratic designs in coloring of perfect taste applied to superb craftsmanship.

The Beauvais factory, established about 1665, and probably directly inspired by Louis again, is considered by many to have excelled even Gobelin in excellence of tapestry weaving and loveliness of designs as produced by such as Boucher, Béhagle, and Oudry. Much of the best Beauvais tapestry was made for covering the seats and backs of chairs and canapés. Suites with original Beauvais covers are among the most desirable articles of furniture extant.

The carpet center of Aubusson produced fine tapestries from the seventeenth century, but they are inferior to Gobelin and Beauvais tapestries. Savonnerie pieces are similarly interesting and fine but not so fine as the best.

It should be noted that the famous Bayeux "tapestry," and indeed many similar antique pieces, was not a tapestry at all but needlework embroidery on a band of linen.

There flourished at Mortlake in England from about 1620 to 1700 a factory that made fine and interesting tapestries.

It is possible to collect a wide variety of old textiles, even of old items of clothing, but such are perishable and often disfigured by age and difficult to maintain and display. The soundest objective, for those who have the taste, is lace, chiefly because its thread is not susceptible to the moth. Some collectors keep specimens of old lace in books or folios. Alençon is a fine needlepoint lace; Brussels is notable for its fine needlepoint sprigs and flowers; Chantilly is a silken variety; Cluny is a netlace with darned stitch; Honiton is delicate with sprigs and figures; Valenciennes or bobbin lace is one of the best and most valuable of all, distinguished by the fact that the pattern and ground are made at the same time.

In the nineteenth-century lace at once became a machine-debased product and so popular that it was put aside by wealthy people as an investment in much the same way as gold, diamonds, pearls and furs today. Lace was indeed an heirloom, but unfortunately twentieth-century revulsion to the fashions of grandparents led to much of the treasured lace being lost or actually destroyed. Time and time again in the last thirty years trunks of carefully preserved lace have come into the hands of dealers and auctioneers who, neither appreciating it nor being able to sell it at good prices, have allowed it to slip through those hands. Much must still be in existence, for the eventual profit of the discerning and patient.

10

Pictures

General

Picture collecting as such is a wide and specialized subject, and often comes so near to the present day that it can be treated in this book only as a department of the general subject of furnishing with antiques. The man who takes the graphic arts seriously must either possess a very large fortune or content himself with visits to museums and art galleries. It is still possible to have the best in snuff boxes and some porcelains and many types of old furniture, but the finest pictures of the greatest periods have become altogether too rare and expensive.

It is possible to collect good second-rate pictures, and even less good second-rate pictures that provide suitable wall adjuncts to antique furnishing schemes. But certain facts are worth noting about these.

Thus there is in the lower reaches of the picture trade a manipulation of fashion that is fortunately not found to the same extent in the furniture, ceramics and silver trades. The dealers will concentrate for a few years on certain subjects, particularly in nineteenth-century painting, and prices will soar for those subjects. Suddenly, at the end of their tether as it were, they will switch to another type of picture altogether.

Thus the buyer of unimportant but decorative old pictures would be wise not to buy what is temporarily in fashion, but concentrate on what might be described as "factual" pieces, topographical, historical, architectural, documentary. They may not be the greatest art but they belong to and shed much information on their periods, and they will always have academic and antique value and interest.

The person who buys an old picture should first consider whether it has beauty, if only for himself. Aesthetic conscience quickly answers this question, and a collector without an aesthetic conscience should turn to some more suitable occupation, such as politics or simple lechery. Beauty is infinitely more important than age, name, or monetary value.

'Then the connoisseur should look for technical excellence, good coloring, depth, light and shade, balanced composition.

Finally he should consider price, and should never in any circumstances pay more than a comparatively small sum for any picture that is painted by an unknown artist and has a general subject. A still-life by a good second-class name of the eighteenth or early nineteenth century will have increasing value whereas a still-life of the same period by a completely unknown artist will never be worth much or yield much interest. On the other hand a picture by an unknown artist will be increasingly valuable and of ever-absorbing interest if the subject teaches us about costume or architecture or furniture or an historical event or personage of the period.

It is indeed an excellent idea to choose a particular subject for collection and to stick to it. Thus increasing knowledge is acquired and the collection gradually becomes important in totality if trivial in particular interest. It is best if the chosen subject has an historical connotation. There always has been a steady if unspectacular demand for such work. Pictures of historical, documentary interest, even if not particularly good as pictures, have a much better record than paper shares for financial appreciation and they pay a dividend every time you look at them.

After the acquisition of a picture it is necessary to decide whether it should be restored or repaired. In the case of a picture that should have increasing value in the long run it is definitely worthwhile to employ a firm of expert restorers to remove the stained and cracked varnish and bring to life again the brilliant colors underneath, or to repair the canvas where it may be torn or cut (by invisibly patching the canvas from behind or by "lining," which means backing with a new canvas), or even, when a potentially important piece is badly blistered or flaking, to have the entire paint surface transferred to a new canvas. But the operative words are "a firm of expert restorers." Such work should never be entrusted to an inferior firm, who would probably charge just as much; and the collector should attempt his own home restoration only on pieces of very small value. There are substances on the market that, carefully employed, will remove the dirt from varnish, but the careful employment depends upon manual dexterity and lightness of touch. Too often the use of such substances leaves the picture in a blotchy condition, where the cotton-wool has failed to reach every part of the surface.

The picture trade flourishes on fashions in frames as well as in names and subjects. If an average picture is transferred from an old-fashioned frame to a new one in the current mode it will superficially acquire greater value and will look better. It will similarly acquire a new distinction if framed more suitably. A small, plain picture looks much more pleasant in a narrow, plain frame than if it is imbedded in ancient gilt. Similarly, a large battle scene will appear more at home in a frame of ornate giltwork than in a narrow surround of thin black wood. Generally speaking, the more important the picture the more important should be the frame, and once again good pictures should be framed only by leading experts. Picture dealers make their fortunes by buying old pictures in the mode and spending as much again on having them cleaned and reframed by specialists. When the pictures come back from those specialists they can scarcely be recognised by comparison with the dirty, ill-framed pieces originally brought home from the saleroom.

The hanging of old pictures is similarly a distinct technique, in which the expert knows best. Thus walls should first be rendered plain, particularly without patterned papers or tapestry hangings or appliqué ornaments. The placing of the pictures should be in careful relation to the positioning of the furniture, and it should be remembered that the most important position in a room is over the fireplace, and the best position from the view point of light is opposite a window. If the proportions of the room are beautiful then the pictures can be hung symmetrically on the walls. If the room is strangely proportioned or otherwise misshapen then it may be best deliberately to hang the pictures on different levels asymmetrically. No wall should be overloaded; and the best height in small rooms is eye level. Supports should be invisible, from wire that hangs on long screws inserted in plugs. Should the district or house be unduly damp then the pictures must be kept away from the walls by corks attached to the backs of the frames at the bottom.

Good pictures cannot be properly appreciated without electric lights that, affixed to the top of the frame, illuminate the piece throughout justly. The effect of this is to restore to the picture the same light as it had when it was painted. Artists paint either in the open air or in studios with roofs of glass; and their work cannot be appreciated thereafter in rooms with side lights from ordinary windows, or at night with the sombre illumination of modern so-called reading lamps.

The Dutch School

Should the collector desire more than furnishing or bread-and-butter historical pictures, and possess the means to purchase what are generally regarded as Old Masters, he might well be advised to concentrate on the Dutch School, wherein prices are still not too absurd, and the essentially sober character of the work should enable its value to survive all future changes in fashion. Several van Goyens could, for example, be purchased for the price of a single badly painted Post-Impressionist or wholly speculative modern.

The Dutch School has two parts for the discerning collector, that of the expensive seventeenth century, and that of the comparatively inexpensive nineteenth century. Fine Dutch painting began in the fifteenth century with Tot St. Jans, and there were masters such as Van Oostzanen and more in the sixteenth century. But the artists of the seventeenth century produced the finest work of all as a result of a kind of national euphoria that followed the martial triumphs of the Dutch over the occupying Spanish (and also of the intermingling of quicksilver Spanish blood with their phlegmatic, painstaking own). The school was characterized by superb draughtsmanship and painting, by a photographic realism, and by an overriding preoccupation with and skill in the depiction of light, derived from the physical atmosphere of Holland with its basis of scintillating sand. And especially, as in the case of the greatest master, Rembrandt, with light and shade in conflict or chiaroscuro. There was also a kind of pictorial hardness, the product of native character, as opposed to the more sensual but also more muzzy quality of the neighboring but quite different Flemish school. Dutch paintings are the pictures of Puritans, and are like northern ecclesiastical interiors; Flemish paintings are the pictures of half-Catholics who have been overliberated aesthetically by Rome.

The leading subjects of the Dutch school are portraits, interiors, conversation pieces, seascapes and architectural. Outstanding masters and their dates are Frans Hals (1580–1666), Rembrandt van Rijn (1606–1669), Jan Steen (1626–1679), Vermeer (1632–1675), De Hooch (1629–1683), Ruysdael (1628–1682), Hobbema (1638–1709), and others of importance include Seghers, van Goyen, Terborgh, Metsu, Cuyp, van de Velde.

The eighteenth century was not so much a bad as a dull period in Holland. Flower pieces of the period are good, and much painting ingenuity was shown, but the great spirit had departed. Very strangely it returned in the nineteenth century in the form of what is generally known as the Dutch Romantic School. Purists would date this from about 1750 to 1850, but the best work was done in the first half of the nineteenth century; and the so-called Hague School continued to paint well for long after that.

Although the school is called Romantic it was essentially a movement of naturalistic painters in Holland whose desire was to depict with poetic accuracy the architecture, people, animals, plants and scenery around them. No superimposition of classical motifs or alien patterns was there, and absolutely no "metaphysics," only a rigidly faithful effort to put on canvas what was seen by the eye. The school inherited the skills and methods of the great seventeenth-century painters, but eschewed much of the seventeenth-century exuberance and experimentalism. They were a sober lot, but how very, very good as painters, with scarcely a charlatan among them!

The principal subjects were (1) conversation pieces and portraits, at first formal in the eighteenth-century manner, then increasingly naturalistic in the first and second quarters of the century, and overinfused with humanistic sentiment as the century proceeded, (2) animal and still-life and flower pieces, beautifully composed and executed, (3) church interiors, often bleak but always perfect in drawing and color, an immortal and unique record, (4) town views, the summit of this school's achievement and its most characteristic product. In these town views each brick is perfectly painted, each line of cement, but the artists also capture the spirit of Dutch domestic architecture in a kind of poetry that is great. Vermeer taught them, but they were pupils who developed an art to the extreme of excellence (after which we have had to wallow in the deluge ever since!).

Other subjects were (5) landscapes of similar accuracy and enshrining poetry with the accent on snow scenes of a thoroughness never attempted before, and on the best tree painting in the history of art, and (6) seascapes with ships, many of them of great interest to the specialist and lover of such scenes, but perhaps not so notable generally as the other genres.

Biographies of over four thousand artists of the period are given in Scheen's monumental *Honderd Jaren Nederlandsche Schilder-en Teekenkunst* (compiled in hiding from the German occupiers during the war), and nearly all of these artists painted fine pictures that are worth collecting. It is quite impossible to indicate more than a few leading strands in this extraordinary tapestry.

A good example of the eighteenth-century type is P. J. van Liender, born in Utrecht in 1727, died in Utrecht in 1779. His formality was often extreme, and his work can have the static but charming quality of an early colored print. He is important for the earliness of his work in the school, and good examples are increasingly rare and valuable.

One of the most characteristic and "best-selling" painters of the middle period was J. H. Verheyen, born in Utrecht in 1778, died in Utrecht in 1846. He was prolific of town views in which he combined meticulous brushwork with splendid pictorial composition and often a very nice sense of color. Although a great number of his paintings must be in existence, and it was possible to buy them a few years ago for no more than a thousand dollars, yet the market is starved of them now, and dealers will pay increasingly high prices for good examples.

In contrast might be cited a painter of equal if not superior merit to Verheyen, whose name remains less known, and a purchase of whose pictures might prove still more remunerative in the long run. This is George Gillis Haanen, born in Utrecht in 1807, died in Bilsen in 1879. A large view of Utrecht by this painter is among the finest Dutch townscapes ever done, meticulously accurate in detail yet expressing the spirit of the scene with a brush that might have been dipped in enamel.

Possibly the best painter's painter of the school was B. C. Koekkoek, born in Middleburg in 1803, died in Kleef in 1862. Few men ever painted trees so well. His landscapes have a life and a light far beyond the photographic, and they are infinitely more beautiful than anything from Barbizon down to the present day. Already Koekkoeks have soared in value compared with others of the school, and this painter could eventually command higher prices than many

Old Masters and Impressionists whose present inflated values rest upon uneasy foundations. (B. C. Koekkoek should not be confused with the several others of his family, who are inferior to him.)

Less expensive as yet but of considerable interest and prolificacy are the three Spohlers, of whom J. J. Spohler, born in Nedelhorst den Berg in 1811 and died in Amsterdam in 1866, painted town views of great charm and of particular appeal to the modern taste, in that he often eschewed accuracy for what might be describeed as the impressionistic method.

And finally—the great Cornelis Springer (born in Amsterdam in 1817 and died in Hilversum in 1891). He is the painter of Dutch and Belgian town scenes par excellence. His early pictures are typical of the painstaking work of the period. In the middle of his career he painted large town scenes, as of Leiden and of Brussels, that combine the best of the ultraphotographic and the impressionistic methods. At the end he was rather too interested in recording essentially sentimental impressions. But the best Springers, already worth several thousand dollars should eventually equal the more important Old Masters, in value as they certainly equal them in achievement.

The Dutch Romantics nearly always signed their work clearly, and worked more often on panel than on canvas.

Among the great number of Dutch Romantics worth collecting are such as J. ten Compe, P. C. la Fargue, J. F. Valois, J. H. Prins, J. A. Langendijk, B. J. van Hove, H. G. ten Cate, J. C. K. Klinkenberg, Ch. Leickert, F. M. Kruseman, H. van Hove, W. Verschuur, W. Roelofs, and S. L. Verveer.

The Dutch Romantic School represents the burgeoning of an enormous artistic endeavor, particularly in Utrecht, The Hague, and Amsterdam, comparable only with that of the Dutch and Flemish seventeenth century—and the moment of its full recognition profitably awaits.

Terms Used in Painting

Jargon is used more in the picture world than in any other department of collecting; and it might be as well to give brief explanations of the leading terms employed by the dealers and connoisseurs. Thus a picture done *alla prima* has been executed all in one setting, while the oils are moist; and *asymmetry* is the opposite to symmetry in that the main features of the composition are not grouped together in an equalized fashion. *Bloom* is the misty cloud formed by moisture in the air on the surface of varnished pictures, removable by a soft, damp cloth and then a dry, soft cloth. The term *broken color* is used for a method of coloring which, by laying small strokes of differing tones alongside each other, makes it appear from a distance that the tones merge in together.

A *capriccio* is a sportive fancy, rather like a rhapsody in music. It was particularly popular with the Italian eighteenth-century school, as seen in the little masterpieces of Guardi. On the other hand, a *cartoon* is a full-size drawing used as the first draft for a large mural or very large picture. And *chiaroscuro* is special use of contrasting light and shade in a composition.

A *cradle* is an attachment of wood fastened behind a panel picture that has begun to crack. *Diptyches* and *triptyches* are altar paintings on two or three hinged panels. *Encaustic* is a method of painting with hot wax; and a *flat* is an edge of material between picture and frame, usually of canvas or wood or velvet, the purpose of which is to break the abrupt transition between picture and frame—and also to enhance the importance of what is essentially an unimportant picture.

The world knows frescoes simply as murals, but painting in *fresco* means to the professional the application of water-colors to wall or ceiling before the plaster is dry. And *fugitive pigments* are colors that fade either from chemical instabilities or from reacting overstrongly to other pigments. *Genre* paintings are those that portray scenes from everyday life; and *gesso* is a mixture of plaster of Paris, whiting, or some kindred material with glue, that was used by the early masters in preparing their panels: they would employ the coarse *gesso grosso* at first, and then complete the work with a fine *gesso sottile.*

Glaze on a picture implies the laying on of a thin coat of transparent color that has been mixed with an oil for dilution, while *gouache* is a method of painting in opaque colors ground in water and thickened with gum and honey, together with the use of a stiff bristle. The term *grisaille* is used for a gray monochrome composition; *impasto* is the laying on of thick paint with palette knife; *imprimatura* is a thin undercoat applied to the canvas or panel before the picture is painted; and a *lay figure,* far from having ecclesiastical significance, is a model with adjustable limbs that is used by the artist for poses or for working on costume: it need not be life size.

The fastening of canvas to a wooden panel with some adhesive is known as *marouflage.* A composition completed by using only one color, in various depths of tone, is *monochrome.* And an *oleograph,* alas, is a reproduction of an oil painting by the process of actual printing with oil colors, a process that, with the technological skills of our age, increasingly deceives the trusting.

The term *pastiche* is used to describe a picture that attempts to revive exactly an ancient style; and the connoisseur mutters something about *pentimento* when he suspects that there is a faint outline of an old painting under the one he studies—an old painting that may emerge awkwardly in time.

The preparatory treatment of canvas or panel before oil painting is *priming;* and to *scumble* is to soften a stroke or slash of color by rubbing gently with a paper stump or even the finger. On the other hand *sgraffiato* is the scraping through layers of paint to get back to the priming or undercoats, and *stipple* is that method of painting whereby, as a result of holding the brush vertically, small round blobs of paint appear on the canvas.

The *stretcher* is the frame of wood with wedges that is used to stretch the canvas before painting. And the term *support* is employed not for the easel but for the ground on which the various media are worked.

Tempera is usually a mixture of egg white, glue, and casein, but literally means the mixing of pigments with egg yolk; and *trompe l'oeil* is the result of that skill in a painter which enables him to portray natural objects so well that to the beholder they appear as the actual object portrayed.

Prints

Collectors must be increasingly content with prints in these days of penury and scarcity, and should know at once that a print is an impression or printing produced from engraved blocks, metal plates or from stones, of which the most important feature apart from its authorship is its "state," or age in terms of whether it was printed in the youth or middle age or dotage of the block, plate, or stone.

Thus "first state" prints are the first impressions taken off before any inscription or lettering appears in the title space, and these should not be confused with "trial proofs," that have interest value only and represent impressions taken by the artist to guide him in his work.

The "second state" is when the inscription or title is added, and/or the artist's name or publisher's imprint. There are several intermediary states, as for example the "open-letter proof" when the title is etched in outline only; and thereafer the state of the "state" refers generally to the wearing of the plate.

"Impression" is another matter. As a printer can usually obtain some three impressions from a single inking, so these became progressively less brilliant.

Probably the earliest prints were simple woodcuts, first used in the thirteenth century for the making of playing cards. The earliest print bearing a date is known as the "Brussels print," from the year 1418. A design was drawn on the prepared surface of a piece of wood and then those parts not to be printed were cut away. The block thereafter was inked and impressions taken from it.

Engraving is the term generally used for cutting wood and metals and subsequently printing from blocks, but it has come to refer specifically to printing of pictures from incised metals.

Etching is a more sophisticated form of engraving, and involves first the coating of a copper plate with a waxy substance. The artist exposes the copper by drawing on this wax with his needle, after which the plate is placed in acid, that eats away the copper only where it is exposed. Dry-point etching is not true etching at all, but involves just scratching the design straight on to the copper; and soft-ground etching is a method that gives the effect of pencil or chalk drawing by placing a thin paper on wax mixed with tallow on the plate and drawing with a pencil on this paper. When the paper is taken off it drags away the tallow where the pencil was impressed and in the subsequent bath the acid goes through the ground to the copper.

Albrecht Dürer (1471–1528) was the early master of etching; and Rembrandt was probably the greatest exponent of the method.

During the twenties of this century there was a boom in etchings, and no wall was complete without them. To "come up and see my etchings" was a plaintive and characteristic cry of the age. Since then our eyes have ceased to find great pleasure in this type of exquisite print, so the forward-looking collector might well consider a comparatively inexpensive collection of fine etching as a certain investment.

Plain line engraving on copper has been practiced from earliest times and seems to have been a development of the goldsmith's art. Outstanding among the early engravers was Ivan Meckenham (1440–1503). The process has always been a simple matter of drawing on a plate with a burin, then printing from the plate, although the great masters of the art would achieve their special effects by making sharp or broad furrows of differing depths. Steel engravings date only from about 1820 and tended to clutter up the nineteenth century with a remorseless sameness of mechanical black and white effect. Steel plates are too hard to produce real beauty in a print and they rust.

Aquatint engraving is a nice method of reproducing the effect of a water-color painting, by coating a copper plate with solutions of rosin in rectified alcohol and then, when the plate is dry and showing a granulation, actually painting on the surface with a brush and acid. The acid bites into the pores of the rosin. To achieve "color" effects the process is repeated with weaker solutions, and exquisite shadings were achieved by the great masters of the art such as La Prince (1733–1781), Goya, and, in England, Paul Sandby (1721–1809). There is little fear of being deceived by faked acquatints as the art is too exacting for our less meticulous and hurried days.

The mezzotint similarly belongs to a vanished age. The great practitioner was Ludwig von

Siegen (1609–1680), and his method was to raise a burr on a copper plate with a tool called a rocker. Then with another tool called a scraper the burr would itself be rubbed away here and there to produce a design in an infinity of subtle tones once the plate was inked and prints taken from it.

Stipple engraving means simple engraving in dots instead of lines, but once again it was a very difficult method save for the most skilled artists, such as the notable Jean-Charles François (1717–1769).

Lithography is nowadays one of the principal methods of reproducing pictures, but the principle was developed by Alois Senefelder as long ago as 1792. It is basically a very simple method, but again requires a great artist or craftsmen to bring out all its possibilities. The antipathy of grease and water is the secret. A polished Bavarian stone has the design drawn on it with a greasy chalk and is then washed in nitric acid and gum. Before each printing the stone is made wet and then inked. The ink, being itself greasy, adheres only to the greasy chalk marks of the design and reproduces only that part. Chromo lithography is when separate stones are used for each color.

But the term color print for the collector should refer specifically to the true color-printing done chiefly between the momentous years 1770 and 1815. Modern color-printing, when not achieved by lithography, is a matter of using several halftone and/or line blocks. The color prints of the late eighteenth century were produced from a single copper plate, on which the printer had applied all the colors by hand. Nor is this method to be confused with the great deal of hand-coloring of steel and other engravings that was done in the nineteenth century, which involved taking an old or young print, finished on its paper, and daubing the lines with water-colors. The last method is used to this day by dealers who buy old atlases, extract the maps, and hand-color them for framing and wall adornment.

It should be noted that old prints as well as paintings can be usefully restored if given only to first-ranking experts. Even the brown spots from dampness called "foxings" can be removed. Damp is the principal enemy of the print—damp and the unscrupulous modern printer who reproduces the originals by photographing them and thus making new blocks. The experienced collector will accordingly learn about old paper so as to be able to detect the forgery immediately. There are, however, some forgers who have taught themselves how to make old paper.

In collecting prints it is again wise to specialize in one subject, such as sporting, nautical, historical, architectural, animal, political. The sporting print is the aristocrat of the genre and perhaps the most attractive still, although the finer examples have been priced almost out of existence.

Maps

The poor man's antique picture, and the important investment of the rich man tomorrow (if there are any rich men tomorrow and indeed if there is any tomorrow) is the early map. It combines a strange archaic beauty, that cannot be exactly analyzed, with a historical interest that particularly appeals to the true antiquarian in the collector. At the moment it is, on the whole, relatively inexpensive. An excellent example can still be bought for the price of a child's bicycle, and, considering the great age of the article and the fact that the atlases from which it is extracted are becoming finally denuded, there may well be such a steep price rise before long as to bring this collector's price into the class of silver, paperweights, and other items of high finance.

The earliest collected maps are those by Christopher Saxton, who seems to have been born in the region of 1542 at Tingley near Leeds. He went to Cambridge, then came to London and obtained the patronage of Thomas Seckford. This worthy man gave Saxton the money to travel all over the British Isles and make the necessary surveys for the compilation of a great atlas of county maps that was dedicated to Queen Elizabeth. Saxton was still living in 1606, but the date of his death is unknown. The atlas of Saxton is the archetype of all successors, and is beautifully antique with its quaint decorations, elaborate cartouches, little churches, ships, and mythological creatures of the sea. The lettering is particularly fine. Saxton's atlas was hand-colored as originally issued in 1579, and no English maps subsequently were tinted so well. Often they were printed in black and white, and the color on them has been applied since.

After Saxton came two excellent engravers, William Hole and William Kip. Hole worked in London between 1600 and 1646, and was a pioneer engraver on copper. Kip's activity was between say 1598 and 1635, but little is known of him. They issued between them in 1610 and 1637 a series of maps copied from Saxton's atlas but in a different style that is characterized by fineness of engraving. These maps can still be acquired quite inexpensively.

Next came the most important name in early English cartography, that of John Speed, important because he enlarged the pioneer work of Saxton and his atlas ran into many editions. He was evidently the great businessman as well as artist. The best old English maps available to collectors have invariably been Speeds because of their availability combined with their beauty of execution. It is believed that Speed was born at Farndon in Cheshire in 1552, and it is known that he was admitted to the Merchant Taylors' Company in 1580 after following his father's trade as a tailor. He married in 1582, may have lived and worked in Moor Fields, London, and we do not know when he died. His first atlas was issued in 1610, although not probably distributed till 1611, and under the names *The Theatre of the Empire of Great Britaine* or *The Generall of Great Britaine*, subtitled *The British ilands, Proposed in one view in the English Map*, it was *Performed by John Speede*, but *Graven by I. Hondius and are to be Solde by I. Sudbury and George Humble in Popes head Alley in London. Cum privilegio Regis 1610.* The great atlas continued to be issued until about 1770. It can be seen from a study of the book that Speed had made himself a considerable antiquary and historian. Each map has a complete description of the relevant county on the back and is therefore best hung in a glass-backed Hogarth-type frame. Speed copied Saxton, but added original decorations and town plans that in some cases are the first ever made of those towns.

Samuel Pepys twice refers to Speed. He says on 20th. June, 1662: "I turned to the Forrest of Deane, in Speede's Mapps, and there he [Sir John Winter] showed me how it lies." And on September 19, 1666: "I and the boy to finish and set up my books and everything else in my house till two in the morning, and then to bed; but mightily troubled, even in my sleep, by missing four or five of my biggest books, Speed's Chronicle and Maps."

Speed's individual maps are gradually becoming more expensive, but can still be acquired for less than a reach-me-down suit.

Inevitably the Dutchmen had to jump in at this point. Two in particular, Blaeu and Jansson of Amsterdam, took Speed's atlas and carefully copied it. John Blaeu was born at Amsterdam on September 23, 1596, the son of a surveyor, globemaker, and publisher whose business he inherited and continued. Ht died in 1673. His first great set of maps was issued in 1645; Jansson's came out the following year. These Dutch children of Speed produced maps that can be recognized because they are less exuberant than those of the master, and, in the case of Blaeu's, far better colored. Much of the Dutch work was issued in colored state, and no colored maps are quite so fine. There was a fire at Blaeu's premises in 1672, and most of the copper plates were destroyed. This probably hastened the mapmaker's death a year after.

Blaeu's colored maps should never be hung in the direct light, as the exquisite hand-colors can fade. They were never intended to be hung.

English successors to Speed included Richard Blome, a paper-ruler who graduated to writing books on heraldry and topography. He issued his set of small decorative maps in 1673 from "Mr. Kid's in the corner of Lincoln's Inn Fields, near New Market," and they may still be collected without undue difficulty or expense. They are crude by comparison with Speed's, but extremely decorative in their archaic way. Then Robert Morden, who worked at The Atlas, Cornhill, from 1668 till 1703, was a bookseller-publisher who dabbled in cartography and issued decorative but unimportant maps that can be identified by the titles inserted in ornamental cartouches.

John Ogilby was a Scotsman, born in 1600, who twice lost all his money and stock-in-trade, once in the Irish rebellion and again in the Great Fire of London. He made the first road survey of England and Wales. John Seller was Hydrographer to Charles II, James II and Anne, and issued charts and maps at the sign of The Mariner's Compass, Wapping, and elsewhere in London. Herman Moll was a Dutchman who made and sold maps in London from about 1688 till 1732; and Sir William Petty, born in 1623, a savant who helped to found the Royal Society, was notable for his survey and maps of the counties of Ireland.

The eighteenth century saw a decline in beautiful mapmaking allied to an increase in cartographical accuracy. The modern, uninteresting but undeniably most useful map was born. The earlier tradition was maintained for a while by such as Thomas Kitchin and Emanuel Bowen, who from 1749 till 1755 issued in particular some large, decorative maps that are notable for their scenic cartouches that contain details of the economic life of the relevant county. Bowen's address in 1720 was "Next ye King of Spain in St. Katherines," and in 1722 it was "Opposite the Bolt and Tunn Inn in Fleet Street," but the poor chap maintained the tradition of the great artist-craftsman by dying poor and blind, while his son Thomas, who inherited the business, ended in Clerkenwell workhouse.

The most important cartographer of the eighteenth century was John Cary, born about 1754, who set up as an engraver and seller of maps and prints at Arundel Street, Strand, in 1783 or thereabouts. His subsequent Strand premises were destroyed by fire; and he moved afterwards to St. James's Street, dying in 1835. The feature of his maps was the fine engraving and superb lettering for place names—the only lettering on English maps to be compared with that of Saxton—combined with a scientific method that is almost modern.

The last of the decorative mapmakers was Thomas Moule, who, as late as 1836, issued a series that is suitably fantastic and in the great tradition although anachronistic and a precursor of typical Victorian pastiche. Born in 1784, Moule was another writer on heraldry and topography who combined this with bookselling, although he possessed the inestimable advantage of a government sinecure. He was "Inspector of Blind Letters" at the General Post Office.

A minister of the Scottish Kirk, one Timothy Pont, amused himself in the seventeenth century by making the first cartographical surveys of the Scottish counties, and Blaeu used this pioneer work as the basis for his 1654 Scottish Counties series, that are especially worth collecting.

Mapmaking has indeed ever been a cannibalistic and derivatory calling. As late as 1910 a Scottish firm was issuing early motoring maps taken directly from the eighteenth-century originals of John Cary.

For decorative purposes and antiquarian interest there are few better choices than the 1675 road maps of John Ogilby. They were executed in strips, just like the itineraries issued by motoring organizations today, but also possess pictorial beauty together with the charm of great age (provided that they are purchased from a leading specialist dealer who will give a written guarantee of that age).

The collector is again advised to choose a particular subject, learn all about it, and not stray from it. He could buy maps of his own country, or county, or even specialize in sea charts, such as the early tracings of Lucas Waghenaer (1588), and of Jansson, van Keulen, Blaeu, and that Captain Greenvile Collins who in 1681 began the seven-year official task of surveying all the coasts of the British Isles. The charts were published as a whole in 1693, and subsequently went through many eighteenth-century editions. Although practical in intent and made for the everyday use of mariners, they were executed with great artistic skill and never failed to embellish their facts with such charming delights as rocks, and buoys, and anchorages, and churches, trees, mansions, and windmills for sea marks on the coastal hills.

A popular printmaker's subject in the seventeenth and eighteenth centuries was the "Prospect," as was equally the "Panorama." Thus it should be possible to purchase still, quite inexpensively, such an item as "London, the glory of Great Britaines Ile, behold her Lanschip here and true Pourfile," which is a colored line engraving showing the City, Westminster, and Southwark, with a numbered key to all places of interest as they were in 1647." Or "A Grand Panorama of London from the River Thames. An historical record of the appearance of the Great Metropolis in 1847. Folded into cloth covers with gilt lettering." Or a colored plan of West India Docks, 1800, that specifically shows all the inns of the district. And a nineteenth-century paper cut-out view of the Thames Tunnel, that extends to give a panoramic effect and includes a small view of the steamship *Great Eastern*.

11

Books

General

Books are still safer to collect than any other item, in that their faking or reproduction is too expensive except in the most important cases, and they are basically so repellent to marauders that they are less likely to be taken from the collector by thieves or officials than objects that have more obvious value. But they are increasingly expensive to collect for those very reasons; and it is wise to concentrate on a particular and if possible recherché department. Important incunabula and such later items as First Folios of Shakespeare are only for people who have vast sums of money to invest. If an out-of-the-way subject or type be chosen, then, the collector can inexpensively browse in the secondhand bookshops and in the unregarded back rooms of antique shops, and can amuse himself by buying bulky lots for a few shillings or dollars at country sales, extracting the volumes that he wants and reselling the rest to a dealer for at least what he originally paid.

Knowledge about books can chiefly be obtained only by handling and reading them, although it is possible to impart certain items of information that can be memorized by the would-be bibliophile: for example, that Aldus Manutius was an Italian typographer of the fifteenth century, founder of the Aldine Press at Venice, who not only gave us italic type but also pioneered book production in the modern sense at comparatively low cost for simple editions. His descendants continued his fine business but eventually lost it.

Or that the Ashendene Press was one of the rash of "arty" private presses that signalized at the turn of the century the beginning of modern preciosity in printing. There was a time when subscribing to and collecting the work of these presses was almost a national sport among the wealthy, who were bitterly to regret it when the bottom fell out of "moderns" before the last war, although there is today a distinct revival in interest and prices, for great, showy books from the Doves Press of T. J. Cobden-Sanderson and Emery Walker, (people who became portentously mystical about it, but did produce the superb Doves Bible), and the Golden Cockerel Press founded by Robert Taylor in 1920, taken over by Robert Gibbings in 1924, and notable during the Gibbings period for its books illustrated with rather mannered woodcuts, and of course the extraordinary Kelmscott Press of that muddle-minded if hard-working dreamer of idle dreams William Morris, whose books such as the Kelmscott Chaucer still have considerable value and fame but are overdecorated in the worst possible taste.

Then it is necessary for the bibliophile to have an exact knowledge of certain terms used in his kind of collecting, terms such as "backstrip" to signify the covering of the spine, "blocking" to indicate designs on covers printed or blocked by hand in color, or "blind" *sans color*. It must be known similarly that buckram is a good strong linen for binding, that "calf" is a brown leather binding material more frequently made from cow than calfskin, and that a "cancel" is a page or smaller inset subsequently inserted in a book to the delight of the ungodly, as it is not part of the original printing.

"Chain lines" are impressions on handmade paper, ideally, although unfortunately on machine-made paper also, that were made by the wires in the trays where the pulp was laid. They vary in width importantly according to the date of making. And to "collate" is, in bookbinding, to bring together the signatures, but in bibliography is to compare books or books and MSS.

A "colophon" equally has two bibliographical meanings (1) material printed in a book which outlines by whom it was produced and how, and (2) a drawn device that serves as a publisher's trademark.

A "cropped" book is one so mishandled in the guillotine that its text or illustrations or margins are impaired; and "cursive" is calligraphy in the running script of modern handwriting as opposed to "uncial," which is calligraphy in capital letters.

The "dust jacket" is the detachable paper cover of a book whose function is to protect the real cover. It may be a temporary phenomenon of our time, often costing far too much to produce—and often rashly destroyed by ultraconservative book buyers who do not realize that book jackets will one day be very rare.

Then a modern book is, alas, often only as strong as its "end papers," because these largely affix the binding to the book; in better days they were not so important but often decorated.

"Folio" is the largest-sized volume, printed from sheets folded once only; also it is another name for the page number. "Fore-edge paintings" derive from the work of the eighteenth-century Halifax bookbinder John Edwards, who developed the method of fanning out the fore-edge of a book and painting a picture on that part which appeared different when the fanning was contracted. This in due course became a favorite Victorian pastime that played its part in the foundation of the motion-picture industry.

A "foxed" book is one afflicted by the brownish-yellow stains or spots that are caused by damp; and when a book is "fresh" it is not so much curious as in essentially good condition, a little less than "mint," which means exactly as new. A "curious" book is one that breaks the sexual conventions in its contents. Then the "frontispiece" is the page opposite the title page; the "half title" is usually the first page on the book proper, with title alone printed on it and the frontispiece on the "verso" or other side (the "half title" can also be called the "bastard" without offense); the "head" is the top edge of a volume; and the "headband" is a piece of cloth or leather around the top of the "spine" or back, built to resist those who pluck too hastily at the contents of bookcases.

The "mull" in a book is the coarse muslin glued on the spine in the binding; and a "page" technically is only one side of a "leaf." The "recto" is the page on the right that immediately appears to the reader on that side, with the aforementioned verso on the left. A "signature" is a folded sheet for gathering, marked with a letter at the foot of the first page; it is usually sixteen pages, but can be eight or thirty-two.

The term "snag" is used by bibliophiles to indicate a torn page, and when a book is

(Courtesy of Martin Breslauer, 2 Weymouth House, Hallam Street, London, W.1.)
A very important Persian illuminated manuscript of the Diwan of Jami the fifteenth-century Persian poet, dated, 1497, have eleven miniature paintings as above, in the Turkman style, executed in Shiraz. Actual size.

described as "soiled" it is dirtied, as by fingermarks, but not foxed, when it is described as "stained." Meanwhile a "sound" book is at least complete and undamaged, although not necessarily fresh or mint. The "state" in bibliography is different from the "state" in print collecting. It implies the slight changes of type that occur with each printing or impression. Inevitably a comma is dropped or a line goes slightly out of true. And, while an "impression" is a printing from the same type, an "edition" involves change in that type.

An "unopened" book has not had the edges of the pages cut by guillotine, and cannot be read until a paper-knife has slit those edges open. But thereafter it is still "uncut," which means untrimmed by guillotine.

It should be noted that the term "first edition" has come to mean the initial impression at one single printing of the book, although technically the subsequent impressions from that type belong to the first edition so long as no change is made in the type.

When the edges of a book are wavy or crimpled they are described as "gauffred." The "hinge" is where the pages join in the middle; and an "opening" in bibliography is a pair of facing pages. A "plate" properly is a book illustration that has been printed from a metal plate such as a halftone or line block.

A "gloss" refers to mutilation of a book by handwritten commentaries into, around, above, or below the text, whereas a "glossary" is a printed and therefore respectable gloss, decently placed at the end where, with any luck, it will not be read.

"Gothic" is black-letter type, the first ever cut and based on the involved handwritten script of the monks. Its illegibility led to its being replaced by "Roman," upright, serifed, clear, like the lettering of the ancient Latins, except in much German, and in newspaper titles, and in the advertisements of antique dealers.

Gothic type was used by Johann Gutenberg, born at Mainz in 1400, died in 1468, who was probably the first European to print with movable type cast in molds. It is believed that the theory was worked out or obtained indirectly from China by one Andreas Dryzehn, who is known to have made an agreement with Gutenberg to teach him certain "secret arts." Gutenberg's Bible of 1456, sometimes called the "Mazarin" because the first copy to arouse attention was found in the library of Cardinal Mazarin at Paris, is the earliest known European book printed from movable type.

Then it should be clearly understood that the term "incunabula" means books printed prior to 1500, being derived from the Latin for swaddling clothes, and that another father of the modern book and European printing was Nicholas Jenson of Paris, who not only introduced printing into France but did much to establish Roman as a more desirable type face than Gothic. Meanwhile William Caxton (1422-1491) went to Bruges and then to Burgundy and Cologne, where he probably learned the infant art of printing. Everything comes out of Germany! Caxton's first book *Recuyell of the Hystoryses of Troye* was printed by him at Bruges 1474-1476. It is the first English printed book. Caxton returned to England immediately after and set up his famous press at Westminster, printing some ninety-six books in all.

Each nation claims to have invented printing. The Dutch insist that the first European printer was Lourens Janszoon Coster, an innkeeper of Haarlem in the fifteenth century, but unfortunately none of his work survives. Meanwhile Bohemia had printers by 1468; Andreas Hess was printing in Hungary by 1473; Hochfeder brought the craft to Poland in 1475; and in 1482 Stephen Koblinger was printing in Austria and John Snell in Denmark prior to setting up a press in Sweden a year later.

In the sixteenth century we have the pioneer New World printing of the book *Breve y mas Compendiosa doctrina,* done in Mexico, and the virtual invention of modern publishing, particularly of pocket editions, by the Elzevirs in Holland, and the great work of Christopher Plantin, born 1514, died 1589, who not only started a printing works at Antwerp that lasted three hundred years, at one time the largest in the world, but also designed one of the finest type faces that we still use.

Wynkyn de Worde was an aptly named Englishman who was apprenticed to Caxton and took over the press after his master's death, producing many fine books in Fleet Street eventually.

During the eighteenth century John Baskerville decided at the age of fifty to produce perfect books from the most elegant and legible type. He set up his press in 1750, and spent the first seven years in perfecting ink, type, and paper. We remember Baskerville not so much for the many fine books he printed as for the type face he designed and cut, that is still without a peer.

Yet at the same time Giambattista Bodoni was designing type faces in Italy that we like to use to this day; and William Caslon (1692-1766) was similarly providing the printer of the future with much of the modern basis of his craft. It could be said that the craft of printing developed in the fifteenth century, and of book publishing in the seventeenth, but that the more beautiful aspects of printing as we know it today originated in the work of eighteenth-century pioneers.

A few final facts may be useful. Thus the "horn-book" was an eighteenth-century device for teaching the young, consisting of a piece of wood with reading matter affixed and then a covering of transparent horn to resist aggression. A "missal" is a Roman Catholic prayerbook, especially interesting when early and illuminated. "Morocco" was originally leather for bindings made from goatskin. The variety known as "Levant" with large grains is the superior kind, and "French" with fine grains is inferior. "Parchment" is the skin of animals prepared for printing or writing, developed first at Pergamos in the second century B.C.

"Muniments" are document or deeds, while "original binding" is a very important term to the collector as it should mean exactly what it says for value, whereas far too many eighteenth- and nineteenth-century books were re-bound after being first issued in paper covers, or deprived of their initial hard covers and re-bound in gaudily tooled leather so that they would look nice in parvenu bookcases. The "book plate" was a device of this period, when a label with the owner's name and coat-of-arms was pasted inside the cover of a volume to add to or detract from the value of the piece according to the extent of the owner's notoriety.

With regard to book paper, it should be understood that there are basically two kinds, laid and wove, the first showing by lines that it might have been handmade, and the second showing an even but granulated texture. "Art" is paper that has been made glossy and weighty by the admixture of chalk, and belongs to the modern period of halftone illustrations. The history of paper starts with the ancient Chinese, goes on to the twelfth century in Spain, and does not start in England until the fifteenth century. "Papyrus," origin of the word paper, is an early writing material made from the pith of a sedgelike plant, and a "palimpsest" is a twice-used sheet of papyrus.

It is essential for the bibliophile to understand the use of those clumsy numerals that probably did as much as anything else to bring about the decline and fall of the Roman Empire. In Roman numerals 1000=M, 500=D, 100=C, 50=L, 10=X, and one=I with V for 5.

"Sheepskin" is a binding material that resembles calf but is softer, and a "slip case" is a cardboard box with one open end to contain a book or papers.

In bookbinding the term "full" indicates that the covers and "spine" or back are all of one material; "half" binding means that only the spine and corners of the cover are bound with the superior material; and "quarter" binding comprises leather or the superior material on the spine only.

"Vellum" is fine parchment, originally from the skin of a calf, but also means a manuscript written on this material, or a paper made in imitation of it.

Miniature Books

Very small and very large articles have always fascinated middle-sized man. When Swift invented his Lilliputians and Brobdingnagians he recognized this trait and made good use of it; when showmen produce their dwarfs and giants they also cater to a taste that is as common in civilization as it is in savagery (if the two terms are not interchangeable). Thus numerous miniature books have been published throughout the ages, some marvels of manual dexterity; and there was once a craze for them that caused their production in large quantities. The fragility of these masterpieces of the printer's, engraver's and calligraphist's art has made them an easier prey to time than larger books; and those of ancient provenance that still exist at the present day are valuable rarities.

There are three distinct classes of miniature books, those in manuscript, those printed in type and as such combining the skill of the type designer, cutter, printer, and binder; and those produced by a photographic process from an ordinary-sized book. Printed miniature books are the collector's true prey. According to Cyril Davenport, a former official at the British Museum, they should not exceed three by two inches, measured on the printed page, to be of bibliographical value.

Probably the first miniature book ever printed was Peter Schoeffer's 1468 *Diurnale Moguntinium,* only 65 by 95 mm., not truly miniature by modern standards, but remarkable by comparison with the enormous first books of the incunabula period, such as Gutenberg's *Fragment of the World Judgment,* that had a type area of 100 by 220 mm., and also remarkable that it was produced at the very beginning of the history of European printing.

Nicholas Jenson printed a beautiful miniature book in 1474 called *Officium Beatae Virginis,* on vellum, and a copy is in the British Museum. Then the Newberry Library in Chicago has, among many other early small books, a remarkable miniature printed in Basel in 1491. The type area is only 41 by 58 mm. Basel went on to print many miniature books, as did fifteenth-century printers of Venice, Naples, and Cologne.

The oldest-known miniature book printed in the English language was the *Hours of the Blessed Virgin* of Julian Notary, a Frenchman who came to London in the fifteenth century and set up a press there at the Sign of the Three Kings, Westminster. This rarity, printed in absurdly small black letter, was an 1½ inches long and 1 inch wide. The date of issue was 1500.

Seventy-four years later there was published by W. Seres, of London, a book called the *Tablet for Gentlewomen,* as interesting for its quaint contents as for its size, that was 2 by 1½ inches; and in 1616 a copy of the Bible called *Verbum Sempiternum,* measuring 1½ inches square, was published by a London printer named J. Beale. Thereafter many miniature books were printed in England. Religious works were a popular subject for the miniaturist, who tended to work as much for the glory of God as for themselves; and many Thumb Bibles, as they were called, came off the miniature presses. Most of these were square in shape, bound in plain calf, and printed in black letter, the type size being usually the old Long Primer. A very small Bible was that published by W. Harris of London, in 1774. It measured 2½ inches by 2 inches, and had an engraved title page.

In the eighteenth century miniature book production was brought to a fine art by two famous Scotsmen, Robert and Andrew Foulis of Glasgow. Robert was for many years printer to the University of Glasgow, where he cut some beautiful types, including a small one in nonpareil, or 6-point, as it is called in modern mechanistic times. Collaborating with his brother, he also produced an extremely fine Greek type, and it was this that was used in the well-known Foulis miniature Greek series. Many volumes, including Anacreon, Pindar, Epictetus, and others of the classic authors were published, none of which exceeded 2¾ inches by 1¾ inches. They were neatly bound in blue morocco, gold-tooled, and the few copies existing today are eagerly sought after by collectors. The Foulis brothers also designed a famous 7-point Latin type.

Between 1770 and 1860 there was a craze for almanacs of all kinds, shapes and sizes. The most popular of these quaint books were the miniature productions. An idea of the contents can be obtained from the title page of an almanac published in 1799, that measured 1⅛ inches square, and that was bound in black morocco: "The Almanack explained. Note. Under the title of every month is the change of the Moon, and every month contains three columns. 1. Days of the month. 2. Saints' Days, Etcr. 3. Time of high water at London Bridge. Printed for the Company of Stationers."

Most of the almanacs were published by the Company of Stationers. Some were bound in silk, others in colored paper, while not a few were equipped with a miniature flap and silver catch, so that they could be fastened and unfastened like a purse. The most famous of these miniature reference books was the *English Bijou Almanack,* that was first issued in 1836, and continued yearly until 1884. The *Bijou*—aptly named, because it measured only ¾ by ½ inch—was bound in colored paper, and was "Poetically Illustrated by L. E. L."—well known to delvers into the queerer cracks of the early Victorian era as the much overated Letitia Landon.

The smallest, and one of the oldest miniature books extant, is a foreign production, printed by an Italian in 1615, and called *Galileo a Madame Cristina di Lorena.* It measures only 15 by 10 mm., approximately ½ by a ¼ inch, and can yet be read fairly easily with the unaided eye.

This is the definitive test of the miniature printed book. Those often indecipherable to the average eyesight are usually printed by the modern photographic process, and from the point of view of the bibliophile are comparatively worthless.

There are many collectors who specialize in miniature books solely, and there are some antiquarian booksellers who issue catalogues in the genre. For anybody fortunate in the possession of the taste, the time and the money it is doubtful whether there could be a more congenial hobby, as the small volumes take up little space, and generally are of pleasing appearance. Some bibliophiles have miniature bookcases constructed to accommodate their finds. In the British Museum there is one of these bookcases, a replica Chippendale type, that contains a fine collection gathered from several parts of the world.

12

Coins

General

Coins are best to collect for those who want portable and permanent wealth, as well as an antiquarian interest. Stamps are more portable, but are ephemeral by comparison, and of course they have as yet no antiquarian interest whatsoever, being typical productions of the modern, paper age. The best coins, those of gold or silver, have intrinsic as well as aesthetic and historical value. They, more than any other human artefact, will buy their owner his supper when the world is in ruins and all else fails. They cross jackbooted frontiers easier than Chippendale-type commodes or heavy gold bars. And, from the early years of human history, there have always been thousands of them, buried, secreted and lost in every age, being turned up anew in every age. Even when counterfeited they have value as well as interest.

Coins are so multifarious in their variety that there is a type for every kind of collector, from the richest to the poorest, from the most historical-minded to the most mercenary. Roman coins, as a single example, can still be bought very cheaply or very expensively according to type and condition, as hoards continue to be discovered after nearly two thousand years whenever a new European road is built or an old site is re-excavated. It should be remembered that until recently it was not possible to keep wealth in the form of book entries: the principal accumulation was in the form of coins, and these usually ended by being replaced in the mother earth from which their metal originally came.

It is a curious fact, however, that coin collecting in the modern sense is rarely based on commercialism or greed. The typical numismatist starts not as a miser but as a little boy who likes to have a few old coins in a box for examining and collating and showing his friends. Nearly always he begins indiscriminately, because there is so much for him to collect at such low price.

Therefore it is extremely important in this branch of collecting that the beginner should learn to discriminate, which he can best do by choosing a distant subject and adhering to it, meanwhile learning about those two all-important factors, rarity and condition.

Because a coin is very old it is not necessarily valuable. There are so many of certain types of even the most ancient coins that prices for them must be low for a long time to come. The great value of rarity depends upon how many of the particular coin were originally struck, plus how many come on the modern market. Quite recently it was possible to acquire a Roman silver denarius (the original "d." of the English "£.s.d.") for as little as a dollar. This would have been struck before the time of Christ. And a few cents would have enabled the collector of the year 1950 to purchase a third- or fourth-century bronze coin. As this book is being written the prices rise in response to international inflation of paper currencies, but still some ancient coins have little more than their original face value after so many hundreds of years.

"Condition," after rarity, is of supreme importance in coin collecting. Numismatists use the abbreviation "F.D.C." ("fleur de coin") to indicate complete perfection or mint state. Coins in this condition are the most rare and usually the most valuable, no matter their type. An "F.D.C." copper coin of comparatively modern times might be worth more than a Greek gold coin, *if* the Greek gold coin were in bad condition, which means badly damaged or hopelessly worn. Most coins are in what the numismatist calls "F" condition, that signified originally "fine" but generally indicates "distinct if worn."

Yet the whole subject of "condition" is not one that can be codified or dismissed in a few sentences. It is more of an art than a science, and different numismatists or specialist dealers will disagree heartily on what constitutes value in the condition of a coin. Each type has its individual range of conditions. Once again, handling, reading, and length of experience are the factors that make for success or failure in building up a technically and financially worthwhile collection.

One golden rule of thumb is that a coin in obviously bad condition should never be bought, provided there is money for a better one. The imperfections loom larger in the eye as time passes, and there is growing dissatisfaction with the piece; also there will be disappointment with price if the collector ever wishes to resell. And, as a corollary to this, the infant numismatist should disabuse himself of all thought of improving the condition of a poor coin by restoring, repairing, or above all cleaning it. More coins have been ruined by collectors' hand-applied abrasives than by hundreds of years of normal wear plus the raging blasts of many great wars. If coins obviously require cleaning they should be taken to experts and the work should be paid for.

Certain terms used by the numismatists require learning by heart. Thus the "obverse" of a coin is that side which normally shows the monarch's head, and the "reverse" is the side opposite to the obverse. A "blank" is a circular, empty piece of metal, or the coin before striking, while the term "flan" is used to describe the whole piece of metal after the striking.

The "type" of a coin is its main, central design; the "legend" is the description; the "field" is the flat part between the main design and the edge; and the "exergue" is the part beneath the main design, usually separated by a horizontal line, and normally occupied by the date.

The "die" is the block of metal with cut design that is impressed into the blank coin to print or "strike" it; and the term "die variety" is used to indicate slight variations of design in coins of one type. A "mule" has the current type on one side and a previous type or generally obsolete design on the other side or is a piece struck from two dies not usually employed together. "Graining" means the crenellations round the edge of coins, known to the populace as "milling," a device introduced to stop the populace from paring away useful lumps of the metal and bringing about their own private debasement of their coinage (an occupation for which they could scarcely be blamed as it has always been the principal sport of kings and successor governments).

The collector who wisely decides to specialize has a wide range of opportunity. He could, for example, opt for a coin of each English, or French, or German, or Italian, or Austrian, or Spanish, or Russian monarch. This could gradually be extended to include a good example of every denomination of the national monarchs chosen. Or he could specialize within this framework to acquire, say, English crown pieces from 1551 till 1937, choosing either dates or types, perhaps choosing both. A similar interesting collection could be made of English shillings from Henry VII to the present day.

English copper coins and bronze coins from the reign of James I to what pass as copper coins today, with a subcollection of Anglo-Saxon sceats; English gold coins; Scottish or Irish; Anglo-Saxons struck at any of the as many as sixty different mints of just Edward the Confessor's reign; Greek coins; Romans (the denarii are particularly attractive and inexpensive to the beginner); coins of the Jews, the Popes, of Napoleon, in fact of any specific people historically or relating to certain classes or rulers; those of the innumerable little states of the Holy Roman or German Empire from the fifteenth century to the nineteenth; Oriental coins and large ones and very small ones, and tokens, curious currencies such as Swedish plate money, cowrie shells as used for exchange purposes in Africa and southern Asia—the collector can choose among these and many others, but that he should so choose, and carefully as regards his disposition and his purse, is all-important.

Ancient

The term "ancient coins" usually refers to those of Greece and Rome in the heyday of their civilizations. It was in Lydia of Asia Minor or by the Greeks of Ionia that the earliest coins were struck, or the earliest that we so far know. It should be possible still to acquire a Persian gold daric of Artaxerxes II, 359-338 B.C. that closely follows the style of the original Lydian coins, with the design on the obverse only. It would show the great king crouching in warlike attitude with bow or shield in one hand and spear in the other. Or a coin still available that stems from the Ionian original type would be a silver tetradrachm of the Chalcidian League in Macedonia, 392-358 B.C., with beautiful head of Apollo on the obverse and the characteristic lyre and Greek inscription on the reverse. The Greek silver coins are indeed among the finest ever made, excellently engraved: and the most valuable are those of around the period 410 B.C. The whole range dates from as long ago as 700 B.C. to the Roman era, and examples could be collected from nearly every town of that considerable ancient world, all around the Mediterranean and farther afield.

It has been said that the collector can easily start with the Roman denarius. This was a small silver coin that was issued in vast numbers both in the Republican and in the Imperial periods. It was the currency that manured Roman expansion; and its original value, indicated often by the mark "x" on it, was ten asses, referring not to the folly of those who sought to build up a fortune in those days but to the earliest Roman coinage, that was of bronze, cast and not struck, called "Aes Grave." A still earlier type, rather bullion assessed by weight than coinage for counting, was the "Aes Rude." It is usually agreed that the "Aes Grave" series started about 222 B.C., and it endured so long as the Romans were a nonimperial people, content with leading self-contained lives on their own produce.

When the Romans got tired of humdrum hard work they began to attack their neighbors, both with sword and with salesman. These neighbors were often Greeks with fine silver coinages, so the Romans had to graduate from bronze. The authority on the subject is E. A. Sydenham, and he has specifically stated: "About 269 B.C. the Roman Republic began to issue didrachms, essentially Greek in style, bearing various types and the name ROMA or ROMANO, but without any indication of their place of mintage. There is little doubt, however, that they were struck at mints that had previously been striking Greek didrachms. Later in the third century these 'Romano-Campanian' didrachms, as they are commonly but somewhat inexactly called, were superseded by quadrigati, which are uniform in type although they exhibit minor varieties of style. The quadrigatus remained current down to the end of the Second Punic War. But during the war a new coin known as the victoriate was introduced, which outlived the quadrigatus and was itself eventually superseded by the denarius (187 B.C.)."

The Roman Republic ceased to mint copper coins from approximately 80 B.C., save for the issue of Julius Caesar in 45 and 44 B.C. With the coming of the Empire all was changed. Augustus firmly controlled the minting of all gold and silver coins himself, but less valuable issues were the prerogative of the Senate. They can be identified by the "S.C." on them, which stands for "Senatus Consulto"; they date from 23 B.C.; and until 4 B.C. approximately they bear the name of their makers. The principal Roman coins of this great period are as follows:

The gold coins consisted of the aureus equal to 25 silver denarii, and the quinarius equal to 12½ silver denarii. The silver issues were the denarius equal to 16 asses, and the quinarius equal to 8 asses. The orichalcum or yellow bronze pieces were the sestertius equal to 4 asses and the dupondius equal to 2 asses; and the copper coinage consisted of the as. equal to 4 quadrantes and the quadrans equal to ¼ as.

Among these the yellow bronze coins can be the most interesting and valuable, notably the sestertii issued in the two centuries after the birth of Christ. Their types bear careful study and can be extremely beautiful. High prices are paid for such sestertii in finest condition. The collector might equally cherish the bronze dupondii and the copper asses. They are smaller but often display a similar perfection of design and minting.

The collector would be well advised to acquire the catalogues of B. A. Seaby, Ltd., London, in order to learn not only about current values but also about the extremely interesting histories of the various great coinages. Thus the Seaby *Catalogue of Roman Coins* quickly condenses the unfortunate facts about Roman gold and silver issues: "Nero lowered the weight of the gold and silver coins and reduced the fineness of the latter. Successive emperors, always pressed for money, carried on the evil process, until by the reign of Caracalla the denarius was barely 40% of silver. This emperor further debased the coinage by introducing a new coin of similar metal, bearing as obverse type his head wearing a radiate crown, which we know by the name of antoninianus. The new piece, although only equal in weight to 1½ denarii, was tariffed as being the equivalent of two."

This inferior coin, the antoninianus, was progressively debased and ended as a piece of bronze or copper with the faintest of silver coating, and naturally it ended by driving the good denarius completely out of circulation and becoming itself the chief currency of the equally debased empire. This was towards the end of the third century A.D. The emperor Aurelian did his best to improve the Roman system of currency, but his denarii were of plain bronze (if interesting to numismatists because they tend to be rare); and the last silver denarii were those of Gordian III.

The wonderful name "barbarous radiate" applies to the badly minted antoniniani of Victorinus and the Tetrici, Gaulish emperors, as copied by outlying, private mints of the increasingly anarchic empire. Often these are found today in western European and British hoards. They are smaller than the official coins, badly designed, and the scholars have not yet been able to disentangle and codify the many varieties.

The Roman coinage throughout the whole history of the republic and empire was so immense and involved that it provides something for every kind of purse and interest. Often the copper coins of low denomination are important and sometimes the silver coins have little value at all. It is impossible to dogmatize, but perhaps the best target is Roman gold coins of the high periods, such as those of Vespasian. They have outstanding beauty and great, ever-increasing value.

British

British coins have natural interest for the English-speaking peoples of the world, but, like those of ancient Rome, they appeal to the international collector, whatever his language, because so many of them have been issued over such a long period of history. There is a continuity in British institutions that no other modern nation can boast. All other countries, save the new, colonial lands, have suffered so many invasions and revolutions, that their coinages have been ruined time and time again and indeed their treasures have been dissipated. The treasures of Britain are at last being despoiled, this very day, by bloodless invasion and social revolution, but it is not too late yet to participate in the rape.

A collector who wished to accumulate a range of British coins from the very beginning would start with the gold staters of the ancient British tribes. They are crude in shape, usually without inscription; and the designs on them depict animals, plants, or are geometrical in the Celtic manner. Shakespeare's Cymbeline was in reality the chief of the Catuvellauni tribe known as Cunobelin. It is possible to buy today a stater of this tribal leader, in comparatively fine condition still although a little squashed in shape, for the price of a well-tailored man's suit. It would have on the obverse a prancing animal with the letters CVN, and on the reverse a head of wheat with the letters CAMV.

British coins of the Roman occupation period are not usually valuable. There are always considerable numbers of bronze coins on offer, that were widely minted in the fourth century A.D., but good prices are not paid for them as yet. Perhaps the most interesting pieces of the Roman era are those minted in London and great Colchester for the usurper Emperor Carausius and the Allectus who succeeded by murdering him. The bronze antoniniani of these blackguards have their image on the obverse and some Roman deity on the reverse, and are worth little, but the gold pieces in their rarity cost several hundreds of dollars, and the silver pieces are similarly rare but much less expensive.

After the Romans came some inelegant copies of the imperial coinage; and the natives did not find their numismatic feet until approximately the year 750, when they invented the ubiquitous and long-lasting penny, which was, bless its heart, at first made of solid silver. A penny of Aethelred the Unready would be a good representative piece for the collector's cabinet, with a somewhat characteristic head and shoulders of the dithering monarch and his name on the obverse and a cross and more crude lettering on the reverse. Canute and Edward the Confessor issued similar silver pennies that can be still acquired for a couple of dollars today, but the collector should be warned against frequent forgeries of the rarer early Anglo-Saxon pennies.

When William the Conqueror crossed to England and took over the country he did not so much conquer the British as to be himself absorbed by them and their strange ways. Thus he continued to use the silver penny as the only item of coinage, and his successors did not attempt to introduce other denominations until some two hundred years later. This was when Edward I invented the fourpenny piece or groat, the halfpenny, and the farthing. All were of silver in those resplendent days, and in 1257 Henry III went so far as to issue a gold penny, worth twenty of the silver variety, that remains one of the finest and most valuable coins ever minted. The value is partly due to the fact that the populace hoarded the coins and melted them down, or even sold them at high prices to the Continental buyers who were already on the prowl in London. Only a few specimens are now in existence, and they are worth well over $2,500. The Edward I groat of 1379 is similarly rare because it was not a success as currency. It is sometimes found as an integral part of early jewelry, or in newly unearthed hoards, but is not too expensive considering its scarcity, whereas the silver pennies of the whole period have small value.

Edward III issued the first proper British gold coinage, but once more abortively, as the gold proved again to be too much for the natural cupidity of the people, and the coins tended to disappear as soon as they were minted. The experiment lasted for only a few months, and, as a result, gold coins of this 1344 issue are among the rarest and most valuable in the whole canon of British money. An example would be worth from $2,500 to $5,000 at present. The name florin first appeared with this issue, which was in florins, half florins and quarter florins. Edward III, a great coiner, also introduced a silver half groat, worth two pence. His florins are in appearance very similar to the modern British coin of that name, solid and beautifully designed, the coin of coins, and, of course, *gold*.

They were, however, not modern coins at all in method of manufacture, being handmade and hammered out. The British coinage as we know it now started in 1662, when the mints of Charles II underwent a technological revolution with the introduction of the mill and screw press. The coins thus produced were known as "milled," to distinguish them from their predecessors; and at the same time the denominations still in British use today were permanently established, although the principal denomination was the five-shilling piece or crown. It was a noble coin whose value was vitiated by the great number struck; and the wise collector buys only crowns that are rare because of some peculiarity. Thus those of 1674, 1675, and 1666 are less frequently found than the others. The silver in them came from the Africa Company, and this is recognized by an elephant below the effigy of the king. The rarest coins of the period, although they are not worth much, are the shillings that have a plume under the king on the obverse, or in the center of the reverse. Shillings and half crowns of the seventeenth century are generally so common as to be almost literally "two a penny." It is, however, worth looking for the 1704 and 1705 coins of Queen Anne, the shillings of George I that have the letters "W.C.C." (signifying Welsh Copper Company) under the king's head and shoulders, and all issues of William III wherein the reverses display plumes or roses. Silver coins from 1816 onwards must be in rare F.D.C. condition to be worth more than their face value save during periods of currency scare: and throughout the eighteenth, nineteenth, and twentieth century freak coins have been minted that command premium prices, but not really high prices so far. Remember always to look for what are known as the "provenance marks," symbols such as that elephant and those plumes and roses, placed below the king's portrait: they indicate the geographical origin of the silver.

It should be noted that increasing value attaches to many of the coins of the first Queen Elizabeth. They were mainly gold coins in that rich age of Britain's glory; and there were two great series, the first of which consisted of nearly pure gold: there was the sovereign of thirty shillings, the scarce ryal of fifteen shillings, then the ten-shilling angel and its half and quarter. The second series was made of 22-carat gold, with the original pound of twenty shillings, the half pound, the gold crown, and the gold half crown. No one thought of striking copper or base-metal coins in those days and the other Elizabethan issues were of nice silver, even to the extremely small halfpenny and the often misshapen but beautifully designed three-farthing piece.

During Elizabeth's very long reign from 1557 till 1603 more denominations were issued than in any other British period. Therefore Elizabethan coins are plentiful and cannot as yet have very great value. They undoubtedly present a considerable opportunity to the farseeing collector, who would be especially wise to acquaint himself with the mint marks of the reign. These will be found at the beginning of the inscription, a device changed frequently. The mint marks are important because Elizabethan coins are dated only in the cases of the sixpence, threepence, three half pence, and three farthings. Nor do the issues of this period bear a mark of value save in the cases of some of the silver half groats or twopences. They were distinguished from each other by their size, and the age was so fiercely religious that it was considered more important to devote space to pious inscriptions such as POSVI DEVM ADIVTOREM MEVM than to plain and useful statements of monetary value. It should be noted that there was a brief attempt in Elizabeth's reign to introduce machine milling of coins. This was in 1561 when a Frenchman named Eloye Mestrell tried to establish a pioneer horse mill in London. The workers arose and said they would have nothing of it, and the machinery was used a little and then had to languish a hundred years before it could be permanently employed.

ELIZABETHAN MINT MARKS

1558-1561	Lis
	Cross crosslet
1560-1561	Martlet
1561-1565	Pheon
1561-1566	Star (milled coins)
1565	Rose
1566	Portcullis
1566-1567	Lion
1567-1570	Coronet
1568-1570	Lis (milled coins)
1569-1571	Castle (milled coins 1571)
1570	Pierced mullet (milled coins)
1571-1573	Ermine
1573-1574	Acorn
1573-1577	Flower (eglantine)
1577-1579	Greek cross
1580-1581	Latin cross
1582	Sword
1582-1584	Bell
	A.

1584-1587	Escallop
1587-1589	Crescent
1590-1592	Hand
1592-1595	Tun
1594-1596	Woolpack
1595-1598	Key
1597-1600	Anchor
1600	O
1601	1
1602	2

A curiosity of the British coinage that might commend itself to the collector is the George II twopenny piece. Towards the end of the eighteenth century the quality of coins had become so inferior, and so much counterfeit money was in circulation, that Matthew Bolton, a manufacturer of Soho, submitted to the government a series of designs that, if used, should make it impossible for the forgers to operate profitably. The designs were accepted for a twopenny piece, that in perfection of die sinking, nicety of proportion, beauty of general appearance and uniformity of weight has few equals in the whole range of world coinage. Unfortunately it was too large and heavy for everyday use and it was manufactured for only one year, 1797, but that very circumstance has made it increasingly rare. There was a time when jewelers used the twopenny piece for mounting, but soon the coin will be valuable. It weighs exactly two ounces, and was often employed as a weight on their scales by shopkeepers, innkeepers and other traders. There is a fine head of the king in Roman style on the obverse with the surrounding words GEORGIUS III D.G. REX, and a nice seated Britannia on the reverse with the inscription BRITANNIA 1797.

Seventeenth-Century Tokens

Britain might well have been proud of its almost exclusively silver and gold coinage in the early days, but this caused considerable inconvenience to the community. A gold standard always stultifies trade. There was among the early British a great scarcity of small change under gold and silver. James I tried to improve matters by giving a patent for striking copper coins to Lord Harington, and Charles his successor spread the privilege to other patentees, but the system did not work because the manufacturers of the little, worthless coins refused to exchange them for silver when they were handed in. They were rogues. The public lost confidence in the issues, and the system was finally abolished by Act of Parliament in 1644.

Then came Cromwell and the Civil War and such a breakdown in means of exchange as had rarely been known before in Britain and has not, thankfully, been known since. The silver and gold coins disappeared into private hoards. The people for a while had literally no means of effective currency. But man is pathetically adaptable; and towns, tradesmen and even private persons began to revive an ancient but hitherto illegal custom, the striking of their own coins, or tokens. Perhaps there were as many as ten thousand of these spontaneous, naive but necessary issues, mainly round in shape but sometimes square, heart-shaped, diamond-shaped, octagonal. The most were in copper or brass, although lead was used. When the North Countryman talks of money as "brass" he is unconsciously remembering the tokens. They were thin and clumsily made, save when devised and struck by former workers at the royal mints. Mostly they had the value of halfpennies or farthings, but a few were made of penny value.

The people used these tokens for the simple wants of everyday life; and the tokens were honored in bulk and silver equivalent by their manufacturers, and also by a new race of "farthing-exchangers" that inevitably sprang up. These took a commission on the transaction. Shopkeepers would devise a wooden box of compartments into which they sorted the tokens from different sources and of different values. They would use some of these for change, and would exchange the bulk at the end of a trading period for good silver.

Throughout the so-called Commonwealth the private token was the principal means of small exchange, but when the emergency was over the strange phenomenon stopped almost as quickly as it had started. Charles II introduced his proper copper coinage in 1672, and the token rapidly disappeared into the national lumber room, not to re-enter until demanded eventually by the inquiring numismatist. They had become illegal with the issue of the 1672 royal coinage, but really disappeared only because their necessity had itself departed. Some private mints still operated in the eighteenth century, but a final law of 1823 killed the amateur coiner once and for all.

Tokens have no particular beauty and lack all intrinsic value. Their interest is wholly antiquarian and historical, but that can be a very real and informative interest indeed. Inscriptions on seventeenth-century tokens have enabled historians to identify forgotten local features, such as the old beacon on a long-demolished bridge at Bideford, or a type of Thames water taxi that had three oarsmen aft and a small passenger cabin forward. Examining these crude pieces is like using a time machine. One token has the inscription ALTHOUG BUT BRAS YET LET ME PASS 1669. That was the year of Rembrandt's death. Another, similarly heart-shaped, has the words THOMAS COTTON OF MIDDLEWICH HIS HALFPENNY. Another, suitably square-shaped, proclaims IN BEWDLEY SQUARE DEALING. Also square is the token of THOMAS DEDICOT GROCER HIS HALFPENNY; and the round token of ANTHONY SEARCH has in the middle the cursive words "plaine dealing is best." Another round one has a spreading tree in the middle, surrounded by the inscription IN FEVERSHAM IN KENT.

At a time when the usual victims of revolution were the poor it was common to find private charity in the form of inscriptions on tokens such as "Remember the Poore," and "The Poore's halfpenny," and "To be changed by the Overseers for the Poor." Then we find tokens issued by the Mayors of Gloucester and Lincoln, by the Churchwarden of Guildford, the Corporations of Southampton and Romsey, the Constables of Taunton, and even by the Sword Bearer of Hereford. They were issued both at the North Gate and the Buttis Gate of Colchester, and other times we see the names of husband and wives, tavern and shop signs, references to trades and professions, puns and pieties.

It is indeed rather pleasant as well as informative to have among the golden splendors of a coin cabinet such a simple token as WILL WAKELIN 1663 HIS HALFPENNY. It somehow helps to preserve a sense of historical proportion.

13

Childish Things

Dolls

Anything that has survived the hands of children and is still in reasonably good condition must be both well made and worth preserving. The perfect example is dolls, ephemeral and unimportant playthings that were yet so often little masterpieces of craftsmanship and the nimble finger that extensive collections of them have been made, and there are even museums for their study. The collector's motives might be antiquarian or curious, sentimental or historical; the outcome is nevertheless an assembly of certain charm and not inconsiderable value.

It stands to reason that the best-preserved dolls are those made of wood, and the oldest of all belong to this type, originally a small whittled stick that was the child of a totem pole, surviving till recent times in the form of the peg doll, which emerged in thousands from the nineteenth-century turner's lathe. They tended at first to be made in the shape of a cone, and finally they were all wasp-waisted like skittles. Paint was used to indicate facial features and hair. They were given jointed shoulders, arms, legs, and even fingers and toes. Ball-and-socket joints are modern. The aristocrats of the genre are finely hand-carved specimens from forested countries such as Germany.

The second type of doll usually found in collections is the wax, which originated in antiquity but has its European beginnings towards the end of the sixteenth century. These were made in three different ways, by modeling from a piece of solid wax, by melting the wax and pouring it into a shaped mold, and by smoothing the wax on to a solid base of wood or metal. The oldest wax dolls were made by the third method, and, in the nineteenth century, bases of papier-mâché and various kinds of "composition" were used.

The early dolls of this type had head and shoulders only of wax; the bodies, arms and legs were of wood or cloth stuffed with sawdust. As the years passed some daring innovator thought of making the hands of wax. Meanwhile much attention was paid to the matter of the hair; and the connoisseur will judge his doll by the type and condition of the hair primarily. Crude wax dolls have the hair modeled in the wax. The best have human hair inserted in small clusters, or along a center parting, while the very best have each individual hair stuck into the head. This was done with a hot needle. Substitutes were often used for human hair, such as wool and other animal excrescences, silk, and flax. Eyelashes and eyebrows have sometimes been inserted hair by hair, to shade glass eyes that would miraculously move.

China dolls are the third type and are mainly nineteenth century. They are understandably rare survivors of that era and can be valuable, especially those made by two French firms, Jumeau and Bru. Some of the best French specimens are among the finest dolls ever made. Other beautiful china dolls came from Germany. They were mostly imported in the nude to England and America and suitably clothed there. Often "English" china dolls were assembled from parts imported from several countries. The best clothes were made by the young owner's mother or grandmothers.

The dating of dolls depends upon many factors that can be briefly mentioned. Thus "baby" dolls were rarely made prior to the nineteenth century. Before that the dolls were nearly all adults. Styles of clothing and hair styles can help in dating, but it must be remembered that the clothes of an old doll would often be brought up to date. Then dolls that walk, talk or open and shut their eyes cannot be any older than 1820, and the moving eyes were controlled by string or wire till approximately 1870 when the weight principle was introduced.

Rag dolls were made of sheepskin until about 1850, when kid was used. And the first celluloid doll was introduced to an astonished world in about 1860.

There is a theory that modern dolls as such originated in the eighteenth century when they were brought from Paris to demonstrate the latest fashions; and in that sense they might have been the precursors of what we now know so curiously as models. The eighteenth-century French dolls were indeed called mannequins, or lay figures, and Britain herself had an export trade in mannequins to the America that was eventually almost to deify the doll.

Furniture and Toys

The dolls required their houses and furniture. Sometimes these were so elaborate and beautifully made that they were carefully preserved after their young owners had been allowed to play with them "nicely" a few times. During the eighteenth century some magnificent dolls' houses were made to accurate scale with every kind of contemporary household article within. They are worth a great deal today, not just in monetary value but also for the information they give about styles of furnishing. The nineteenth-century houses and equipment inevitably tend to become more machine-made and mass-production in character, but are still very fine and interesting.

Sometimes an eighteenth-century dolls' set of table china will be found that was made at Meissen or Chelsea; during the Victorian era these came from all the well-known manufacturers of pottery and porcelain, but mostly from the less important Staffordshire makers of such substances as ironstone china.

It is important to remember that dolls' furniture and china were not the only miniature household items of their kind. Very similar small pieces were made to act as travelers' samples, pieces that ranged from tiny chairs to single cups and saucers of Tom Thumb size. These can be distinguished from the children's toy pieces by their far superior quality.

Toys generally comprise a subject in itself. They seem to have been provided by a special industry only in the seventeenth century. The "modern" toy dates from that time; and children before then probably enjoyed themselves just as much with sticks and stones and self-devised playthings. A collector would once again find his greatest interest and value in the eighteenth century. He would still find charming Noah's arks, boats, bugles and drums, even mechanical dancing animals of that period, together with tops and cup-and-ball games—and the ever-popular rocking horse, that was an instructional as well as a pleasure toy in those days when equestrianism was as essential and as important as motoring is today.

Early rocking horses are now rare, but those of the late ninteenth and early twentieth centuries are still so abundant as to keep several specialist dealers in being. The author once found a Hampshire dealers' garden filled with rocking horses, but none of them in such resplendent condition as two he saw in the window of one of the most expensive boutiques in Brussel's boulevard de Waterloo.

The early toy trains and motor cars will one day be lengthily discussed in a book such as this. Today it is more important and still possible to write about collecting miniature furniture, that was made not for the dolls but for the children themselves. This goes back to the earliest known periods, and the collector will find that the cradle and the chair are throughout the most common items to be preserved. It might be easier and infinitely cheaper to find a pre-Tudor cradle, for example, than any other item of pre-Tudor furniture. These articles were preserved from generation to generation almost as heirlooms. And it might be poetic justice that the best survivors are the rough-hewn oak examples that were originally made by the village carpenter, with enormous built-in strength to resist the usage of many future generations, rather than the beautifully decorated and finely constructed cradles of the nobility. Children's beds as such have rarely survived. The cottagers would not have special beds for children, and the nobility has always tended to wear its beds out quickly and to regard them as utilitarian articles to be broken up after a time and replaced. The early children's beds that do survive tend to be cane-sided. The sides slide up and down like those of modern cots.

Chairs are different. It seems that throughout the ages indulgent parents have taken delight in having small chairs made for their children's use. Doubtless the idea has been that if the child has its own chair it will occasionally sit in it and be quiet. Also there is something rather quaint about a chair in miniature—and craftsmen undoubtedly liked to make them. Thus a collection could be made of small chairs of all the great periods. Some have very considerable value indeed, when evidently from the workshops of London cabinetmakers who followed the designs of Chippendale, Hepplewhite, Sheraton, and the brothers Adam.

"High" chairs and "pot" chairs generally are in a different category. They were not lovely copies in miniature of famous styles but strictly practical devices for holding children while they were being fed and when they evacuated. They were not preserved very carefully, and would not be collected along with miniature children's furniture as such.

Curiosities, and, alas, great rarities, include children's hairdressing chairs, on which the children sat back to front with the forehead resting on the rounded top rail, and the "baby cage" to teach walking (sometimes with a circle of wood that went around the infant body).

Ship Models

The child that is always in the mind of man has been responsible for a wide variety of model craftsmanship throughout the ages. This has sometimes risen to the heights of art, especially in the making of ship models, that have been a characteristic product of peoples for whom the sea has been a thoroughfare to fortune and relief from insular boredom. Such models have been found in ancient Egyptian tombs. Later, they were made for launching on Good Fridays to propitiate the sea gods and ensure favorable weather. Until recently fisher boys of the British Isles would send toy boats to sea for that traditional purpose.

The collecting of ship models as such might have begun with the great courtesan Madame du Barry at the Court of Louis XV. For some reason or other she liked to have such models on her ormolu cabinets and marquetry commodes and gilded consoles. Perhaps her first customer was a matelot. What Madame du Barry did soon became widely fashionable; and what was originally a pastime of sailors, making such models from rough materials with hand knife and nimble fingers in order to while away the time on long voyages became a speciality of the greatest working craftsmen.

During the Napoleonic period large numbers of unfortunate men languished for lengthy periods as prisoners of war, and it strangely became a custom among them to make model ships from bone and ivory, but particularly from bone that was probably a plentiful product of those wars. The prisoners were mainly French and languished during the years 1793–1815 in unsavory hulks amid the shipping of Portsmouth, Devonport, Chatham, and such ports, and in prisons notably at Portchester Castle, Norman Cross, Peterborough, Taunton, Tonbridge, and Perth.

Many of these were among the finest craftsmen of Europe, for Napoleon in his final desperation conscripted the most skilled men to fill the ever-depleting ranks of his so-called Grand Army. They were quickly taken prisoner because craftsmen are by nature unfit to be good soldiers and sailors and rarely fight to the death. They included hundreds of the best ivory carvers from Paris, Dieppe, and West Africa, as well as Breton jet carvers, and not a few great Parisian jewelers and watchmakers, together with similar skilled people from the occupied cities of Europe.

In the hulks and prisons they quickly organized themselves into groups and working parties. The aristocrats were known as "Les Lords," and the craftsmen were called "Les Laborieux," while the rascals were despised under the generic name "Les Raffales." The object of "Les Laborieux," under the direction of "Les Lords," was to obtain money for the purchase of amenities by the sale of handmade objects to jailers and the local population. For some reason or other they tended to concentrate on ship models, perhaps under the influence of nautical companions who already knew the tricks of this particular trade. They had all the time in the world, essential to the making of objects of beauty. A carver might devote six months to the fashioning of two inches of bone in an elaborate pattern. And they were even rewarded with what amounted to miniature fortunes for what they made, so that some of them after the wars could retire with comparative riches to France, or stay in England and set up in permanent business, the founders of jewelers' or manufacturers' dynasties with grandchildren in the peerage.

One prisoner of war at Forton Camp in Hampshire was Germain Lamy. He got to work with a fellow prisoner and constructed a 74-gun ship—measuring only six inches in length. This he sold for £40, a lot of money in those days; and when Lamy returned to France in 1814 he was reputed to have a fortune of some 17,000 francs.

The French were, between 1812 and 1816, joined in the English hulks and prisons by many American seamen captured in the American War of 1812. They had often had experience on whalers of what was known as "scrimshaw work," the carving of whalebone and whale teeth and walrus tusks. They entered with characteristic energy into the ship model game, specializing in frigates, the most common ships of their navy.

The prisoners displayed extraordinary ingenuity not only in the fashioning of their miniature ships but also in the preparation of materials. Bones kept from meals and probably bones smuggled into the hulks and prisons were wrapped in wet clay and thus softened. Tools were made from pieces of scrap metal, and were provided by hopeful dealers on the outside. Portchester Castle to this day has a small hole in the thick wall through which the tools were passed from outside, and through which the completed articles were passed from inside. Hinges and rivets and mast strappings were made from such personal trinkets of the sailors and soldiers as gold earrings and even gold teeth. Sails would be made from infinitely thin layers stripped off an old cow horn. They would be hammered between leather to the consistency of tissue paper. Anchors would be fashioned out of rusty nails; and copper nails, when extracted from barrels and from the very fabric of the prisons, would be used for making tiny guns. The men would pull at their beards, pigtails, and ever-balding heads to secure hair for the construction of delicate rigging. The bases for mounting the ships would be fashioned by the cabinetmakers among the prisoners from timber that originally formed the underparts of chairs, tables, and beds. These bases would sometimes have carved bone rails and stanchions. Those from the prison at Tonbridge can be notable for bases finished with the traditional "Tonbridge work," colored and inlaid straw (from mattresses).

The models would be made in exact proportions to their originals, but to a scale of about one in a hundred. Even the bolt eyes would be reproduced, sometimes so small as scarcely to be seen with the naked eye. It was as if the prisoners wanted to set themselves almost impossible tasks to stop madness from tapping them on the shoulder.

If a prisoner-of-war ship model is carefully examined it will be seen that it is constructed exactly like a real ship. The skeleton frame and keel and keelson are there, covered properly with the right number of curved planks to make the "skin," each plank of cunningly whittled bone that is riveted to the frame with real rivets of copper or gold. Cabin and deck furniture even to coils of rope and capstans and figureheads that are themselves separate works of art have been constructed with a skill that even Fabergé and his craftsmen would have envied. As for the rigging, that is quite incredible. In the best models it is more exact, more workable even, that the rigging of real ships. All minute parts are there, the blocks, deadeyes, lanyards, cleats, splices; and the guns run in and out on springs and in extreme cases could even be fired with powder that was concocted by the prisoners from elementary chemicals.

These models are objects of beauty and have great value today, but are primarily triumphs of the human spirit, that continue to give some hope to the philosopher who would otherwise see no future at all for the human race.

Of course their rarity has been increased in recent times by the destruction of war. During the blitz, one London collection of some fifty models was completely destroyed. The Trinity House collection was similarly lost, including the finest ship model ever made, that of the *Loyal London.*

Moreover, the models cannot be faked. They can be copied superficially, but the result lacks nine tenths of the ingenuity and beauty that came only from the special circumstances and the horror of those hulks and evil camps.

The prisoners also made chessmen, dominoes, miniature spinning wheels, tobacco boxes, and other articles of bone in their characteristic, meticulous manner; but only with the ships did they transcend the everyday and rise to the heights of inimitable art.

After which it is somewhat of a descent from the sublime to discuss ships in bottles, but the subject has interest and the articles are collectable by those who could not possibly afford the genuine bone models. They were chiefly made from about the middle of the nineteenth century until the end of the sailing ship as a commercial proposition, being again an occupation for seamen during long voyages. The actual insertion of the ship into the bottle was, curiously enough, the simplest part of the operation. The most difficult was the preparation of the background or scenery inside the bottle, which was done by inserting an adhesive with a long brush and then using another long brush to apply materials such as paint and putty and sand.

The hull of the model ship would be carved of wood or cork and painted, then supplied with spars and other rigging, the masts of which would be hinged so that the vessel could be inserted flat through the neck of the bottle with cottons attached to the rigging. Glue would have been brushed on the "sea" inside so that the ship would adhere to it, and when this was dry and the ship firmly attached the cottons would be pulled to elevate the masts, then burned off and the cork tightly inserted.

Infinitely finer than the ships in bottles were the Victorian glass ships that were mounted on tempestuous glass seas under glass containers or bells. The feature of these was the spun glass rigging, and there would perhaps be dark blue glass for the bulwarks, and possibly a lighthouse of cream glass.

For the very wealthy man who takes an interest in ship models there is always the silver "nef," or indeed the silver-gilt "nef," variously a large, elaborate model as such, particularly by one of the leading nineteenth-century silversmiths, or a silver receptacle in the form of a ship, sometimes on silver wheels, that was a development of the great salt cellar of early times. Such "nefs" are very lovely, but require a lot of cleaning in acidulous metropolitan atmospheres. Lacquering them is only putting off a much more evil day.

14

Fakes

General and Oak

Fakers have throughout the centuries been of two kinds, those who have done it primarily out of pique to compensate for their failure as artists or craftsmen, and those who have responded to the demands of an overheated market. The first type do not concern the collector so much as the second type. Forgers like the recent Dutchman van Meegeren, who painted what the art experts continually passed as genuine Vermeers, and the late nineteenth-century Russian gold-smith Rouchomowsky, whose elaborate gold tiara of the ancient Scythian kings was purchased by the Louvre after "authentication" by the greatest "experts," and the nineteenth-century Eng-lishman Thomas J. Wise, who set himself up as a bibliographer and then printed short works by famous nineteenth-century writers that were sold for large sums to specialist collectors (and continue to be sold for large sums to specialist collectors of fakes), were themselves great artists manqués whose object was to demonstrate their skill primarily; and they concerned themselves with the forgery of works that in any case would be beyond the reach of the average connoisseur.

The dangerous deceivers are small craftsmen, cabinetmakers, potters and picture restorers, also dealers and manufacturers, who realize that the market is desperately short of certain antique items. This occurs especially at times when people are frightened of paper investments and rush unthinkingly to buy any kind of solid works of art or old articles. The small craftsmen and busi-nessmen often start honestly enough by making reproductions of popular items. They copy old brass and copper, use original moulds to reproduce nineteenth-century pottery and porcelain, make smaller and lighter copies of heavy old furniture, issue facsimiles of pleasant, early engrav-ings. After a while unscrupulous dealers and collectors sell these reproductions as genuine. The currency begins to be debased; and eventually a craftsman or businessman here and there seeks to extricate himself from financial difficulties by using his newly discovered skills in the making of "old" articles as such. A new trade or occupation begins, especially, as said, at times of eco-nomic crisis, and particularly when the collecting public is undiscriminating and willing to buy anything so long as it gives itself a hedge against inflation, devaluation, and the rapacious tax col-lector.

It is an especially good trade because collecting has always been regarded as a "take it or leave it" hobby, and the laws against forgery, misrepresentation and conspiracy have rarely been enforced in this essentially anarchic, undercover situation. The investor who finds himself landed

176

with a forged share certificate has immediate remedies and takes them: the forger of such a document inevitably goes to prison. But the collector who discovers that his small Sheraton-type table is a fake, or who watches the nice piece of Liverpool creamware in his cabinet as it turns yellow, very rarely makes a fuss for fear of exposing himself as the self-deluded fool that he is. If he does make a fuss he may obtain redress from the perhaps innocent dealer who sold him the piece, and the dealer probably takes the matter no farther with his supplier for fear not only of offending him and others but also—and most important, this—of arousing that derision which is one of the outstanding emotions of his trade. Many dealers take more satisfaction from tripping up fellow dealers than from making money. It is a unique, very human business.

Certainly the police rarely go into antique shops except to check whether the dealers have acquired stolen articles, or whether early closing days are being observed. As the law has been unable to crush the saleroom system of the "ring," so it has evidently long since given up any thought of checking whether antiques offered are genuine. This applies even to important works of art. An American millionaire of our time, a man of great power, complains that his important collection of pictures has been demonstrated as largely consisting of forged canvases. The trail goes back, of course, to Paris, and suddenly there is a bewildering argument of "experts." Will that millionaire ever see his money again?

Undoubtedly he should, and so should anyone who spends large sums with a first-class dealer and finds subsequently that the articles bought are not genuine. But the smaller collector who follows his hunches in little shops and salerooms should not, perhaps, expect any redress if he goes wrong. Certainly it is most unlikely that he will get any. And the really obsessed collector is usually the first to cover up his own mistakes, which he rightly regards as an essential part of his education.

Then, as regards the actual terms "fakes" and "forgeries," they should be taken only to comprehend deliberate and near-criminal attempts to reproduce period pieces and pass them off as genuine of their period. They should not be used to cover "restorations."

If the invidious terms did cover "restorations" it would be an end of most "antiques." No article can survive the passage of time without some damage or wear and tear. Even hand polishing is a form of restoration. Loving care alone enables the mutable to survive; and the world may be defied to produce, say, a piece of period furniture that completely lacks a new piece of wood here, a touch of stain or a modern screw or nail there.

A clever craftsman may find in a lumber room the ruin of a Jacobean daybed. He replaces a broken rail with a newly turned one, provides a new cane back and seat. His finished product is still a Jacobean daybed if an imperfect one, not a fake or forgery. It enters that class only when it has been built up from scratch as a new piece in Jacobean style. It may not be an antique as defined at the beginning of this book, but it is not a fake, and is a deception only when sold as "mint" or "unrestored."

There are a few, necessarily very wealthy collectors who seek only the completely genuine, that is, pieces which appear to have undergone no kind of restoration whatsoever and belong absolutely to the moment in the time claimed for them. They form a minority. Their collections would not always please the general public, who might be disappointed at the sometimes drab and uninteresting appearance of the "completely genuine." It is, for example, always amusing to introduce ladies who "simply rave over old oak" to a few authentic, "unrestored" pieces of the Tudor period. They refuse to believe that such black old chests and gnarled, clumsy, pitted old short-legged stools have any value at all. They are certain some mistake has been made. The modern eye is too accustomed to machine-turning and electro-polishing and miniature proportions.

What the average collector wants to know is how to increase his knowledge so that he may not be duped by those who would fabricate an old article from new or "breakdown" material and sell it to him as a genuine product of a certain period. The term "breakdown" introduces what has been discussed before, the "cannibalism" that is practiced by fakers. They purchase, say a number of old oak pews from a derelict church, and fabricte their "genuine Tudor" articles from the brokendown timber.

Consider, however, that this is not necessarily the most heinous of sins, provided that the craftsmen are good ones, and that they do not insist too loudly that their articles are absolutely genuine of the period, and that they sell either to other dealers or to customers who would not appreciate a completely genuine piece anyway. The expert dealer or collector would never be deceived; and the ordinary but careful collector need not be, if he obeys certain rules.

The first rule is to learn about the subject from books and from frequent visits to museums where genuine period articles can be seen, and to shops and antiques fairs where period articles can be seen. Acquaintance with the real soon breeds an instinctive awareness of the spurious. Further rules may perhaps be gleaned from the remarks that follow.

Remember always that furniture was crude and sparse in Tudor and Tudor-Elizabethan times, the luxury of perhaps a hundred thousand gentry, if that; and also that the wider range of Jacobean furniture suffered a sad reverse during the Cromwellian period, when great quantities of it must have been destroyed by the Puritan iconoclasts (as in our time Chinese antiquities have been deliberately destroyed by the vicious young Red Guards of philosopher Mao).

Genuine old oak is either blackened and pitted with usage, or polished to a quite unique patina, once seen never forgotten, a patina that cannot be reproduced on rubbed-down oak by modern polishing substances and methods. Fakers attempt to forge the blackness by use of a very dark stain. Scrape this with a penknife on some unimportant part and the rubbed-down wood will be revealed underneath. As regards the patina, this is like that produced on the seat of a wooden chair by generations of sitting. It has no glassy or sticky surface. It is in and of the wood and cannot be faked.

There are two ways of determining whether the old oak article was really made during the period claimed, and not put together at a later date from genuine period wood by the process of marriage after cannibalism. The first way is to examine the joinings. These joints should be tenon and mortise, fastened together by squared and crumbling or hopelessly jammed wooden pegs. The second way is by matching the moldings, those strips of wood applied as surrounds to sides or panels, and by similarly matching such items as pedestals and ornaments. In the piece that has been fabricated from old materials (put together cunningly to make a new piece) it will almost always be observed that some mouldings or ornaments do not match in design or age or color with others. Similarly, there will be something wrong with the proportions of the piece. It will look strange, like the face of a dark woman who has dyed her hair blond. The faker cannot achieve natural symmetry in his forged piece, because his design has been dictated by his material.

Finally, price. A genuine Tudor or even Jacobean item of furniture should be available only from a very important dealer at an extremely high price. Do not consider that you have a find if you discover in some dingy antique shop a fine wainscot chair that is priced within the limits of the normal purse. If that chair were genuine it would be out of the class of the small antique dealer and he would long since have passed it on, at a high profit, to one of the great specialists or their representatives who call on him almost daily. A small antique dealer knows that he cannot sell really important articles save to the trade and he very seldom attempts to go out of his class, except when he is trying to put over a fast one.

If, however, the collector is offered what is described as a genuine Elizabethan wainscot chair by a first-class dealer for a very considerable price then he can be reasonably certain that it is either genuine or will always pass as genuine in the trade. And he can be sure that if the chair is subsequently proved to be a forgery then the great dealer will, for the sake of his reputation and livelihood, give the money back. Britain, America, and some European countries are filled with spurious oak at quite cheap prices (as it ought to be). Genuine oak must be paid for, heavily.

French and Eighteenth Century

The same applies, only even more so, to fine French furniture and works of art of the great periods, which are either extremely expensive and found only in important shops, or comparatively cheap and faked. At the same time it must be said that nineteenth century and even modern reproductions of furniture from "les belles époques" are often finer in appearance and craftsmanship than their originals, and should constitute a first-class investment as well as a lasting joy to behold in the home. On the whole French and European antiques, after being faked in vast numbers throughout the nineteenth century and during the first quarter of this century, are being reproduced less frequently now than English antiques. Experts in that trade will explain broken-heartedly that craftsmen can no longer be found to labor long hours in dingy workshops at the fabrication of works of art for less pay than they would get as factory hands or minor functionaries. Dealers from the Continent continually cross to England with their commissions for such work, because much "restoration" and/or faking is done in England by amateurs of the former middle classes who have been brought down to this kind of occupation by the social revolution there. They are willing and even like to work with their hands, and it may be their salvation.

Indeed, it is true that much of the best French reproduction furniture has always come from outside France, not only from England but also from Holland, Italy, and, in recent times, Spain. In the middle of last century the firm of Town and Emanuel, Bond Street, London, made an industry of producing tables and cabinets in the style of Louis XV and Louis XVI. There was a great demand for such pieces at the time, and good London firms of cabinetmakers executed them not as deliberate fakes but to the orders of customers. They may possess a masculine quality that misses the extreme elegance of the true French masterpiece, but their value is by no means negligible, and they are beautiful articles of furniture as such, much more beautiful and sensible than anything in so-called "contemporary" style. Similarly, the French reproductions that have become a recent industry in Spain will probably have considerable, lasting value.

It is important to examine the mounts of period French furniture. To be genuine of the period these should bear scraping to the basic bronze or brass or ormolu. There has been in modern times a great Parisian industry in the faking of these mounts, whereby "galvanos" or electrogilded ornaments have been produced in vast numbers. An even cheaper method is simple gold lacquering. Both methods can be unmasked by the point of a penknife.

In examining French furniture one should look particularly for "mutton dressed up as lamb." It has been a profitable custom to take an old chair or cabinet, plain and homely or "provençal," and to enrich it with ebony veneering and ormolu mounts. Look for any discrepancies between type of framework and outside decorations. Respond to the innate instinct of the connoisseur, that says at once: "There is something wrong with that piece."

Marquetry has not suffered so much from the faker as plain furniture for the obvious reason that it is so much more expensive and difficult to forge. Indeed, a well-faked article of marquetry is in itself a thing of permanent value, being the product only of consummate craftsmanship. Moreover the style has never been very popular in the lucrative markets of America and England. It is only in living memory than prices have soared for the finest marquetry articles, such as grandfather clock cases and cabinets of the period of William and Mary. It has just been said that faked marquetry is in itself beautiful and valuable, but this does not apply to the Dutch variety. For some reason or other the Dutch fakers of their coarser style of marquetry have invariably been unable to conceal the too bright colors of the woods inserted, and the product tends to have a staring, orange appearance that is most undesirable.

The collector should be especially careful of small pieces, that may appeal to him as suitable for the diminutive modern home. Most early marquetry furniture was made for large salons in the days of spaciousness, and in itself is bulky. Also the collector should look dubiously at lightweight construction, lack of weight in the veneer, and walnut that does not possess the ultrafine figuring and lovely, silken tone of the early periods. Restored genuine movements of old clocks are often inserted in faked marquetry cases, or in cases made from brokendown genuine pieces. The marriage, fortunately, is seldom a happy one, and the way the movement is attached to the case is invariably modern in method and screws.

Then there has been such a vogue in recent times for English eighteenth-century furniture, particularly work in the schools of the great drawing masters Chippendale, Hepplewhite, Sheraton, and the brothers Adam, that it stands to reason the forgers have been very busy here. They have been aided by the frequent simplicity of the styles. It is easier and cheaper to reproduce a very plain Chippendale-style or Hepplewhite-style country chair, or a clean satinwood cabinet, than, say, an ornate Empire chair of the French ebonized wood and ormolu school. Faking is always more prolific among the clean-cut pieces and increasingly difficult with the schools that relied for their effects not on purity of line but on superfluity of decoration. That superfluity of decoration just takes too long to fabricate these short-hour days.

But once again the fake in eighteenth-century English furniture can be quickly detected by the collector who, in the process of time or by natural taste, has developed an instinct for observing awkwardnesses and discrepancies. Only the very skilled expert can state definitely that a piece was made in the workshops of the Chippendales, but furniture that is truly of the period has certain features that the modern forger cannot reproduce. One of these is solidity. That was the time of opulence and easy availability of fine mahogany. The modern reproduction of the eighteenth-century piece invariably tends to be skimpy and trashy by comparison with the genuine article. To make one of the arms of their chairs, for example, craftsmen in the Chippendale school must have used a block of West Indian mahogany at least five inches in thickness, to obtain the wide curve. Such thickness of timber would be too expensive for the faker today, and in any case he would probably be working in an inferior, redder mahogany.

Then the carved work of the eighteenth-century schools has a sharpness of edge, a surety of touch that stands out immediately, the modern reproduction being soft and uncertain by comparison. And painted furniture of that period should always reveal the old, faded, and flaked paint under the new paint of subsequent restoration. It is almost axiomatic that eighteenth-century painted furniture which is covered with new white and blue and gold paint is faked, for the simple reason that no dealer of any consequence would have a genuine painted piece restored to that extent. Anyway, remove a little of the new paint and look underneath. Invariably brand-new beechwood will be revealed, without a trace of the old paint that should be there. Or, if there is old paint, be sure about its age. That of the eighteenth century should be very discolored and flaky. Several highly respected firms of London cabinetmakers in the nineteenth century met a contemporary demand for painted wood furniture by reproducing it in large quantities and most skilfully. They also reproduced much satinwood furniture, and the product is infinitely newer in appearance than the genuine eighteenth-century piece. Satinwood, like unstained wood, gradually changes color with age, becoming ever dirtier and deeper in tone.

There is a method of faking in connection with eighteenth-century furniture that has frequently been discussed in this book: the method that involves marriage or cannibalism. A single dilapidated article of the period may be taken to pieces and parts of it carefully copied in old mahogany from another period source. The whole is then reassembled to make two pieces, each of which is sold as genuine of the period. Once again the trick can be detected by careful examination of details that cannot be hidden, such as methods of joinery, fittings, staining and overpolishing. When the various parts are put together it is nearly always necessary for the faker to apply some super-dressing to equalize color, and this can be discovered by careful scraping with the infallible penknife—or by just looking at the piece in bright sunlight and suddenly noticing the inevitable tonal difference between the unnaturally wedded parts.

The small collector is, however, advised to remember that the total number of genuine pieces of the Chippendale, Hepplewhite, Sheraton, and Adam schools in existence in increasingly reduced by the years, and that the good reproduction or fake is often in itself a beautiful and valuable article. Moreover, if he was himself deceived into believing that his acquisition was genuine then subsequent purchasers of the article might be equally satisfied, especially as the years will pass and genuineness is largely a matter of age. The acid test is beauty.

It may be added in regard to eighteenth-century furniture with decorations in the form of paintings of the Angelica Kauffmann type that the important features to determine authenticity are the style and patina of the paintings. Very often badly worn paintings are rubbed off and newly painted. The result is naturally much brighter than the original could be. Also the fine patina of the original is destroyed and replaced by the equivalent of French polish. Old paintings on furniture are as if coated with gelatine, displaying the mellow surface of a Stradivarius violin. The restored article "stares" in well-merited reproach. And if the painting is wholly new it is invariably so badly painted as to require only a cursory glance of disgust. Angelica Kauffmann (who, by the way, was a Swiss from Chur who came to London in 1766 and worked for the brothers Adam, and left England in 1782) was a very fine artist who was elected to the Royal Academy soon after her arrival in London. So were most of the others who painted scenes on English furniture in the eighteenth century. Their modern copiers are hopeless daubers by comparison.

Miscellaneous

A few sentences may be offered about the detection of fakers in other types of antiques. Lacquered furniture has been generously faked in modern times, and is rarely genuine when offered in the fine, "mint" condition of the work to be seen in some sumptuous furniture shops, particularly those of European countries. First-class dealers do not sell such reproductions, that can be made sometimes from genuine old bureaus, cabinets, chairs, and screens coated over with lac and painted with patterns by clever forgers. Carefully note whether the interior color of the cabinet matches with the outside; it should and rarely does. Strip away a minute portion of the lac, if possible, and see whether the wood beneath is mahogany. It should not be. Remember that blue lac is the most rare and valuable. Examine hinges and escutcheons to make sure that they are genuine of the William and Mary or Queen Anne periods. Above all, just consider whether the lacquered surface looks old or new. The fake nearly always tells its own story if it is regarded with a steady eye.

The subject of metalwork has been dealt with in the relevant chapter of this book, but some recapitulations may be useful here. Patina is again the important feature to look for, particularly in bronze and copper. Either it is there or it is not. Get used to it by studying genuine articles in museums; thereafter the collector will never be deceived by brummagem reproductions. Examine underparts carefully. The modern, usually machine-made article is neither rough and crude nor indelibly tarnished by age underneath. Old rivets or their lack provide useful evidence. Massive appearance and clumsiness of construction again characterize the genuine old work.

Should an article involve a great deal of money it can be subjected to scientific modern tests that will be arranged by museums or important firms of dealers. Alas, such tests are too expensive for all but the finest pieces. It should be remembered, however, that a strong magnifying glass can enlarge a surface by some thirty times, and that it is possible to acquire hand microscopes that enlarge by as much as a thousand times.

15

Buying and Selling

Acquisition

The best way of acquiring antiques is through a great-great-grandfather, or an even more remote ancestor. Then they would have been bought brand-new and absolutely right of their period. Unfortunately few people today can look back to such worthy progenitors, or intervening generations have lost the antiques through philistinism, greed, or to pay the tax collector. Consequently the would-be possessor of beautiful old articles must buy them for hard cash in shop, saleroom, or privately from other owners.

If the purchaser is unsure of his knowledge or flair then he should buy only from very important antique dealers, preferably those whose businesses have been long established in the centers of the greatest cities. Many dealers may be described as the last freebooters of the modern world, acknowledging no code save that of the jungle. They can appear like an exotic plant overnight in a fine shop of a noble thoroughfare, or in a centuries-old building of some ancient town, and may impress with their manners and charm with their tongues. Anyone can thus set himself up almost anywhere. So it is essential for the greenhorn to buy only from firms that have been noted for excellence of their antiques and probity of their methods for a long time. Membership of trade associations, although it does not guarantee the aforementioned qualities, is a reassuring factor always.

The above remarks apply if the collector lacks knowledge and confidence but desires to invest his money wisely and not lose it under any circumstances: and money in this context means a considerable sum. They do not apply if the buyer of antiques has considerable knowledge and skill, or if he is interested only in buying junk with the thin residue of his pocket money. With knowledge and skill it is possible to defeat the most swashbuckling dealers at their own mean game. This is especially so when a collector of, say, Italian majolica, goes buying in shops that principally deal in furniture, or a collector of, say, English furniture, goes buying in shops that principally deal in old china. A friend of the author's found a pile of old copies of *The Illustrated London News* in a general antique shop. He bought them for the price of a movie ticket, and when he got home he found that some previous owner had kept a valuable seventeenth-century map between the pages of one of the magazines. That map is now worth a considerable sum. If the magazines had been offered by an antiquarian bookseller they would never have contained the map.

Another friend of the author's visited a gaudy antique shop run by a wispy spinster in an old house on the edge of sand dunes on the remote coast of Scotland and he bought there, for a modest sum, a piece of faience that the woman described as Norwegian pottery. When the buyer arrived home and consulted his books he found that his flair was confirmed. The piece was faience of Strasbourg, about 1770, and had the authentic Hannong mark in blue under the glaze. Its value was considerable then and today it could be worth the price of a lengthy holiday.

A silver expert was prowling about in Switzerland and paused to gaze in the elaborate window of a so-called antique shop, wherein most of the antiques were recent reproductions of French furniture and hideous vases from Japan. He saw two tarnished spoons and bought them very cheap. His eye had detected the early eighteenth-century marks on them. They turned out in fact to have been the work of a London silversmith of the Queen Anne period, worth at least ten times what had been paid.

The author himself once visited a suburban house in a town of the north of England where an old picture dealer was in retirement. Dingy rooms were high-stacked with frames and canvases, among them a small panel on which, under layers of thick varnish and dirt, could be faintly detected a painting of a Dutch town scene. The old church tower could be recognized as that of Delft. The dealer said the picture had no importance and could be bought for a few pounds. It was bought and cleaned in London for a few more pounds. The cleaning revealed an excellent little example of the work of J. J. Spöhler, complete with signature, and the picture is now worth many times the original expenditure on it.

This is an amusing game, not a matter of collecting old articles carefully, or of investing money shrewdly. If it has its ups then it has its corresponding downs. The author visited a provincial antiques fair and saw an attractive Sunderland resist jug on the stand of a dealer whose specialty was old silver. The dealer was a quiet, elderly man with a pleasant family and considerable business interests in the town. He said he knew nothing about the pottery but had often seen the jug in the window of a cottage and had at length gone in and persuaded the cottager to sell it to him. He said that he had just liked it and had bought it on instinct, although it was not his line.

The patter was so good and convincing that the author bought the jug. It looked very good on a window ledge in his house, but unfortunately the light was too strong from that window. Within a few months the jug had changed color from pink and cream to pink and yellow, as if it had been roasted. Beside other jugs in a Sunderland collection it was an obvious fake. As much money was lost on that as had been gained on other, wiser acquisitions.

It is indeed worth emphasizing that antiques cannot be bought successfully according to formula, but the beginner can at least work out for himself what should be the average prices of certain common articles of average quality. Dealers who want to remain in business do definitely adhere to such a level of prices. It will be found that an oak corner cupboard of average size and quality will be offered at pretty much the same price by all but fools in antique shops ranging from San Diego to St. Louis and from Boston to Tucson. The same applies to the prices of average quality copper articles, and davenport desks, and early maps, and chandeliers and Battersea or Bilston boxes.

But for rare and important pieces the price range can be as wide as their terms of rarity and importance. Some items labeled "Meissen eighteenth century" have just been seen in an

This antique shop in a small Danish town has been patronized by royalty and by collectors from many parts of the world.

antique shop, and the dealer is asking very high prices for them, which would be justified if they were indeed eighteenth-century Meissen even though they are very dingy and unpleasing pieces of porcelain. Unfortunately they are neither Meissen nor eighteenth century. On the other hand a small white sauceboat with a badly molded sea horse on the handle is offered very cheaply among a tray of assorted old china, and if it is the Cookworthy Plymouth that it could be then the buyer will make a couple of hundred dollars or more for a small expenditure.

To buy in salerooms is definitely dangerous for the beginner unless he is strong-minded enough to rest on low bids. He should get into the habit right away of regarding his sale bidding as a cold-blooded progression towards a low ceiling price and no further. Too many collectors, even old and experienced hands, allow themselves to be carried away by a kind of gambling, competitive emotion that only plays into the hands of others and lands them in inevitable financial difficulties. Possibly it is true at certain times like the present that a collector cannot bid too highly for a rare piece which everyone else is after, but a wise man will watch his step very carefully even in such a case. The beginner will most definitely be sensible to stop bidding if several prominent dealers are working beside him. He is small fry and must be content with small prizes from unimportant sales until such time as his skill, knowledge and capital are sufficient. Meanwhile he must watch and learn.

It will be found by investigation that certain firms of auctioneers locally or in a nearby town have a better class of trade than others. Possibly all local auctions will be worth a cursory visit of inspection, but the best to attend seriously will soon be found. Then the collector will be advised to study all local newspapers and those of adjacent districts within striking distance so as to be apprised in good times of casual sales at private residences. He will take care to secure catalogues early and to attend when the goods are on view. This will be his serious hour, the time for deciding whether or not to bid at the sale and how far to bid. The catalogue should be marked with ceiling price in simple code.

It is extremely important to acquire the art of reading between the lines of auctioneers' descriptions. Even the expert catalogue writers of the great metropolitan auctioneers tend to describe their geese as swans. Country auctioneers use names such as Canaletto and Sheraton and Sèvres with the noxious lavishness of condiments used by inferior chefs. On the other hand, they have an often sublime capacity for overlooking the truly important. Apostle spoons have been found among lots described as "kitchen cutlery," and piles of old books still repay the attention of the expert.

Possibly the best way for the expert to buy today is privately. He studies small advertisements in local paper, or inserts small advertisements himself, and sometimes he finds treasures still in private hands that the owners are understandably nervous of offering at sales or to the trade. One of the difficulties here is that such private sellers can have a hopelessly inflated idea of the value of what they offer, or are even dealers in disguise themselves. Many unfortunate descendants of noble or wealthy families in England and on the continent of Europe have, for example, developed a shrewd technique of privately advertising articles for sale from their collections, articles they have themselves recently bought for that purpose, which, in the atmosphere of their fine old houses command prices that could not be obtained in humble shops.

A legal point worth remembering as a buyer is that people often offer valuables and antiques for sale when they possess no title to the property in question—when they have stolen the goods, or are part owners only (as in the case of some heirlooms). If there is any doubt in the buyer's mind as to the vendor's status he should require him to sign a receipt that contains the words, "I hereby warrant the above articles to be my own personal property, over which I have full and unconditional right of disposal."

The friend of an aristocratic family once wanted to give the earl and his wife an anniversary gift of silver, and by a remarkable chance found in a silversmith's an eighteenth-century piece actually engraved with the arms of that family. The silver was bought and proudly presented, but the earl's face darkened. "Good heavens!" he exclaimed. "That is mine and should be in my safe." The countess hurriedly left the room; and it was found that for some time she had been secretly selling off the family silver in order to keep a boy friend happy. (A side moral here is, of course, that you can never count your silver spoons too often.)

Antiques buying is best conducted on a cash basis, not only because the collector who buys on credit is liable to overspend what he can afford, but also because antique dealers themselves have to pay each other and the auctioneer on the nail. A useful discount will nearly always be given for cash, and should be demanded. There are many antique dealers who mark their goods with prices that contain the element of discount, so if the buyer pays the marked price he pays too much. So many foreign buyers like to haggle that the dealers have had to develop their own method of self-protection.

The author once asked a leading Scottish dealer for the kind of advice that he would give to a collector, and wrote down the following reply:

Experience in buying must come the hard way. Book knowledge is useful and visits to museums are to be advised, but it is only by buying one's mistakes that one can ever appreciate values, and be successful in the long run. It is therefore to be recommended that one starts very modestly, so that the mistakes which one must make may not be too costly.

Furthermore, it is unfortunate that the examples which one sees in museums, or which are referred to in the normal reference books, are generally speaking items that are not found by the small collector or dealer. In other words, he is much more likely to find Sheraton-type tea caddies and nineteenth-century Pembroke tables than fine Chippendale-style commodes or Queen Anne kneehole desks. I can clearly remember the story of one man who started in the antique business with a small fortune but no knowledge. By buying his mistakes in the course of ten years he was left without his fortune, but had accumulated some useful knowledge. Eventually the position was reversed, and his knowledge helped him to regain what he had lost.

I think that another point that should be brought up is the advisability of avoiding *bargains*. So often one is tempted by the price at which one can buy an item, and not by its quality. These so-called bargains invariably become eyesores in the collector's cabinet, or what are described as "shopwatchers" in the antique shop, whereas a good item which one likes and pays a fair price for will always be a proud possession that can easily be re-sold at a profit.

Disposal

The most difficult of all problems for private collectors is how to sell their collections profitably. There is no problem with Post-Impressionist pictures (at the moment), or with genuine Louis furniture, or with Tompion clocks or Paul Storr silver. But most people do not possess such items, only quantities of average quality old furniture, china, silver, and pictures that they or their fathers have bought quite expensively at antique shops or in salerooms.

The dealers are a close fraternity and like to make big profits, so will not offer the collector anything like the true resale value for the items that he wants to sell.

The auction sales are plagued by the "ring" or "knockout," a device inevitably developed by the dealers to ensure that the vendors and the auctioneers lose much of the true value of articles sold. The dealers crowd the front of the saleroom and leave the bidding to an appointed member of their fraternity. Sometimes it is quite impossible for members of the general public to participate, and strongarm methods have frequently been used to keep the private buyer at bay. Since the bulk of the dealers do not bid their appointed representative acquires pieces at low prices.

Afterwards the dealers hold subsidiary auctions among themselves in a hotel or similar venue under a respected chairman. The monetary difference between the prices at these "knock-outs" and at the original auction is divided among the dealers present, with a cut for the chairman. There are dealers who make their livelihood this way, traveling around to sales and earning their share of the proceeds at subsequent auctions.

The remedy for the private seller is to put an adequate reserve on what he offers, although that will often result only in the piece being left on his hands with auctioneer's commission to pay, as the "ring" will have crowded out the auction and no one else will have had a chance to bid. Certainly the "ring" will very rarely pay a good reserve price.

How, then, is the collector to sell his antiques profitably?

There are three more or less adequate but by no means perfect methods, of which the first involves calling in several good dealers and asking them what they would give for the articles to be sold. Maybe one or even two of them may offer better prices than the trade average. It may well be found, however, that all will play the same game. They may just say that the articles to be sold are for various reasons worth less than the average price. If this is said then the seller must steel himself to resist the psychological effect of the denigration. On the whole, if he keeps with the dealers he will find one who is willing to pay good prices, always provided that the articles are indeed genuine and of fine quality.

The second method of satisfactory selling is to consult an important firm like Parke-Bernet in New York, and then to offer the articles at auction under adequate reserves. This method is excellent for items of value and importance but not so good for the second-rate as there are expenses involved and, even with the important items, an element of gambling. Should the sale be attended by a buyer with plenty of money and desire to buy then prices may soar. Should that man be absent and the sale be otherwise depressed by some circumstance such as a snowstorm, then prices may never get off the ground.

The third method of selling is to become, if only temporarily, an antique dealer, that is, to advertise the goods for sale in trade magazines and local papers, even in the case of large collection of antiques to open a "shop" in a private house or a real shop, call it "The Thieves' Kitchen" or some such suitable name, and recoup oneself for rent and advertising expenses by charging and trying to obtain high prices. This has been done very often, quite successfully at first, but rarely with great success in the long run for the simple reason that the amateur antique dealer nearly always tries to overreach himself. After selling his own antiques at good prices he considers that he may as well continue and make a fortune. He starts to buy fresh antiques for sale from his professional colleagues, and, lacking knowledge and experience of the trade, tends to fall for their suggestions. In buying the new stock he loses all the profit he made on the sale of his own antiques.

In theory, however, if the owner of a fine collection were to sell it off at high prices in temporary premises after advertising in trade publications, he would be certain of getting his true profit: provided that he put the shutters up immediately the last piece was sold and contented himself with that profit. It is the old story of the gambling table. Amateurs make money from the casino, the stock exchange, or antiques only when they take their profits and leave the table before the law of averages can deprive them of those profits and more. It is quite different with the professional, who has bought a long, hard training, makes a real business of it, and, like the banker, makes money by handling the money of his clients.

How should an antique be prepared for sale? Should it be repaired and polished or not?

This question of whether or not to "touch," that is, partly to restore and clean and polish, has been fervently debated in the trade of recent years, but results in shops do tend to show that the "brighter and better" school of antiques is winning the day. Some old dealers maintain, as all once held, that collectors prefer their antiques "untouched." If the library table has ink stains on the mahogany do not remove them on any account. Leave the dirt in the crevices of the porcelain figures. Let the pewter attain its dull patina and the silver remain tarnished. Allow the missing section of marquetry to remain missing. And go easy with the duster, even, lest a precious flake of gilt may be flicked from the frieze of the fauteuil.

This at the time might have been demonstrated as foolish, in that antiques are preserved by loving care and not by lazy neglect. The best pieces of the past are those kept long in some noble house and daily polished by prim hands. How shocking, on the contrary, to encounter a historic relic in the mud, or an Hepplewhite chair all broken in the basement!

A sense of proportion is required. To remove the green patina from a primeval urn is insanity. To French-polish an antique by modern cheapjack methods is criminal, as it is to regild an early Chippendale-type lookingglass frame, touch up a piece of pottery with new color, or rebind an old book in fresh leather. But to maintain a piece of furniture in the same condition as it came from the eighteenth-century workshop, or to polish brass and copper as it was originally polished by the maker, or to maintain silver as brightly as it was made is commonsense. The beauty is sustained and the value augumented, as will be found when the time comes to resell. The author remembers seeing a collection of Staffordshire figures as bought by a dealer. They were very dirty. Later he saw the same collection in the dealer's window. They had been washed carefully, and looked so beautiful that they might have been porcelain. All of them were sold within a few days.

An important factor in selling is the place of selling in relation to the type of article. The antiques trade knows that old oak sells well in rural counties but does not always please the sophisticated in the cities. The place for French furniture is New Orleans, and of course France and other continental countries and the best districts of New York and London. It will appeal no more in Norway than it will in Nebraska.

What the general public respond most quickly to are small pieces of elegant furniture, colorful pottery as against the great porcelains, drinking glasses, lookingglasses, prints, Oriental rugs, nineteenth-century jewelry, and always small articles of local interest. The furnishing aspect is increasingly prominent as the wealthy class that provided the great collectors is slowly strangled by taxation. The real collectors of today tend increasingly to be little men, interested in spoons, inexpensive old glass, coins, pottery, or china of the more accessible varieties such as Spode, and treen, pewter, pot lids, maps.

A word or two may be added about insurance. All antiques should be adequately insured, and the best method is to consult a broker and take out a policy against fire, burglary, larceny, and some other risks. An inventory should be made of all articles, and their replacement value should be "declared" with supporting invoices or, preferably, up-to-date valuations from experts. Then in the case of disaster there will be reimbursement without quibble. The ordinary householders' comprehensive policy is not wholly suitable for antiques. Insurance against breakages are usually too expensive (except breakages that are automatically covered in the case of fire or burglary). The collector of fragile items such as glass or china should remember that it would often cost more than the pieces are worth to insure them against breakage, which is a reason for always keeping fragile old articles in cabinets beyond the reach of overmuscular dogs and adventurous children or friends.

Why is it that ignorant people must always *handle* antiques, especially in other people's houses? We do not discipline our children very strongly these days, but the world would be a safer place if the young could be taught severely "not to touch." There is a type of human being who must pick up a porcelain figure or a piece of newly polished silver, and a kind of Parkinson's law applies whereby the hand comes off the porcelain figure and some acid on the visitor's thumb almost indelibly marks the silver.

Note also that, according to the law of contracts, a contract for sale of goods 25 dollars or over, or ten pounds or over must be signed in writing by the buyer unless the buyer makes part payment or immediately accepts part of the goods. These goods must be what they are represented to be, otherwise an action for breach of warranty lies against the vendor.

Antique Dealers

This book cannot end on a better note than may be provided by a brief study of the antique dealer as such, a study that is more fascinating to some collectors than the actual collection of antiques itself. It may be doubted if any trade or profession today contains such a variety of individuality as antique dealing, wherein the twin factors of artistic temperament and freedom from rules and agreed conventions promote singularity of character and some most extraordinary juxtapositions, as of a saintly but devious man partnered with his brother, a roughneck, a roisterer and a straight man.

There are aristocrats in junk shops and gangsters in chi-chi metropolitan salons: but it must be agreed that foremostly the average antique dealer is an interesting person to know. Somehow or other the association with fine craftsmanship, objects of beauty, and also with discriminating customers, tends to soften the coarseness of mind and accentuate unusual points of character.

The author in his own experience can, for example, think of tea taken out of long mugs in the dark recesses of an old shop with an elderly woman maybe of Romany descent, surrounded by odd types from the village always, and of learning quite a lot about Derby porcelain in the process. This old woman was a remarkable expert on that subject, but, alas, she was suffering fatally from what she described as "the sugar, love."

Then the author remembers an ex-officer of the Brigade of Guards selling antiques shrewdly under the shadow of a famous abbey while the long-distance trucks eternally thundered by; of an old dealer who could not write his own name but who had trade interests extending across

Europe; of a former admiral who had become a leading authority on pictures, and a former general whose keen commercial sense had made him a byword for bargains in furnishing antiques.

One of the most romantic if not necessarily the most up-to-date antique shops was to be found in the Lanes of Brighton, England, those unique narrow ways where a veritable market abides. This was presided over by a character from books—he had, indeed, appeared in books and films—who showed visitors around with soft but firm intent, cold and implacable if crossed or taken less than seriously, warm and brilliant if in contact with a kindred spirit. The tall, many-paned windows of this shop revealed an amazing variety of stock, ranging from suits of armor to chamberpots. Upstairs there were galleries so piled with glassy and potted treasure that in memory the scene is a kaleidoscope of colored promise.

Or the memory may leap across space and time to a business in London that consists of no more than an untidy room wherein two or three black-hatted gentlemen seem continually to be wrapping and unwrapping articles of tarnished silver till the whole space is a sea of wood shavings and old newspapers.

A lovely manor house in the country may mask a considerable antiques business conducted by excellent folk of the "huntin' shootin'" type, who reveal that their manners may be outmoded and their background effete but the old steely spirit that originally built the estate is still there.

Some of the most interesting antique dealers to talk to are those whose fathers and even grandfathers have been in the trade before them. There are one of two of these shops and families that go back to the beginning of the last century. Such dealers have a quiet assurance of manner that is very different from the sham self-assurance of others, and the knowledge they impart is sound.

There are companies that run antique businesses with many subsidiary shops and a multiplicity of agents and "runners" across the country; there are businesses run in side streets by the impoverished but plucky widows of dead dealers; there are chromium-plated shops, and others unaltered even to the cobwebs since the days of Beau Nash. A famous snob business in the West End of London, that boasts of its concern only with "antiquities" of the most important type, has a moneymaking subsidiary under another name in the Portobello Road where the junk is sold. One of the wealthiest dealers has no shop but spends his time marching into other people's shops, banging his fist noisily on fragile tables till the very silver dances, and saying "How much? I'll give you half, cash."

One prominent name used to be that of a man who worked for India as an engineer over half a lifetime, then served in the inevitable war and afterwards found himself unable to resume his former career. He came to England with a helpful wife and £2,000, and set up as a watch repairer because he had read that it was difficult to get a watch repaired quickly. His mechanical skill enabled him to make parts himself. He was soon employing tradesmen in an old country house, and finding by chance that the best money could be made by buying old clocks and restoring them. Finally he had a branch in the West End of London and would make several hundreds of pounds out of a single ancient timepiece that he had restored to its original beauty and working order. He appeared in television programs, the height of success, and then vanished from the scene, probably with a fortune.

There was a young man in a cathedral city, son of a father who had sold antiques to American millionaires, and who had kept him almost as a day laborer at the cabinetmaker's bench. That young man had eventually broken away from his father and established his own business. He looked like a gangster, but displayed exquisite taste in his choice of furniture, and ended with what amounted to a factory for the "restoration" of "antiques." At the same time he never ceased to be a very kind man.

There was a tobacconist who sold early clocks and fine eighteenth-century porcelain among his cigarettes, and a grocer who, perhaps appropriately enough, dealt on the side in pot lids. A large store in a coast town had an excellent antiques department, which meant more to the owner of that store than all the other, more lucrative departments. Many proprietors of country tea-rooms and restaurants sold antiques, and some hotels developed the sideline. It was curious to stay in one country-house hotel, wherein all the items of the bedroom had price tickets. While shaving it was possible to assess the values of pieces of porcelain and copper and treen, although this could be a dangerous preoccupation when suddenly it was realized that the prices on the tickets were several times the value of the pieces.

There was a partnership between a young man who owned a great factory and the old lady proprietor of a secondhand shop with clothes hanging outside. The wealthy man provided the capital and the old lady did the buying—lovely French antiques that were displayed in a smarter shop down the road.

One of the largest and most successful antique dealers was at that time to be found with an enormous establishment in the far north of Scotland, where he started work at seven o'clock each morning after originally starting work as a barefooted orphan boy, and where he eventually tended to look like a fox-hunting man from the shires; and there was one street in the most fashionable part of London, with money flowing past the doors each day, where the little shops seemed to change hands each week.

It was possible to enter a certain shop in the romantic ways of Edinburgh and to talk with the proprietor and his wife on equal footing, whether the interest was metaphysics or professional boxing, poetry or large cars. The man was a former coal-heaver and his wife had the gypsy ways of second sight and plaintive voice. They sold beautiful and often important old clocks and weapons.

Languishing ladies linger in some shops under fringed lampshades: they tend to be dangerous with sharp tongues and brains like cash registers. In others there are stout women who tell fortunes rather than make them. An exiled Russian "prince" is to be found here; a former "magnate" of Vienna there. One of the most showy and tricky dealers of all, large, fat and with the chilling manners of the popular idea of an aristocrat, would steal away to spend hours of meditation in the local cathedral, in intervals of running a string of women like a string of race-horses.

There was a crude antique business by a coastal creek, and it was run by the former proprietor of a night club. In London one of the most sophisticated galleries was run by a character who prided himself on being a jolly old salt (which, incidentally, he was not). The lady of the manor in a beautiful village ran a small antique shop in that village. A small antique shop in another village was presided over by a coarse man who delighted in spitting, swearing, and calling the most sedate customers "Cock." At the back of this shop he had delightful apartments with a superb collection of his own antiques and a wife and children of the utmost refinement.

The dealers have, of course, tended to change in character with the increasing scarcity of what they describe as "quality goods." When reproduction furniture comes in at the door character is apt to fly out of the window.

But there always will be antique dealers and they will always be at once shopkeepers par excellence and totally different from other shopkeepers. It is said that the race will soon die out because there will be nothing left for them to sell. This is nonsense. If all civilization were destroyed by atomic warfare there would soon develop a lively trade in the buying and selling of the ruins of that civilization, and, if there were no ruins, they would buy and sell each other's corpses, radioactivity and all.

More than two thousand years ago Rome had an entire district that was devoted to the antiques trade, around the Villa Publica: it had all the furniture, china, glass, picture and book dealers that we know today; and the Emperor Caligula, in intervals of being cruel, himself ran great auctions with himself on the rostrum. Members of his court had to attend and had to buy. On one occasion an unfortunate courtier fell asleep, and Caligula nicely presumed that every time the man nodded in his sleep he was bidding. When the man awoke he found that the Emperor had put him down as the purchaser of a small fortune in trash.

Similarly there will always be collectors, whether of cheese labels or of million-dollar pictures. If some people must always buy and sell, others must always pile up hoards of this or that. In both cases the activity is what counts, not the object of the activity. The true collector, if left alone in a desert, would soon begin to assemble odd grains of sand.

The true collector is like that rich young man of Paris who devoted all his time, energy, and money to the acquisition of rare editions of La Fontaine. He finally reached the state of almost perfect bliss, when he needed but a single book to complete his collection. This was the unique copy of the *Contes* illustrated with unpublished drawings by Fragonard.

The young man advertised and made inquiries and at length discovered that the volume did exist and was in the hands of a certain widowed lady. The young man obtained an introduction to this lady and offered to pay her almost any price for the book. Alas, she was rich and saw no reason why she should sell. Did she realize what a weapon she had in her hands? Possibly she did, because very soon the young man, driven to virtual madness by the situation, suddenly realized that the widow's property would be his if he married her, which he did.

On the wedding night he neglected his bride, rushing instead to her library for a gloating examination of the book. He opened it and his heart nearly stopped. Something was wrong with the all-important illustrations. He rushed them to a strong light and found that they were nineteenth-century reproductions.

That young man fell into a swoon from which he never awoke.

Or there was that famous bibliophile the Comte de la Bédoyère, who after years of collecting suffered a fatal aberration in 1847. He decided one day that he had had enough and should sell his library. But no sooner had the aution sale begun than he regretted his decision. He could not bear the idea of his precious books falling into the hands of other people, and he began to bid furiously for them. He topped every price, and, at the end of the sale, retained possession of all the items—less commission and expenses.

The writer of this book, neither collector nor dealer, has made a study of what we call antiques and works of art because the subject as such has always fascinated him. It teaches so much about men today and men yesterday, and indeed about men tomorrow. His own artistic skill, if he has any, consists in the manipulation of words, and he would prefer to write in verse if only it were acceptable in an age of prose. Verse is so much more economical. It enables a man to say in a sentence what a whole chapter is otherwise required to say. Therefore to end characteristically he will write down two sets of verses, which need not be read:

The Chase

How sad the days, how dull the hours
When finally at last
The house is done, all rooms arranged,
And treasure-seeking past.

As he must feel who comes to end
Of busy working life,
And sighs amid achievement's wealth
For former toil and strife.

Until—an opportunity
Once more to enter race,
And boredom instantly away
Is vanished from his face.

As when the news is brought of piece
Available to buy,
And off we run with eagerness
To purchase it or die.

Across nine shires, by day and night,
As if the flaming goal
Were Golden Fleece awaiting there,
Not what the butler stole.

Our life renewed, grim cares forgot,
Past acquisitions naught,
As down the roads of hope we run,
Still youthful and untaught.

Best medicine a man can have,
And for a woman too,
To leave all else and run away
The chanceful gods to woo.

A piece of delft, a set of chairs,
A Guardi or a pot:
It's all the same, so long as it
Is what we haven't got.

The Artist

Whoring round Haarlem in search of a guilder
I got this quick job from a fat jerry-builder,
To paint his new house with some figures outside,
That I did in a week with old Vermeer as guide,
And handed it over for price of a drink,
That just about saved me on starvation's brink,
A picture that now is worth more than the house,
And graces the salon of smug English louse,
Who speaks of The Master in tones so refined
I stir in my hell and drink myself blind.

Bibliography

(NOTE: Good antiquarian booksellers in the United States should be able to procure most of these English books still, as they have been published mainly in the last twenty years, and they will often be found in public libraries).

Furniture

Dictionary of English Furniture. MacQuoid & Edwards. (Country Life.)
Sheraton Furniture. R. Fastnedge. (Faber.)
Regency Furniture Designs. J. Harris. (Tiranti.)
Chippendale Furniture Designs. R. W. Symonds. (Tiranti.)
Hepplewhite Furniture Designs. R. Edwards. (Tiranti.)
Sheraton Furniture Designs. R. Edwards. (Tiranti.)
Georgian Cabinet Makers. R. Edwards & M. Jourdain. (Country Life.)

Ceramics and Glass

Marks & Monograms on Pottery & Porcelain. W. Chaffers. (Reeves.)
Handbook of Pottery & Porcelain Marks. J. P. Cushion & W. B. Honey. (Faber.)
The Collectors' Encyclopaedia of English Ceramics. B. & T. Hughes. (Lutterworth.)
Pictorian Pottery & Porcelain. B. Hughes. (Country Life.)
An Illustrated Encyclopaedia of British Pottery & Porcelain. G. A. Godden. (Herbert Jenkins.)
English Pottery Figures. R. G. Haggar. (Tiranti.)
Monographs on Pottery & Porcelain. (Faber.)
The Collector's Dictionary of Glass. E. M. Elville. (Country Life.)

Silver and Jewelry

English Goldsmiths & Their Marks. Jackson. (Macmillan.)
Victorian Silver & Silver-Plate. P. Wardle. (Herbert Jenkins.)
Hester Bateman. D. S. Shure. (W. H. Allen.)
Old Sheffield Plate. E. Wenham. (Bell.)
Greek & Roman Jewellery. R. A. Higgins. (Methuen.)
English Victorian Jewellery. E. Bradford. (Country Life.)

Objets d'Art

English Painted Enamels. T. & B. Hughes. (Country Life.)
Paperweights. E. M. Elville. (Country Life.)
Snuff & Snuff-Boxes. H. McCausland.
The Art of Carl Fabergé. A. K. Snowman. (Faber.)

Bygones

Collecting Copper & Brass. G. Boothroyd. (Arco.)
Chats on Old Copper & Brass. F. W. Burgess. (T. Fisher Unwin.)
Old Pewter. H. H. Cotterell. (Batsford.)
Antique Pewter of the British Isles. R. Michaelis. (Bell.)
Old Clocks & Watches. F. J. Britten. (Spon.)
The Grandfather Clock. E. L. Edwardes. (Sherratt.)
The Story of Watches. Camerer Cuss. (MacGibbon & Kee.)
Collecting Musical Boxes. A. W. J. G. Ord-Hume. (Allen & Unwin.)
Gun Collecting. G. Boothroyd. (Arco.)
Horse Brasses & Other Small Items for the Collector. G. B. Hughes. (Country Life.)

European

The Complete Guide to Furniture Styles. L. A. Boger. (Allen & Unwin.)
The Concise Encyclopaedia of Continental Pottery & Porcelain. R. G. Haggar. (Deutsch.)
European Ceramic Art. W. B. Honey. (Faber.)
Dutch Silver. M. H. Gans & T. M. D. de Wit-Klinkhamer. (Faber.)

Oriental

A Short History of Chinese Art. M. Sullivan. (Faber.)
Ancient Chinese Bronzes. W. Watson. (Faber.)
Chinese Jade. C. S. Nott. (Batsford.)
Japanese Decorative Art. M. Fedderson. (Faber.)
The Japanese Print. J. Hillier. (Bell.)
The Netsuke of Japan. E. Ryerson. (Bell.)

Victoriana

Victoriana. V. Wood. (Bell.)
Victorian Pottery. H. Wakefield. (Herbert Jenkins.)
Victorian Porcelain. G. Godden. (Herbert Jenkins.)
Victorian Pottery & Porcelain. G. B. Hughes. (Country Life.)
19th Century English Furniture. E. Aslin. (Faber.)
Victorian Furniture. R. W. Symonds & B. B. Whineray. (Country Life.)
The Pictorial Pot Lid Book. H. G. Clarke. (Courier Press.)

Carpets and Textiles

Oriental Rugs. H. Haack. (Faber.)
How to Identify Persian Rugs. C. D. May. (Bell.)
French Tapestry. R. A. Weigert. (Faber.)
English Needlework. A. F. Kendrick. (Black.)
Victorian Embroidery. B. Morris. (Herbeert Jenkins.)

Pictures

The Dutch School. H. S. Degener. (English Universities Press.)
Honderd Jaren Nederlandsche Schilder-en Teekenkunst. P. A. Scheen. (Boeken Periodek, The Hague.)
Old Prints. A. Hayden & C. G. E. Bunt. (Benn.)
Antique Maps. P. J. Radford. (Radford.)
How to Identify Old Maps & Globes. R. Lister. (Bell.)
Decorative Printed Maps. R. A. Skelton. (Staples.)

Books

Books & Book Collectors. J. Carter. (Hart-Davis.)
Book Auction Records. (Stevens, Son & Stiles.)

Coins

Coin Collecting. L. Brown. (Arco.)
Catalogues of Coins. (B. A. Seaby.)

Childish Things

English Dolls, Effigies & Puppets. A. K. Early. (Batsford.)
The Golden Age of Toys. J. Remise & J. Fondin. (Patrick Stephens.)

Index

Adam, 24
Adams, potters, 38
Antiques dealers, 190
Arita, 117
Arquebus, 78
Arras, 141
Art Nouveau, 131
Asia Minor Rugs, 138
Astbury, 38
Aubusson, 138
Auction sales, 186
Axminsters, 138

Barometers, 76
Baroque, 88, 100
Bateman, Hester, 52
Battersea, 59
Baxter, George, 131
Bayeux Tapestry, 141
Bayonets, 80
Beauvais, 141
Bellarmine, 39
Belleek, 130
Bells of glass, 42
Berlin, 98
Biedermeier, 98
Billies and Charlies, 124
Billingsley, Wm., 33
Bilston, 60
Birdcase clocks, 73
Birmingham silver, 44
Blaeu, 151
Blome, 152
Blunderbusses, 79
Bone models, 172
Books, 154
Books by cabinetmakers, 19
Boulsover, Thos., 55
Boulton, Matt., 55
Bourne, 39
Bow, 31
Bracket clocks, 74

Brass, 70
Bristol glass, 127
Bristol porcelain, 35
British coins, 165
Brown Besses, 79
Buying, 183

Cabriole leg, 21
Candlesticks, 70
Capo-di-Monte, 101
Care of pictures, 144
Care of rugs and carpets, 140
Carolean, 21
Carpets, 135
Cary, 152
Cassone, 99
Caughley, 35
Celadon, 111
Chairs, 19
Chaise-longues, 126
Chelsea, 30
Chess sets, 65
Chester silver, 46
Chests, 21
Children's furniture, 171
Chimney ornaments, 40
Chinese carpets, 137
Chinese periods, 109
Chippendale, 18, 22
Clocks, 73
Coalport, 34, 129
Coats-of-Arms, 50
Coins, 161
Colebrookdale, 34
Colt, Samuel, 80
Copeland, 129
Copenhagen, 105
Copper, 70
Credenza, 100
Cromwellian, 21

Damascening, 80

Danish furniture, 105
Dantesca, 99
Dates, 29
Davenport, 37
Davenports, 125
Dealers, 190
Delft, 103
Dental antiques, 85
Derby, 31, 129
Dogs, china, 124
Dolls, 170
Doulton, 39
Dresden, 96
Drinking glasses, 41
Drug jars, 39
Dublin silver, 47
Dutch marquetry, 101
Dutch school painters, 145
Dutch silver, 101
Dutch silver marks, 103
Dutch styles, 101
Dwight, 39

Edinburgh silver, 46
Elers, 38
Empire Period, 90
Enamels, 58
Exeter silver, 46

Fabergé, 66
Faience, 91
"Fair Hebe," 39
Fakes, 30
Famille Noir, 111
Famille Rose, 111
Famille Vert, 111
Farthingales, 21
Finger bowls, 41
Firearms, 78
Fire backs, 73
Fireplaces, 72
Flintlocks, 78

Frames, 144
French, 88
French fakes, 179
Frog mugs, 39
Fromanteels, 74
Fürstenberg, 98

Glasgow silver, 47
Glass, 40
Glass ships, 175
Gobelins, 141
Goss, W. H., 130
Graham, George, 74
Grandfather clocks, 74
Greek coins, 163
Gunmakers' marks, 81

Hallmarks, 48
Hannong, C. F., 93
Hats of glass, 127
Hepplewhite, 21
Hokusai, 117
Hole and Kip, 151
Horse brasses, 86

Imari, 117
Intarsia, 99
Irish silver, 47
Italian styles, 99

Jacobean, 21
Jade, 111
Jansson, 151
Japanese, 114
Japanese color prints, 117
Jelly glasses, 41
Jelly molds, 71
Jewelry, 55
Joiners' work, 21

Kakeimon, 117
Knibb, Joseph, 76
Knock-out, The, 188
Knole, 21

Lace, 129, 141
Lacquer fakes, 182
Latticino, 41
Leeds, 39
Lighting of pictures, 145
Liverpool, 39
Locks, 84
London silver, 44
Longcase clocks, 74
Longton Hall, 35
Louis styles, 88
Lowestoft, 36

Mahogany period, 22
Majolica, 101
Manton, Joseph, 79
Maps, 150
Marieberg, 105
Martin ware, 130
Masons Ironstone, 39
Matchlock muskets, 78
Meissen, 96
Military chests, 127
Ming, 111
Miniature books, 159
Mint marks, 167
Minton, 36, 129
Monteiths, 42
Mortlake, 141
Moule, 152
Musical boxes, 76

Nailsea, 42
Nantgarw, 33
Neale, 38
Needlework, 127
Nefs, 175
Netsuke, 117
Newcastle silver, 46
New Hall, 36
Norwegian furniture, 105
Norwegian glass, 105
Norwich silver, 46
Nymphenburg, 98
Nyon, 108

Oak period, 21
Ogilby, 153
Ormolu, 95

Palissy, Bernard, 91
Paperweights, 64
Papier maché, 124
Persian rugs, 138
Pewter, 71
Pharmacy jars, 39
Pinxton, 36
Pistols, 80
Plymouth, 33
Porcelain, 30
Porcelain marks, 34
Pot lids, 131
Pottery, 37
Pratt, 38
Prayer rugs, 136
Prices, 25
Prints, 148

Quare, Daniel, 74
Queen Anne, 18, 21

Ravenscroft, 41
Regency, 22
Registry marks, 133
Resist, 39
Restoration, 21
Ridgway, 39
Ring, The, 188
Road maps, 152
Rockingham, 36, 39
Rockinghorses, 171
Roman coins, 163
Romantic pictures, 145

Sales, 186
Savonarola, 99
Savonneries, 138
Saxton, 151
Scandinavian, 103
Scottish silver, 46
Sea charts, 153
Seamen's chests, 127
Selling, 187
Seto, 114
Sèvres, 93
Sheffield Plate, 54
Sheffield silver, 44
Sheraton, 22
Ship models, 172
Ships-in-bottles, 174
Silver marks, 43, 48
Snuff boxes, 61
Staffordshire figures, 40
Strasbourg, 93
Sunderland, 39
Sung, 111
Swansea, 36
Swedish chandeliers, 105
Swedish coins, 105
Swedish furniture, 103
Swedish silver, 103
Swiss ceramics, 107
Swiss furniture, 107
Swiss prints, 107
Swiss stained glass, 106

T'ang, 109
Tapestry, 141
Tea caddies, 65
Toddy lifters, 42
Tokens, 168
Tompion, Thomas, 74
Tonbridge Work, 174
Toys, 171
Tsuba, 114
Turners' work, 21

Upholstery, 21

Venetian glass, 41
Verzelini, 41
Victoriana, 121
Victorian silver, 47
Vienna, 98

Walnut period, 21
Walton, 130
Warming pans, 70
Watches, 74

Waterford, 41
Wedgewood, 37
Whatnots, 125
Wheel-locks, 78
Whieldon, Thos., 37
William and Mary, 18
Wiltons, 138
Windsor chairs, 21
Wood, Ralph, 37
Woods, 28

Worcester, 32, 130
Wormholes, 16

X-shaped chairs, 21

Yards-of-Ale, 42
Yorkshire chairs, 21
York silver, 44

Zurich, 107